WORKERS'
PARTICIPATIVE
SCHEMES

Recent Titles in
Contributions in Labor Studies

WORKERS' PARTICIPATIVE SCHEMES

The Experience of Capitalist and Plan-based Societies

HELEN A. TSIGANOU

Contributions in Labor Studies, Number 35

GREENWOOD PRESS

New York • Westport, Connecticut • London

Library of Congress Cataloging-in-Publication Data

Tsiganou, Helen A.
  Workers' participative schemes : the experience of capitalist and
plan-based societies / Helen A. Tsiganou.
    p.   cm. — (Contributions in labor studies, ISSN 0886–8239 ;
no. 35)
  Includes bibliographical references and index.
  ISBN 0–313–26479–1 (alk. paper)
  1. Management—Employee participation.   2. Comparative economics.
3. Comparative government.   I. Title.   II. Series.
HD5650.T85   1991
338.6—dc20   90–19916

British Library Cataloguing in Publication Data is available.

Library of Congress Catalog Card Number: 90–19916
ISBN: 0–313–26479–1
ISSN: 0886–8239

First published in 1991

Greenwood Press, 88 Post Road West, Westport, CT 06881
An imprint of Greenwood Publishing Group, Inc.

Printed in the United States of America

The paper used in this book complies with the
Permanent Paper Standard issued by the National
Information Standards Organization (Z39.48–1984).

10 9 8 7 6 5 4 3 2 1

To George

Contents

Preface

Participatory decision-making forms are part of our lives as they relate to politics, religion, or community activities. Yet, there is an overall tendency to ignore the significance of participation in one very central part of our lives, work. There is no doubt, however, that interest in work and efforts to democratize it, including participatory reforms, has increased over the course of the last twenty years in many countries around the world.

This book can perhaps be best understood as part of a long personal research effort to understand and explain the origins and dynamics of worker participation from a comparative perspective. In its attempt to present a comprehensive picture of the variety of the workers' participation schemes, the book examines a number of countries never studied together before. But the book is distinctive not only in its extensive coverage of national workers' participation schemes but also in its attempt to develop a broad comparative framework for understanding the development of workers' participation in its various forms.

The purpose of the book is to explain the diversity of workers' participation schemes in broad comparative sociological terms and to establish why worker participation reappears in reform efforts initiated by various actors such as rank and file workers, union leaders, and political elites.

Undoubtedly, the issues explored in this book are of considerable importance, reappearing in the popular media and business press, whether under the guise of competitiveness and quality strategies for the United States, Japan, Western Europe and Scandinavia or as part of recent attempts to reform entire economies, as in the Soviet Union and Eastern Europe. It is hoped that the book's broad comparative perspective will contribute to the understanding of the evolution of worker participation, as well as the broader social, economic and political conditions of democratization in the twentieth century.

In writing the book I have incurred a number of debts that need to be acknowledged. I would like to thank the publisher's reviewer who provided many useful suggestions and constructive criticisms on the original manuscript. I would also like to thank all the people at Greenwood Press who contributed to the smooth production of this book, especially Cynthia Harris, Catherine Lyons and Betty Pessagno. Stephen Fielding, Augie Diana, Paula McCabe and Elaine Doll read earlier versions of the book, and their comments and criticisms were most helpful. Other individuals to whom I owe thanks include Thomas Shapiro, Michael Rustad, Litsa Nicolaou, and especially Professor Carmen Sirianni for his continuous support, insightful comments and constructive criticisms. Finally, this book would not have been possible without the love, patience, emotional and technical support of my husband, George.

Introduction

Over the course of the twentieth century, worker participation has attracted considerable attention as a major political, social, and economic issue in many countries around the world. Interest in managing production in less bureaucratic ways and in making worklife more meaningful and satisfying by allowing workers to participate in the decision-making process has increased in the last twenty years in particular. This interest is reflected in the growing number of worker participation schemes that have emerged in most Western industrialized countries, in Japan, as well as in Eastern European and Third World countries.

Worker participation schemes range from consultative arrangements in the United States and Japan, to employee representation on the board of directors in Scandinavia, codetermination plans in Germany, producers' cooperatives in England and the United States, workers' councils in Eastern Europe, and self-management in Yugoslavia. Along with this growth of worker participation schemes, a considerable amount of scholarly research and writing has been done on this issue. Over the years a number of theoretical formulations have been developed to explain the diverse participatory forms, but no single satisfactory theoretical approach to worker participation exists inasmuch as there is no single channel available to promote it.

As studies have shown, this diversity of participation arrangements shows differences in important dimensions such as the range of issues that participation schemes might cover (e.g., immediate working and pay conditions or long-term policies); the organization level at which participation is introduced and takes place (e.g., shopfloor, board of directors); the basis of participation schemes (e.g., formally prescribed versus informal participation arrangements); and the nature of participation (e.g., direct participation or through representatives) (Brannen, 1983; Cordova, 1982; IDE, 1981a; Stephens and Stephens, 1982).

These diverse arrangements simply elucidate different historical periods, economic and technological differences, national traditions and cultures, as well as differences in the political and industrial structures in the countries where worker participation schemes have been developed. Finally, they point to the differences in the orientations and goals of the industrial relations actors within each country. In that respect they shed light on the conflict over the distribution of power within industrial relations systems and the degree to which the decision-making power has been transferred to workers (Brannen, 1983; Poole, 1978, 1981).

In this work we use a historical comparative approach to examine worker participation plans in two major contextual settings: first, the developed capitalist countries of the United States, Japan, and the European countries of Sweden, Norway, England, Germany, and France; and second, the centrally planned socialist countries of Yugoslavia, Poland, Hungary, Czechoslovakia, China, and the Soviet Union. The goal is to explore the origins and explain the diversity of worker participation schemes across these specific national contexts, although occasional references are made to schemes in some Third World countries.

Through this study we hope to enhance understanding of the diverse nature of worker participation schemes. Specifically, we address the following critical points: the conditions under which these plans emerge; and the reasons that account for the similarities or differences among them in the national settings examined. Why, for instance, do countries that face similar problems or have similar political and economic systems differ in regard to the participation schemes they develop? Who are the main initiators of these plans? What is their ideological orientation and power? Under what socioeconomic, political, and labor market conditions do these actors initiate participation schemes and how might their underlying goals in introducing worker participation plans be constrained or facilitated by those conditions?

In order to address these issues and give some meaningful answers to the questions raised, we first study the origins and history of worker participation within a given national environment. Contemporary phenomena and problems are rooted in the past and cannot be fully understood and analyzed unless their historical origins are explored. Having delineated a historical account of participation within each country, the next step is to draw on the specific national experiences regarding participation schemes and make cross-national comparisons. The analysis indicates that the labor market conditions of each country, the overall nature and structure of its industrial relations system, the strength and orientation of its labor movement, the educational levels of its working class, and, finally, economic and political circumstances as well as international influences are the most important factors explaining the diverse nature of worker participation arrangements in the countries under consideration.

As is apparent, not only the number of cases examined, but also the number of variables considered are quite substantial. The book is not in any way a systematic, detailed, country-by-country comparison of worker participation on all these variables. Rather, it is a long-overdue attempt to explain the enormous diversity of worker participative schemes through comparative analysis. Without doubt cross-national research is important in its own right; in the past few years its significance has begun to be recognized in the field. As Melvin Kohn (1989: 19) correctly argues, "we are . . . well beyond needing to demonstrate that nations and cultures differ; it is time to explain these differences." Cross-national research is necessary if we want to enrich our understanding of practices, phenomena, and social problems in this country. New meanings and insights can be brought to light by studying similar experiences and practices in other societies. If this book enhances our understanding of the diversity of worker participation in the countries under examination, it would have accomplished its goal.

Chapter 1 examines the origins of worker participation, the motives and goals behind various participatory schemes, and their development and outcomes in the two distinct settings mentioned above. Specifically, in this chapter, the comparative logic and analytical framework of the book is laid out against the background of the existing theoretical and analytical work on the issue of worker participation. The chapter also deals with the variety of meanings and definitions attached to worker participation and their significance in denoting the dynamic of power, not only within the workplace, but also within the overall society. The chapter ends with a discussion of some of the major assumptions of the book.

Part I deals with the diversity of worker participation schemes in some developed capitalist countries, whose economies are market driven. Chapter 2 discusses the Scandinavian approach to worker participation by focusing on Sweden and Norway. Chapter 3 examines the English, French, and German experiences with worker participation schemes. Chapter 4 elaborates on the American and Japanese experiences in this area. These countries exemplify the capitalist type of economy with advanced industry and a democratic pluralist political system. Although they are advanced capitalist countries, their labor relations systems, cultures, and political systems differ one from the other. In that respect, they provide some of the factors considered to have a profound impact on the diversity of origins, developments, and outcomes of worker participation schemes.

Part II discusses worker participation in some centrally planned socialist societies. Chapter 5 covers Yugoslavia; Chapter 6, Poland, Hungary, and Czechoslovakia; Chapter 7, the Chinese experience; and Chapter 8, the Soviet Union. These countries exemplify the centrally planned, socialist type of economy that through reforms are attempting to correct some of their weaknesses. These countries also differ with regard to the centralization of their economy and their political system, and therefore provide us with an explanation of their differing participation experiences. Chapter 9, the concluding part of the book, summarizes the findings of the study and explores issues that emerge as some broad cross-national and cross-sectional comparisons are made.

WORKERS' PARTICIPATIVE SCHEMES

1

The Analytical Framework

Over the years, appeals for participative work arrangements through which workers could exercise some control over their working lives have been informed by a number of debates and theoretical formulations. Some of the theoretical approaches include radical criticisms of both market capitalism and the Soviet-type socialism. They also suggest a number of strategies, such as self-management, economic democracy, and direct participatory democracy, to empower individuals not merely as workers, but also as members of the overall society seeking to transform it into a more just and egalitarian society.

Within the liberal democratic tradition, for instance, we can find inspiration and insights for a democratically run workplace. In John Stuart Mill's model of democracy, participation in every single sphere of societal activity, though difficult to achieve, is perceived as essential in the development of well-informed citizens.[1] Within the participatory democracy tradition, political theorist Carole Pateman argues that representative institutions are not sufficient for democracy. For a truly democratic society to exist, political participation by citizens should be expanded to include all major institutions, including the workplace (Pateman, 1970).

Various Marxist traditions have emphasized the process by which workers under industrial capitalism have become alienated, stripped of their creativity and capabilities, and unable to control their labor power, the production process, and the end product of their effort. Workplace democracy and worker self-management have been perceived as one way to eliminate the ill effects of alienation and transform workers into free, creative human beings.

Neo-Marxist and postindustrial theories also touch on issues of workplace control and worker participation in an attempt to explain the changing power relationships that have accompanied technological change during the post–World

War II period. According to Braverman (1974), new technologies have allowed management to deskill jobs. Through deskilling, labor power can be bought at lower prices, workers can be easily replaced, and management can thereby gain greater control over the design and production process and the overall execution of work. As a result, workplace rationalization and capital centralization are facilitated and the capitalist drive for more control, lower production and wage costs, and thus more profits, can be pursued (1974: 88–124). Because of these developments, Braverman argues, a reverse trend away from participation takes place. From this point of view, participation schemes represent a successful managerial strategy that facilitates workers' coaptation and allows for more productivity as well as more management control over workers. In that sense all participation schemes are illusionary. They do not represent a genuine change in the worker's position within the workplace. There are simply pseudo-participation schemes. Indeed, workers might be involved in some insignificant tasks, be moved from one job to another to avoid boredom, but in reality workers "have the illusion of making decisions by choosing among fixed and limited alternatives designed by a management which deliberately leaves insignificant matters open to choice" (Braverman, 1974: 39).

Within the neo-Marxist tradition, Edwards (1979), too, views mechanisms of technical and bureaucratic control as managerial responses to the struggle over control of the division of labor.[2] Technical control was widely adopted in the 1920s to subdue labor unrest and to increase productivity; it eroded workers' discretion and control over the production process since technologies such as the assembly line provided, according to Edwards, unambiguous direction of what task the worker was to perform next and at what pace. The continuous mechanization soon undermined managerial gains as well. Mechanization might have eroded the need for skills, but it also homogenized the workforce, which consisted mostly of unskilled and semiskilled operators. The conflict between management and workers was merely displaced to the plantwide level, not elim-inated. In the post–1945 period, in response to market and technological changes and in order to compensate for some of the deficiencies of technical control, bureaucratic control was adopted mostly in large corporations to organize white-collar, higher skills jobs. Under bureaucratic control a number of incentives were provided, such as grievance procedures, seniority provisions, fringe benefits, and the promise for a more or less stable employment. As a result, workers learned to identify with the enterprise, become loyal, committed, and, at the end, self-motivated and self-controlled.

As Edwards shows, however, in creating the conditions most favorable to bureaucratic control, capitalists inadvertently established the conditions under which demands for workplace democracy could flourish. Secure employees, expecting to work at the same place for long periods of time, usually become interested in issues of quality and work control and in participating in the for-mulation of regulations and policies in the workplace. If their expectations are blocked, worker dissatisfaction and alienation increase. Workers resist corporate goals more readily, and productivity and efficiency decrease. Edwards mentions that the rising frustration with capitalist control creates the potential for revolutionary change as visions to organize work in alternative ways are materialized in actual experiments of job enrichment, job enlargement, worker self-management, and worker-employer co-management schemes. The capitalists themselves are sometimes led, even forced, to introduce these schemes which promise to increase productivity but also have the potential to undermine their power.

Overall, Edwards is skeptical as to whether the combination of the two elements—growing resentment with the present system and a vision for an alternative—will significantly challenge managerial prerogatives. For this to be accomplished participation should be raised as a mass demand, which in turn requires that the workers' vision and struggle be supported by their unions and by a conscious political movement. Edwards agrees that some of the union leaders, socialist organizers, and other working-class activists have expressed an interest in workplace democracy, and they have perceived workers' control as a possible building block to create a decentralized socialist economy. However, no organized effort has been launched to make workplace democracy an integral part of working-class demands and organizations (Edwards, 1979).

While Braverman is quick to dismiss efforts of worker-management cooperation as coaptive,[3] Edwards at least acknowledges the potential of worker participation for a more democratic society. Their differences notwithstanding, both seem to agree on the increasing influence of managerial control in the workplace. Bell (1973), on the other hand, in his postindustrial theory, suggests a shift of workplace authority away from owners and managers. With the separation of ownership from control and with technological innovations rapidly transforming the workplace, Bell argues, authority has shifted from owners and managers to salaried, professional employees, who possess specialized knowledge (Bell, 1973).

As Cornfield (1987: 332) correctly argues, both the neo-Marxist theories mentioned and Bell's postindustrial theory complement each other to a certain degree. For instance, neo-Marxist theories deal extensively with managerial control of labor in the shop or office, whereas Bell's theory implies the growing influence of professional elites at the companywide level. These two processes are interconnected, however. As Cornfield points out, workplace rationalization through job deskilling, technical or bureaucratic control very often requires engineering, personnel, and legal expertise in order to design and implement these strategies. Therefore, management's increasing reliance on specialized professionals for decision making at the companywide level in the postwar period may very well have derived in part from the continuous effort to rationalize work and thereby control it (Cornfield, 1987: 334).

In spite of their similarities, both neo-Marxist and postindustrial theories have failed to seriously consider and adequately explain the increased participatory reforms during the post–World War II era. The question still remains: What accounts for the increasing interest in participation and the actual development of participatory management in various parts of the world in the post–World War II era? Of course, it would be illusionary to assume that there is only one best model or theory able to explain all participative schemes that exist in a number of complex industrial societies. Instead, the relevant assumptions of the existing models and theories, as well as the study and analysis of the empirical development of participatory reforms, should provide us with new ideas and insights to further explain the complexity of participatory schemes and reforms and thereby build on the existing theoretical formulations. To that end, a brief survey of the empirical developments and patterns of participatory reforms, as well as the theoretical explanations for them, follows in the next section.

EMPIRICAL DEVELOPMENT AND PATTERNS OF PARTICIPATORY REFORMS

For a number of years some scholars have pointed out distinct phases of advance and decline in participatory reforms in several countries. By studying the history of those reforms, we can identify the favorable circumstances under which specific participation schemes have apparently emerged.[4] Sirianni (1983) and Sorge (1976), for instance, show that participatory reforms in some European countries became more intense during certain periods of time, such as during and shortly after the two world wars, as well as during the mid- to late 1960s, with the trend continuing up to the present. It also appears that the development of participation cycles is not uniform or consistent. The cycles, especially since the Second World War, do not present the sharp distinction of progress and decline that characterized the earlier periods. Rich experimentation in the last twenty years can perhaps be compared with similar developments during the 1910s and 1920s. Poole (1978), too, argues that pressures for participation have ebbed and flowed in particular historical periods, while Brannen et al. (1976) show that these waves relate to economic and political crises. For instance, in periods of crisis, such as war periods, or in periods of economic growth and expansion, such as postwar reconstruction, labor market power increases and workers are in a position to press demands for participation. It is during those periods that worker participation movements have developed and been institutionalized. During the 1960s, a new wave of participatory reforms began as affluency and tight labor market conditions in many advanced industrialized countries allowed workers to enjoy full employment, to strengthen their bargaining position, and thus to demand better working conditions. Under those circumstances, workers' expectations regarding workplace control issues were raised, ushering in a new wave of participatory demands and reforms (IDE, 1981b; Garson, 1977).

In a similar vein, Ramsay (1977) argues that workers' participation is not the result of the increased humanistic spirit of capitalism. In Britain enthusiasm for participation schemes was the result of management's response to threats and challenges to its authority and prerogatives, during a period of tight labor market conditions. For instance, the Whitley labor management committees of 1917 were the product of the war-created need for increased production and hence labor-management cooperation. We should also keep in mind that during the same period the power and militancy of organized labor had increased considerably. With trade union membership growing and working-class consciousness at its highest peak, labor was in a very strong bargaining position to press for changes. Moreover, revolutionary and Guild Socialist ideas had sprung out all over Europe, and the events in Russia had made many businessmen fearful of their future and ready to seriously consider workers' demands for participation. These managerial initiatives, Ramsay argues, have to be understood within the framework of antagonistic industrial relations. Based on a Marxist point of view, Ramsay views the relations of production under capitalism as conflictual because of the opposing interests between capital and labor. Through this perspective, participation schemes become illusionary; they are merely means to secure labor's compliance.

If Ramsay's account is indeed accurate, does this mean that the prospects of worker participation reforms within the capitalist system are very grim and that efforts to democratize the workplace are doomed to fail? Are the prospects for worker participation more promising within the Soviet-style economies? These questions are yet to be answered. Implicit in Ramsay's account is the notion that the opposing interests of worker-management will always be resolved on management's terms, since management has more resources and more power. Even when managerial prerogatives have been challenged and management has been obliged to introduce participation schemes, Ramsay argues, management has the upper hand. The reason, he states, is that a whole structural economic and social transformation has to take place in order for a genuine industrial democracy to prevail.

Historically, managerial interest in participation has been mainly a reaction to prevailing unfavorable circumstances. When labor is in a strong bargaining position or when adverse economic conditions prevail, management has come forward mostly with participatory solutions, at least in the West (Brannen, 1983; Poole, 1978; Ramsay, 1977). But Ramsay's analysis, like Braverman's, is determinist and not particularly helpful in explaining the diversity of participation schemes in terms of structure, functions, and power given to workers during the various cycles. As Poole (1981) correctly points out, a distinction should be made between the integrative and consultative types of participation envisaged during war periods, and conflictual forms developed in periods of class tension and industrial unrest. It would be logical to assume that during adverse economic and political times and in order to smooth out conflicts, more integrative schemes of worker participation will be developed, while during periods of labor militancy more transformative types will be introduced. As this book shows, because worker participation entails some power redistribution toward the workers, it has been and it will always be implicated in power struggles not only in the workplace, but also within the larger society. Management, especially in the

United States, has often used participative schemes to undermine worker solidarity and union power (Parker, 1985; Parker and Slaughter, 1988). In most
capitalist countries participative innovations involve two basic assumptions: first,
an increase in productivity and reduction of industrial conflict, and second, the
placement of ultimate decision-making power in the hands of owners and/or
managers (Jenkins, 1973; Zimbalist, 1975).

But the participative process is not static, and whether or not integrative or
transformative intentions of participative efforts will materialize depends on a
number of factors. In some cases participation schemes have been introduced in
order to integrate workers; yet once workers were given control over their work
they demanded more power at the same or other levels of the organization
(Espinosa and Zimbalist, 1978; Kochan, Katz, and Mower, 1985a; Sirianni,
1987b; Zwerdling, 1980). In 1968, Peru introduced participative schemes as part
of the revolutionary plan to stabilize the society, eliminate the conflict between
capital and labor, stimulate the initiative and qualifications of workers, and
increase productivity. The overall goal was to equalize deep societal differences
by weakening the power of the capitalist class and raising the standards of living
of the poorest groups (Stephens, 1980). This goal could have been accomplished
by integrating workers into the system through participation schemes. The participative arrangements would give some power, income, and property rights to
workers and hence eliminate the destabilizing effect of the capital-labor conflict.

As Stephens (1980) shows, however, the government's initial plans did not
work out. Instead of integrating, participation schemes helped mobilize union
activity and intensify the conflict. In contrast to the promised prerogatives,
participative schemes did not provide workers with the opportunity to exercise
real influence, and workers responded to such limiting options. It was expected,
for instance, that workers' representatives would bring up questions regarding
wages, working conditions, or personnel issues to the board of directors. However, it was illegal for them to defend workers' rights. As a result, there was
no mechanism to resolve conflicts or to ensure the implementation of legal
provisions regarding workers' participation and monetary rights. Consequently,
workers turned to their unions to defend their interests, to provide legal expertise
and experience, and to pursue real participation goals. From the start, the participative efforts and reforms met the hostility of Peruvian capital. Such a reaction
sharpened the differences between capital and labor and intensified the conflict.
Workers, seeking to protect their rights, escalated their demands to include
participative rights not only within the workplace, but also within regional and
national state decision-making bodies. Yet in other countries, as in France,
managerial resistance and worker lack of power led to apathy and no escalation
of demands within the works committees. As Stephens (1980) suggests, in
contrast to France, participation rights in Peru were linked with ownership and
cash distribution rights. This might explain workers' interest and escalation of
demands for more participation rights there.

To explain such differences as a broad rule, we need to remember that each country is part of the world system, and therefore it has been influenced by developments in it. An equally important consideration is each country's specific economic and sociopolitical development and the major changes it has undergone throughout history. It has been shown, for instance, that although industrialization created common problems in Western Europe, the solutions devised were different because of particular circumstances in each country. As a result, a variety of industrial democracy institutions and ideologies emerged (Sorge, 1976). It would have been difficult to explain the particular variety that emerged on the grounds of different functional requirements of the countries' industrial structures. Instead, according to Sorge (1976: 278), "explanations must therefore be sought in the wider political implications, value systems, beliefs, ideologies held by both trade unions and employers' organizations, as well as those in the country at large."

Similarly, Poole (1982: 195) identifies four dimensions that explain different participation outcomes: cultural, ideological, or value patterns; the structure of bargaining; the power dynamic among industrial actors; and the exercise of strategic choice. The importance of culture in explaining international variations has been suggested many times in the literature. The Japanese economic success, for instance, has been attributed to some unique elements of the oriental culture such as submissiveness to authority, cooperation, and the enhanced sense of communal responsibility. It has also been suggested that the solidaristic cultures of the villages and the cultures of autonomous administrative units in Yugoslavia, established as part of the resistance movement during World War II, facilitated the emergence of ideologies supportive of self-management in that nation. In addition, many of the communist leaders had become familiar with the principles of self-management while fighting in the Spanish Civil War, and their experience helped to strengthen the self-management tradition as well. Others have suggested that it would have been extremely difficult to unite the many heterogeneous and contrasting cultures that make up the Yugoslav nation under one huge centralized nation (Riddell, 1968: 50–51). In contrast to the centralized Soviet-style system, self-management could unite the nation by providing its citizens with a common goal after the break with the Cominform in 1948. Similarly, it has been suggested that the highly legalistic nature of the German codetermination system reflects, on the one hand, the interventionist role the state has traditionally played in industrial relations, and on the other, the cultural inclination of resolving differences and conflicts by institutionalizing them (Schregle, 1978; Sorge, 1976).

With regard to the second dimension, it has been argued that if adequate arrangements for collective bargaining within the plant are made, this tool can be considered a satisfactory form of industrial democracy. In contrast, in cases where provisions for plant bargaining do not exist, arrangements must be made that would allow workers to exercise some influence over matters not covered by regional or industry agreements (Clegg, 1976: 97). The Scandinavian cases of Sweden and Norway seem to fit this description, whereas the German system takes care of the diverse interests by institutionalizing both collective bargaining and codetermination. Collective bargaining, for example, provides the framework for regulating working conditions at the regional and/or industry level, while codetermination makes similar provisions at the plant and firm level.

The power distribution among industrial actors and its effect on the development and outcomes of worker participation schemes have been the subject of a great deal of research. After the Second World War, labor shortages in England strengthened workers' bargaining position greatly. As a result, workers were able to exert strong pressure on management to introduce welfare practices, such as sickness and pension schemes, and to develop personnel departments that would handle workers' grievances and working problems. The subsequent emergence of bargaining arrangements based on the shop steward system reflected workers' increased power during that period (Poole, 1978). Stephens and Stephens (1982) compared participation schemes in France, Germany, and Sweden, and they too concluded that variations in control schemes across societies are due primarily to the strength of organized labor, which is perceived to work at two levels. First, through its political strength organized labor can pressure for legislation to introduce workers' participation schemes, which in turn enables labor to exert more influence at the organization level. Through protective policies at the societal level such as control over investment, the workers' bargaining power increases, and demands for more participation rights can be advanced. Second, through its mobilizing activity at the organization level, organized labor can ensure that legislative measures regarding power redistribution and worker participation will become reality.

Whether or not the state is supportive of participative reforms also has an impact on the outcome of participative schemes. Legislative intervention and supportive policies at the state level define the parameters within which participative initiatives can develop and grow. In a number of European countries both legal and voluntary institutions of workers' participation have emerged. Sorge (1976) explains this variation based on the state's degree of involvement or repressiveness. In the case of nineteenth-century Germany, for instance, he shows that the more the state became repressive the more it got involved in the battle for industrial democracy between employers and workers, since unions were illegal. Consequently, because union activities were repressed, the labor movement became more radicalized. As a result, nonunion, highly legalistic, and institutionalized forms of participation emerged (e.g., legal works councils). On the contrary, in countries such as England, where the state was less repressive, and the suppression of unions was not that strong, the mode of labor representation at the plant level was based mostly on trade unions. In the United States, on the other hand, where the role of the state in industrial affairs has been limited, and trade union membership has been declining, initiatives for workers' participation schemes came mostly from managerial circles within the human relations tradition (Coleman, 1978).

The notion of strategic choice has also been proposed to explain the diversity of national participation schemes. Strategic choice implies the most rational solution chosen at the time decisions to create institutions are made (Sorge, 1976: 282). The diversified institutional solutions devised are explained on the basis of differing national circumstances at the time the innovation takes place. Sorge illustrates this process by discussing the introduction of the first legal works councils in three countries—Germany, France, and the Netherlands. In all these countries the state had followed a repressive strategy. At the time of their introduction legal works councils seemed the most rational alternative since employers were opposing participation, and unions were weak at the plant level.

The existing studies indicate that some of the major factors that have produced the existing participatory schemes are political and economic conditions, the nature and the extent of the participatory program introduced, the actors who introduced it, the work organization and the prevailing technology, the reaction and strength of sociopolitical forces in the society, such as unions, corporate leaders, management, and the state. Undoubtedly, major structural changes in our modern era, especially economic and technological changes, have facilitated the emergence of participatory structures. Such changes entail, among other things, more complex and interdependent industrial roles, and a more knowledgeable and educated labor force. Furthermore, changes in the value system (e.g., emphasis on intrinsic rather than instrumental values), in conjunction with the existence of a more demanding and unpredictable workforce, have been conducive to some institutionalization of worker participatory forms.

COMPARATIVE LOGIC AND DIFFICULTIES

This book covers a wide spectrum of participatory schemes. To date, comparative studies that explain the diversity of workers' participation arrangements have been limited in two respects: Either they cover a limited number of countries to test a specific set of hypothesis or assumptions, or when a larger number of countries are considered, either a descriptive account of the various participative mechanisms is presented (ILO, 1981) or very specific hypotheses are empirically tested (Stephens and Stephens, 1982). Yet no study has been undertaken to examine the issue in terms of the broad comparative analysis employed here. Most of the existing studies treat workers' participation as just another aspect of human relations management and thus ignore the larger political, economic, cultural, technological, and international factors that influence the distribution of power within the workplace. This book differs from others in that it studies a large number of countries and analyzes their participation schemes in much detail.

Another unique feature of this book is that it attempts to determine the effects of those broad societal factors on the origins and development of workers' participation schemes. The book employs a historical comparative approach in developing its broad analytical framework, by drawing on the insights and assumptions of the discussed models, theories, and studies. The goal is twofold: (1) to establish the common factors that influence the development of the various participation schemes in the countries under consideration; and (2) to identify the historically unique circumstances responsible for the diverse nature of the existing participation schemes. At the end some broad explanatory propositions are discussed, which hopefully will expand our knowledge and understanding of the diversity of participation schemes.

Employing a comparative historical approach for a study of this scope poses a number of difficulties and limitations. Many variables and complex factors have to be taken into consideration. Worker participation is a multilevel reality that has to be understood over different time periods and across many different national contexts. Therefore, a direct, detailed country-to-country comparison would have been extremely difficult and time consuming, if not impossible. Furthermore, perfectly controlled comparisons were not realistically feasible, since "societies can not be broken apart at will into historically manipulable variables: and history rarely, if ever, provides exactly the cases needed for controlled comparisons" (Skocpol and Somers, 1980: 193–194). Instead, in order to achieve some kind of control, we considered each country's industrial relations system and the way it had evolved over time with regard to economic, technological, political, and cultural changes, as well as international influences. The purpose was to determine the specific ways in which such developments had impacted workers' participation schemes. The ultimate goal was to come up with some broad assumptions that would explain the diversity of participation arrangements across nations. Since it would have been extremely difficult to establish the validity of the formulated propositions and assumptions, the emphasis was placed on making those propositions as suggestive and explanatory as possible.

As Melvin L. Kohn (1989: 93), an authority on cross-national research, has indicated, such research not only enhances our knowledge, but also extends our power of interpretation. Obviously, by studying one country any conclusions are limited by the political, economic, cultural, and historical context of that particular country. Cross-national comparisons are more powerful in that they can provide us with new ideas and insights to interpret variations in the existing empirical reality. The origins and development of workers' participation schemes in one country are usually analyzed independent of developments in other countries. It is generally assumed that the compared units are independent of each other. As pointed out above, such an assumption is not necessarily correct. All the countries examined here operate within a world system, which affects them on an individual basis but also ties them to each other. Specific historical circumstances have prompted the development of workers' participation schemes in a number of countries, but the development of schemes in one country is not always independent of the emergence of schemes in another.

Such a potential impact needs to be explored and studied, and a comparative analysis is suitable for such an inquiry. The Yugoslav self-management system, for instance, has been studied extensively, and some of its elements have been considered and in some ways applied in other countries. Similarly, because of increased worldwide competition, lower economic growth, and technological developments, some American companies were forced to study and adopt some Japanese management practices, as Japan had done in the past.

The historical comparative method employed here necessitated the use of secondary data. However, the use of secondary data created some problems, as data are fragmented and not uniformly available for all countries. Special attention was also required to filter out the researchers' value judgments and interpretations by examining as many studies as possible on issues that seemed controversial. Another limitation encountered was the lack of extensive comparative studies on worker participation schemes to guide this research. Nonetheless, some very insightful comparative studies do exist, and their assumptions and suggestions have been taken into account in this book. For instance, Stephens and Stephens' 1982 study has been very helpful here. Briefly, they theorized that variations of workers' control mechanisms are due primarily to the different organizational and political strengths of organized labor. They tested their hypothesis first by examining in detail the determinants and effects of workers' participation in three countries (France, Germany, and Sweden), and second by briefly examining the development of workers' participation in other major European countries.

It will be shown here that the political strength and mobilizing activity of organized labor significantly affect outcomes of workers' participation schemes. Schregle's study (1978) compares the various mechanisms through which workers gain control, while Sorge (1976) explains why those mechanisms tend to differ from one country to another. Similar problems and questions are explored in this book, though on a larger scale. Cole and Walder (1984), by comparing participation schemes in the United States, Japan, Sweden, and China, explain why movements to introduce participation schemes have succeeded in some countries and not in others. Because of the ambivalence of the term *success*, we used their insightful analysis to explore, not whether schemes in various countries were successful, but why they were different. Finally, numerous references are made here to the pioneering effort of the Industrial Democracy in Europe (IDE) International Research Group which, among other issues, has examined the association between prescribed (*de jure*) and actual (*de facto*) participation and its economic, social, and psychological impact in twelve European countries.

WHAT DOES PARTICIPATION MEAN?

For a number of years the issue of worker participation has preoccupied intellectuals, social scientists, and economists. It has also become a major practical issue in the agenda of politicians, industrial relations specialists, and management, as well as workers and their representatives. Therefore, in writing about the topic we have to sort out the variety of meanings that have been attached to terms such as *worker participation, worker control, self-management,* and *industrial democracy*. Such terms take on different meanings depending on historical periods, traditions, ideological positions, who uses them, and to what ends. Clegg (1960), for instance, believes that the major precondition for true democracy is the existence of opposition, which in industry is channeled through trade unions. For some, participation implies workers' rights in financial matters. For others, it means having an input in decision-making processes either directly or indirectly. For some Marxists, workers' control implies extensive worker power rather than just simple participation. For Lenin and the Bolsheviks, however, worker control simply meant supervision over production and not decision making.

As Steve Fraser shows, the concept of worker control took on different meanings in the post–World War I period depending on the specific context in which it emerged. It meant the reassertion of craft prerogatives in conservative periods and democratic mass management of certain industries under revolutionary circumstances. Similarly, the meaning of industrial democracy varied ''according to the social grammar into which it was incorporated'' (Fraser, 1983b: 174). For militant shop stewards, for example, industrial democracy meant management of the shopfloor by rank and file. Unions, on the other hand, having been part of the power structure during the war, saw industrial democracy as a means by which corporations or whole industries could be managed by representatives of unions, management, and the public. Management, being seriously concerned about the widespread democratic enthusiasm of the period, attempted to validate its position on the shopfloor by initiating mock ''employee representation'' plans. Those plans were perceived as yet another form of industrial democracy (Fraser, 1983b: 173–174).

Robert Cole also shows how the difference in language used to describe small-group participation in the three countries he studied is not a random phenomenon. Instead, according to Cole, it reveals a great deal about industrial actors and their objectives in initiating the reforms. In Japan, for instance, where management has been in charge of the small-group reforms, the emphasis has been on decentralization of responsibility rather than on industrial democracy or even workers' participation. In Sweden, on the other hand, the focus has been on industrial democracy. According to Cole, this indicates on the one hand that management did not have total control over workplace reforms and, on the other, given the highly centralized nature of the collective bargaining system, that the proponents of small-group activities had some chances in successfully pursuing their goals. In contrast, in the United States, the focus has been mostly on employee involvement and participation instead of the rather ambitious concept of industrial democracy. The unions' strong presence on the shopfloor in the United States preempted the need for industrial democracy at that level (Cole, 1987: 41). Finally, Pateman (1970: 68) makes the distinction between pseudo-participation, which refers to the techniques management uses to persuade employees to accept decisions management has already made, and full participation, that is, ''a process where each individual member of a decision-making body has equal power to determine the outcome of decisions'' (Pateman, 1970: 71).

This is not the place to review all possible uses of such terms. The purpose is to look at the various ways worker participation manifests itself in a number of different countries, and thus the term *worker participation* will be used interchangeably with the above-mentioned terms to indicate how workers might influence the decision-making processes, and thus influence the economic, organizational, and social situation of the enterprises they work for. Any form of worker participation implies the wresting of some prerogatives from management or capital by the workers; therefore, it can have an impact on the distribution and exercise of power between labor and capital. Worker participation includes not only direct but also indirect ways in which workers might influence the decision-making process. Worker participation is a political issue and as such is involved in the struggle for power and control in the workplace and the overall society. This means that some participation schemes might be developed to enhance managerial goals while giving the illusion that workers participate and exercise some kind of power. In some participative schemes, however, workers can exercise power and influence decisions that affect their working lives. Genuine worker participation entails power redistribution not only at the enterprise, but also the societal level to involve workers in the decision-making process, to extend their citizenship rights in the workplace and thereby enhance their power. Worker participation implies respectability of workers' rights, it permits workers to affect outcomes in an equitable way and to expand their power and develop their potential, abilities, and skills. Workers are entitled to these rights and have demanded them throughout this century, not because of capital ownership, but because of mere labor input in the production process.

This conceptualization has long raised fundamental opposition for ideological and practical considerations. Taylorist methods of work organization have advocated scientific measurement, routinization, standardization, and managerial control over the production process on the basis of two requirements that workers arguably lack: (1) capital to invest, and (2) time and skills to master the art of management and thus be more productive and efficient. But Taylorist methods of work organization have been challenged not only in theory but also in practice. Worker participation and self-management schemes in both capitalist and centrally planned societies are living proof of that assertion. This does not necessarily mean that issues of managerial control, efficiency, and workplace democratization have been resolved or that they are easy to resolve.

Any form of workplace democracy is clearly embedded in both the power structure at the enterprise level and at the larger societal level. As the interplay of that power at the micro- and macro-levels is interwoven with issues of technology, efficiency, skills, cultural approaches, and legislative measures, it results in the variety of participation schemes found in the countries under consideration. Consequently, participation schemes can be established at the various levels of the enterprise (e.g., the corporate, plant and department, and shopfloor levels) and they can range from simple disclosure of information, to joint consultation, joint codetermination, to worker self-management and control. With the exception of collective bargaining and the cooperative practices, though references will occasionally be made to both, the focus here is mostly on worker participation as a process by which workers directly or indirectly have the power to influence management decision making at various levels of the industrial production. The definition of participation is deliberately broad to capture the dynamic, variable, and multidimensional reality of workplace democratization, and to allow the incorporation of factors that determine the outcome of participation schemes found in each country.

GUIDING HYPOTHESES OF THE STUDY

Having clarified the term *worker participation* as used here, we will briefly discuss some of the major assumptions that guide this study. First, the labor market conditions that prevail in a given country are perceived to affect the introduction and development of worker participation schemes in that country. Specifically, the greater the demand for labor, the greater the possibility that participative reforms will be considered as one possible solution to adversities and problems. The underlying assumption is that labor power increases, while capital finds itself in a more conciliatory position as the labor market becomes tight because of war, crisis, or economic growth.

Although such an assumption can explain some of the origins of participative reforms, certainly it does not explain why workers' participation has been developed and supported in periods of recession. This phenomenon can be understood only if we consider some other contributing factors. For instance, we have to establish the initiators of participative reforms and determine their goals. Worker participation is a political issue, and the forms it takes reflect and influence the power distribution within the workplace and the industrial sector of a given country. Worker participation schemes with limited worker power have sometimes been introduced by management as a way to deal with adverse economic problems, such as slow growth and low labor productivity. In other words, participation has been used as a way to combat worker alienation and thus increase productivity.

Since advanced industrial countries have to face the hardships of competitive markets, we would presume that participative schemes are perceived as a productivity strategy only in those countries. However, since the mid-1960s market considerations have played a considerable role in state socialist countries and to a certain extent explain the proliferation of worker participation schemes there as well. Participatory schemes became part of economic reforms in state socialist countries as these countries began to try to correct the inefficiencies of their overcentralized system and structural labor shortages by decentralizing economic activities (Sabel and Stark, 1982).

The second assumption of this study relates to the increasing levels of education and rising expectations among workers both in market- and centrally planned societies since World War II, especially since the 1960s. As younger and better educated people join the ranks of the workforce, they expect their work to be interesting, meaningful, and fulfilling of individual and citizenship rights (Kanter, 1978). Workers in both types of systems have become increasingly dissatisfied with monotonous, rigid, tedious work tasks associated with the extreme division of labor and authoritative work structures. Job dissatisfaction, high turnover, absenteeism, and strikes, mostly in European countries, Japan, and the United States, and to some extent in state socialist countries, are manifestations of this trend. The more educated people become, and as they first satisfy their basic needs, the more they pursue self-fulfillment and self-realization needs (Maslow, 1954). Participation, self-expression, and responsibility at work are some basic ways to fulfill those needs. In this book, it will be further argued that worker participation can become a learning experience, enhancing workers' knowledge and power and thus, under certain circumstances (e.g., legislative support, strong labor organizations) escalating workers' expectations and promoting further demands for input and power. How these demands are shaped to produce the diversified participatory forms depends on the prevailing conditions in each country.

A third assumption is associated with certain technological developments and economic changes that prompted the need to modify the power dynamic and authority structures within the workplace toward a more flexible and participatory industrial relations system. Piore and Sabel (1984) have extensively discussed the late twentieth century—the "second industrial divide" as they call it—during which the craft model with participatory demands has reemerged. The craft model, together with the demand for flexible specialization, has been revived in a number of industries from specialty steel production and precision machine tools, to customized textiles, owing to the shifts in the international economy and the saturation of markets for mass-produced goods in the industrial countries. The growing demand for technologically complex, rapidly changing, and specialized production processes also requires more educated, skillful, and autonomous employees; workplaces where flexibility and delegation of authority prevail; and thereby favorable circumstances for participatory demands to develop (Piore, 1985; Piore and Sabel, 1984). It is for reasons inherent to industrial structures and the changing nature of technologies and markets that worker participation schemes might be considered.

A fourth assumption takes into consideration the role of organized labor, and the role of the state, to explain why participatory schemes and practices might develop. Both factors are very influential in terms of the introduction of participative reforms as well as in terms of sustaining workers' gains, enhancing participatory demands, and promoting workers' interests. Employers, management, and/or the state, faced with a variety of economic, labor, or political challenges, might introduce participation schemes. It is interesting to note, however, that countries with roughly the same economic and political bases have established completely different patterns of industrial democracy. The German system of codetermination, for instance, does not have many similarities with the American or Japanese systems of workers' participation. Moreover, the workers' councils developed in Czechoslovakia in 1968 have few similarities with participation practices in Hungary or the Soviet Union. The specific challenges and circumstances at the time participative schemes were introduced in these countries might explain some of the existing differences.

It can also be argued that the types of workers' participation schemes developed, the actual power transferred to workers, and their overall prospects depend primarily on the labor movement's support and its ability to pursue its goals regarding workers' participation schemes. Labor organization strength, which further entails labor bargaining strength, degree of mobilizing activity, and degree of unity and political leverage, are some of the factors that affect the diversity of workers' participation schemes. The stronger and more supportive of workers' participation the labor movement is (under favorable economic conditions), the greater the possibility that certain participation structures will emerge that will further enhance workers' power and interests. Because considerable amounts of freedom and democracy prevail in the advanced industrial countries, it is assumed that such a proposition holds true for those countries.

In centralized planned economies, on the other hand, the state's powerful interventionist role stifles workers' initiative and represses their autonomy. It also severely constrains the freedom of trade unions and the potentially supportive role they could play in advancing participative goals. In both systems, the state can support participatory goals through legislative intervention, policies, and allocation of resources. The strength of the labor movement and its ideological commitment to such goals are crucial determinants of the participatory outcomes. In some capitalist industrialized countries, the unions' initial suspicion of participatory innovations and efforts seems to fade away. In planned economies, as Czechoslovakia in the 1960s and Poland in the 1980s demonstrate, unions can play a decisive role in supporting participative reforms. In both countries participation has been perceived as a means to legitimize their existence and activities and to further their goals.

To a certain extent values, cultural traditions, and the ideological position of the industrial actors toward participation reforms are important factors in determining the origins, development, and prospects of participatory schemes. As discussed before, the Yugoslav system of self-management was supported by ideologies proclaiming the withering away of the state to justify the official position against the bureaucratic forms of socialism during the break with the Soviet Union. Self-management was also promoted because of the unique cultural aspects and experiences of Yugoslav society.

Managerial ideologies largely oppose any expansion of workers' participation that may challenge their prerogatives. The position is justified on the grounds that managerial expertise and proficiency are the most crucial factors for the efficient and profitable operation of the enterprise. However, historical evidence has shown that, under certain circumstances, management can support worker participation, especially when its interests are not threatened. Japan is a case in point here. Because of adverse economic and labor market conditions, and in the name of productivity and profit, management may sometimes be obliged to consider workers' participation. Because of adverse economic conditions, management in the United States, for instance, considered workers' participation more in the 1980s than it had in the previous decade. The case of Sweden during the 1960s also illustrates the point. In response to the tight labor market conditions that prevailed at the time, management initiated a number of experiments to reform the workplace.

Finally, although values and ideologies might affect worker participation schemes, they do not operate in a vacuum. Instead, they reflect and are governed by power relations of the main industrial actors within the social, political, and economic context of each country. The balance of power among the industrial actors and its relation to worker participation are relevant to all country groups examined in this study. However, as the subsequent chapters will show, the state's power and intervention in industrial relations is particularly important within the context of state socialist countries. In these countries worker participation is an important element of economic reform designed to decentralize the economy and introduce market mechanisms. Since economic and political structures in these systems are closely associated, however, economic reforms tend to spill over to political demands. This usually means the demise of participation schemes in cases of outright confrontation with a nonsupportive regime or with the Soviet Union.

The IDE (1981a) International Research Group found that the level of *de facto* participation is associated with the level of *de jure* participation, which suggests that formal laws or collective bargaining agreements play an important role in the development of participation. We suggest that legally prescribed recipes can transfer real power to workers only when other conditions, such as genuine political interest and a powerful labor movement, exist.

NOTES

1. See Greenberg (1986: 13–23); Poole (1982: 182); Sirianni (1987b: 4–5).
2. Indeed, class conflict is one of the key elements in Edwards' analysis. Writes Edwards (1979: 18): "Systems of control have undergone drastic changes in response to changes in the firm's size, operations, and environment and in the workers' success in imposing their own goals at the workplace. The new forms did not emerge as sharp, discrete discontinuities in historical evolution, but neither were they simply points in a smooth and inevitable evolution; rather, each transformation occurred as a resolution of intensifying conflict and contradiction in the firm's operation."
3. Braverman's argument was very provocative, since, first, it accurately described the deskilling processes that took place in a number of occupations, and second, it introduced questions of power and control in the labor process in ways that had not been considered before. But Braverman's thesis also raised important questions and criticisms. Among the major criticisms were that Braverman's thesis ignores workers' struggles and resistance; it overestimates management's power and willingness to control; it ignores the conflicting and different interests of the working class; it exaggerates the extent of

the deskilling trend and thereby underestimates the market and technological changes that demand the upgrading of workers' skills, their increased commitment and responsibility, as well as their involvement in the decision-making process regarding aspects of their working lives. For more details see Brecher (1978, 10: 1–23); Edwards (1979); Hill (1981); Hirschhorn (1984); Sabel (1982); and Stark (1980: 89–130).

4. See Poole (1981a: 23–53; 1982: 190–195) where he describes the assumptions but also contrasts the cyclical or favorable conjunctures school with the evolutionary school.

I

PARTICIPATIVE REFORMS IN MARKET-ORIENTED SOCIETIES

2

The Scandinavian Model of Workers' Participation

THE CASE OF SWEDEN

Demands for industrial democracy as it is known today were first brought up in Sweden, as in the rest of Scandinavia and Europe in the period following World War I.[1] The revolutionary climate of that time allowed the revolutionary wing of the labor movement to raise demands regarding the formation of workers' councils. The workers' councils were to assume an instrumental role in the process of socializing the means of production. During the same period the Social Democratic party (SAP) also raised demands for industrial democracy, as it did again in the post–World War II years (Åsard, 1986; Schiller, 1977). Although labor's position was strong at the time, the Social Democrats were only a minority government in 1920 (Hancock, 1978: 6); therefore, the labor movement was not in a position to enforce its demands. Furthermore, although employers were interested in labor-management cooperation as a means of increasing labor productivity, they were not ready or willing to give up some of their basic prerogatives. Employers would only agree to the advisory power of the councils. Similarly, although the proposals discussed by government committees were influenced by British Guild Socialist ideals,[2] in reality their goal was to buy time and thus ward off genuine revolutionary goals (Schiller, 1977: 65).[3]

By 1920, the revolutionary tide had subsided considerably, and the issue of workers' participation did not surface again until 1946. The labor movement was in a strong bargaining position because of the labor shortage and increased labor demand, and this helped bring back to light the issue of workers' councils. Union membership had increased from 36 percent in 1940 to 44 percent in 1945 (Stephens, 1980: 57). In 1946, the union federations for blue-collar (LO) and white-collar workers (TCO), and the Swedish Employers' Association (SAF), signed the national Works Council Agreement. As a result of that agreement, workers' councils were established.

The councils, like those in West Germany, had mostly consultative powers (Stephens, 1980). They were consulted, and they were given information on technical and financial matters, as well as overall economic issues. Their power was limited, however, and only management could make the final decisions, since it had the right to withhold information which it perceived as harmful for business. Moreover, their members were not allowed to share information disclosed to them by their fellow employees (Bellace and Gospel, 1983: 67). Workers' councils had limited powers because at that time the labor movement was not particularly interested in the issue of workers' participation. Instead, its goal was to secure employment, improve wages and working conditions, and ensure that the Social Democrats remained in power. It was believed that, by instituting broad national policies, economic growth, full employment, redistribution of wealth through the welfare state, and thus more public control over the economy would follow. The pursuit of those goals was not without negative consequences. As will be explained in more detail later, by the 1960s the labor movement and the Social Democrats had to face some serious problems including high labor turnover, absenteeism, and wildcat strikes. During that period, both the LO and the Social Democrats seriously considered the issue of worker participation (Stephens, 1980: 57–58).

Labor-Capital Cooperation up to the Early 1970s

Sweden, more than any other country in the world, best exemplifies two different approaches in reorganizing work and redistributing power at the workplace. The first relates to the reorganization of shopfloor production and organization by allowing workers to engage in autonomous, small-group activities. The second relies mostly on legislation to increase workers' decision-making power, and it will be discussed later on. The first approach is best exemplified in the emergence of the new work structures and the introduction of experiments that took place during the late 1960s. In the Saab-Scania plant, for instance, assembly lines were abolished, and semiautonomous groups were formed. Within those work structures workers coordinated, rotated, and shared a variety of work tasks. Changes like these exemplify the typical aspects of work reorganization projects that took place during that period (Cole, 1985: 565; Poole, 1978: 67).[4]

Let us briefly consider the conditions that facilitated those changes. Labor market conditions in the mid- to late 1960s were extremely tight. As severe labor shortages began to cause serious production problems, employers became interested in innovating work organization and production structures. However, increasing levels of education and the rising expectations that had accompanied a long period of increasing economic growth and affluence made the task of recruiting workers for routine, monotonous, standardized jobs extremely difficult. As young people who had never felt poverty began to understand and value quality of life issues, including work issues, employers had a difficult time attracting them to these repetitious, unpleasant jobs. High turnover and absenteeism rates, as well as an increasing number of strikes, were signs of a workforce that was growing increasingly dissatisfied and alienated (Cole, 1985: 567; Foy and Gadon, 1976; 1974: 269; IDE, 1981b: 54; Jenkins, 1973: 269; Martin, 1977: 66).[5]

Companies considered two options in an effort to cope with these problems: namely, hiring women and recruiting higher numbers of migrant workers. Both alternatives proved to be insufficient and problematic.[6] The next best strategy considered and eventually adopted was reorganizing production, creating new work structures, enriching jobs, and rotating tasks (Cole, 1987). These changes didn't happen in a vacuum: Changes in neighboring Norway during that time provided a framework for restructuring work in Sweden. By the time Sweden was considering workplace reforms, Norway had already begun experiments, drawing on the research of the Tavistock Institute in England. The creation of autonomous groups was under way. Meanwhile, the Norwegian scholar Thorsrud became very instrumental in diffusing ideas related to work restructuring in Sweden (Cole, 1985: 573; Poole, 1978: 66).[7] As a result, a substantial number of highly publicized experiments that complied with the humanization of work principles began to emerge. The goal was to free workers from rigid organizational structures and to make them more knowledgeable, competent, and autonomous.

It was hoped that those changes would help to enhance workers' quality of work life (QWL), reduce high levels of absenteeism and turnover, and therefore increase productivity. Employers, supporting these productivity goals, soon espoused the Tavistock ideas. Through their powerful confederation, the SAF, employers supported small-group activities, training programs, as well as research projects on participatory issues. The Personnel Administration Council, another branch of SAF, also helped in that direction by supervising projects and by linking academic research to the real problems the business world was facing (Cole, 1985).

Unions also played a very active role in efforts to democratize the workplace. As a first step in 1966, and later in 1968, the 1946 Works Councils Agreement was revised. Unions felt a pressing need to revise the agreement since the information conveyed to them through the councils was irrelevant, or it was brought to their attention too late to be effectively used for any kind of action. The 1966 revision of the Works Council Agreement provided that councils had to be informed well in advance of any planned changes. Yet, any piece of information was disclosed as a part of the consultation process, and the employer was the one who reserved the right to make the final decision. Also, in 1966, the two major labor confederations, the LO and the TCO, in cooperation with the SAF, established a Development Council for Cooperation Questions to facilitate labor-management cooperation and to carry out experiments. The council set up a special research group called URAF whose goal was to conduct research, and to initiate and supervise projects and experiments aimed at restructuring work and authority relationships (Cole, 1987; Jenkins, 1973).

Traditionally, unions in Sweden were either hostile or negative to the idea of direct workers' participation. Unlike American unions, whose hostility toward participation schemes is explained by their interest in protecting existing job definitions, the stance of Swedish unions can be explained by their strong commitment to centralized national bargaining. Any increase in decision-making rights among small groups was perceived as threatening to this centralized bargaining system (Cole, 1987: 54). Why, then, did the union position shift in the mid-1960s and early 1970s? To understand this change, we have to explore the unions' structure and organization, their strength, goals, and role within the industrial relations system, as well as the conditions and problems that had shaped their overall orientation to that date.

Unions are exceptionally strong in Sweden. Sweden has the highest unionization rate of any industrialized society. About 95 percent of the blue-collar and 75 percent of the white-collar workers are members of the LO and TCO, respectively, the two major national confederations. Unions are centrally organized, which enables them to effectively mobilize their membership. Their capacity to mobilize it is reinforced by the fact that union membership is concentrated in a few unions organized mostly along industrial and sectoral lines, although divisions among unions on the basis of broad occupational categories do exist. Historically, then, unions in Sweden have pursued goals of industrial democracy through national bargaining with the employers' confederation SAF, which is also highly centralized (Harrison, 1976: 71; IDE, 1981b: 42; Lind, 1979: 21; Martin, 1987: 96–97; Stephens, 1980: 55).

As the 1906 agreement, the so-called December Compromise, illustrates, however, not all issues affecting labor-capital relations have always been subject to negotiation. In exchange for the union's right to organize,[8] the famous Paragraph 32 of that agreement legally confirmed the employer's right to manage. This prerogative remained effective even after the 1936 Act on the Right of Association and Negotiation, which legally established the workers' right to belong to unions and required employers to negotiate with them (IDE, 1981b: 46; Martin, 1977: 60). All matters, with the exception of wage issues and employment conditions, were excluded from bargaining and were subject to employer discretion. The famous 1938 Basic Agreement[9] regulated somewhat the dismissal power of employers, and the various Works Councils' agreements from 1946 to 1968 laid down specific guidelines for joint consultation by forcing employers to inform and consult the unions before their final decisions (IDE, 1981b). Despite all these changes, basic managerial prerogatives, such as personnel policy and work organization, remained intact and outside the scope of collective bargaining. Furthermore, although economic and technological changes could be discussed, employers were not obliged to negotiate with unions in regard to those changes. In cases of disagreement and conflict, and unless the labor court had ruled otherwise, employers reserved the right to interpret negotiated agreements, including the Works Council Agreement (IDE, 1981b; Martin, 1977).[10]

A conscious labor movement policy pursued up to the late 1960s was to some degree responsible for these developments. Unions strove to accomplish two important goals: (1) to improve the working and economic conditions of the working class through social and economic policies, and (2) to ensure that the Social Democratic party remained in power as a prerequisite of a more even distribution of wealth. Both the LO and the Social Democrats are closely associated, ideologically and organizationally, and they are strongly committed to the development of an economically strong and politically democratic and egalitarian society. The overall strategy they pursued up to the late 1960s entailed an economic activity that was largely shaped by government policies in regard to private and public consumption and income distribution. Although the actual production was left in the hands of capitalist firms, the government's task was to maintain full employment and to use budgetary resources, not only to support the private sector, but also to finance public needs such as education, health, and housing. Through progressive taxation and transfers, the government was to maintain economic security and reduce inequality among its citizenry. For their part, unions were to implement a wage policy that would enable workers to improve or at least maintain their share of the growing national income, to reduce wage differences among workers (e.g., workers would get the same pay for the same job regardless of the profitability of individual firms or industries), and to avoid the interunion wage rivalry that could produce inflation. Thus, the rationalization measures pursued up to the late 1960s were designed to facilitate the growth of the more productive companies and industries. This meant that less productive companies closed down and that unemployment, at least at the early stages, became unavoidable.

At the same time, labor market policies were introduced to alleviate the unemployment impact by helping workers to get new jobs in the more productive companies. In summary, from the early 1930s to the late 1960s, unions accepted and promoted technological and structural changes (e.g., measures to shift labor and capital to more efficient and profitable activities) to rationalize the Swedish industry. The assumption was that these changes could promote economic growth and increase the productivity, efficiency, and competitiveness of Swedish industry. Under those circumstances, increased economic growth became the basis of the union wage policies to ensure that workers got their fair share of benefits. The labor market policies of the Social Democrats ensured that workers would not be alone in bearing the consequences of those changes (IDE, 1981b: 54; Jenkins, 1973: 260; Martin, 1977: 62–63, 1979: 9).

This scenario presupposed, and in actuality reflected, a collaborative relationship between capital and labor in which labor enjoyed the benefits of a strong welfare state,[11] while management controlled the running of the enterprise, the introduction of changes, and the adoption of new technology, prerogatives that remained mostly unchallenged until the early 1970s (Mydral, 1981). Under those circumstances the unions' obligation was to defend workers' interests. Participating in decisions that would increase enterprise efficiency could jeopardize such a fundamental union responsibility. Unions would have to face the classic dilemma of dual loyalty running the risk of having their position undermined and their capacity to successfully represent workers' interests seriously eroded. Consequently, labor-capital relations remained unchanged and largely unquestioned until the late 1960s. Joint-consultation schemes were the only preferable forms of workers' participation within the enterprise.[12]

The Changing Labor Relations of the 1970s

The structural changes introduced and the rationalization strategies adopted were indeed successful in increasing the country's economic growth, but not without negative consequences. High turnover and absenteeism rates, recruiting difficulties, as well as growing signs of erosion of rank-and-file loyalty to unions, were all symptoms of bad work conditions and unsatisfactory labor relations. The rationalization of production intensified the pace of work, increased health and safety risks, reinforced the social isolation of workers, and overall diminished worker influence and satisfaction and/or undermined their ability to find and keep a job. The LO leadership was forced to recognize the importance of QWL, not only as a way of supplementing satisfactory wage rewards, but also accommodating the alienated and dissatisfied rank and file (Cole, 1985: 578; IDE, 1981b: 54; Martin, 1979: 11; Stephens, 1980: 49).[13]

SAF supported the work reorganization projects mainly for productivity reasons. Another important consideration was that any erosion of rank-and-file loyalty to unions would threaten to undermine the industrial peace and hurt managerial interests as well. Within the context of joint consultation, SAF also agreed in the 1966 revision of the Works Council Agreement to give equal weight to occupational satisfaction as to the goal of productivity. This period witnessed the proliferation of work reorganization projects and experiments and the increased collaboration between local union officials and management. Such collaboration seemed imperative for both management and unions. Although reluctant to give any of its authority up, management had recognized, to some extent, the need to alter the ways it used authority within the workplace. For their part, the unions, having to face the challenge of the wildcat strikes, as well as workers' participation in the reorganization projects under managerial influence, felt compelled to take part in them. Their influence was limited, however, given the joint-consultation nature of those projects. During that time, a new position began to take shape: If unions were to survive, the scope of the collective bargaining had to expand to include nonwage issues that were exclusively under managerial control (Martin, 1977: 68–69).

Until the early 1970s, all achievements in the area of workers' participation were the result of voluntary or negotiated agreements. Employers' commitment to democratizing the firm was limited, going as far as supporting small-group activities at the workplace level. As the LO sought to expand workers' participation beyond the shopfloor level and called for joint determination at all levels of decision making within the firm, the cooperative relationship soon felt the strain. Since the advocated changes by the LO seriously threatened the basic managerial right of decision making, management did not support those goals. At that point LO created a commission to examine the question of industrial democracy. In its annual Congress in September 1971, it proposed a series of reforms that differed considerably from its previous policies. In the policy statement on industrial democracy, LO called for joint determination instead of joint consultation (Albrecht and Deutch, 1983; Cole, 1987; IDE, 1981b; Martin, 1977).

Access to power at the national level through the SAP to shape the general economic conditions was no longer considered sufficient. The personnel policies introduced (e.g., mostly retraining and relocation assistance) seemed to be inadequate to compensate workers' needs, and the overall impact of technological and structural changes proved to affect workers much more adversely than had been anticipated. If unions were to maintain their legitimacy by claiming to defend their members' interests, workers' source of stress and dissatisfaction had to be eliminated, and workers' physical and psychological needs had to be taken into account. Economic direction and technological change could no longer be left exclusively in the hands of the managerial authority. The circumstances of that period required that unions move beyond cooperation and participation in joint-consultation and work-restructuring projects. They had to defend workers' interests by exercising power over economic, technological, and related questions at all levels of the company.

Given that employers strongly opposed such an idea, and given that previous efforts by unions to gain some power over personnel and work organization decisions through negotiation had failed,[14] it became apparent that the only effective way unions could gain a voice in those matters and expand the scope of collective bargaining would be not just through negotiation, but mostly through legislation (Martin, 1977, 1979). Since both the TCO and the SAP supported the LO's position, the LO was able to pass the Law on Joint Determination. This change in the union position functioned as a barrier to the further expansion and diffusion of restructuring projects. Labor-management relations had become increasingly conflictive, and the shopfloor had become just one of the levels through which the labor movement sought to expand worker and union influence (Cole, 1987: 56). Before we discuss the Law on Codetermination in Work and the other legislative acts introduced to expand worker and union power, let us first consider in more detail the factors that contributed to LO's escalation of demands and its considerable shift of policies.

First, in late 1969 the well-paid miners at the state-owned LKAB iron mine started a long and illegal strike protesting the incompatibility and unresponsiveness of state and union officials, as well as poor working conditions and wage inequality. In addition, during 1970 and 1971 a number of other wildcat strikes broke out in major industries of central Sweden. These were strong indicators that union confidence in their leaders was declining, that the national labor associations were losing touch with the rank and file's demands, and that their overall legitimacy was seriously eroding. The increasing wave of wildcat strikes, a phenomenon foreign to Swedish society, as well as high turnover and absenteeism rates, soon conveyed the message to the LO and SAP leaderships that something had to be done about nonwage issues in order to ensure their members' loyalty and support.

Second, the strikes helped to initiate a national debate regarding the meaning of work, the role of the unions, their centralized nature, and the prospects of restructuring authority relationships and work organization structures. Increasingly, workers and their local unions became very critical of the centralization of authority of the national labor confederations. Undoubtedly, the centralized nature of the Swedish labor movement allowed unions to be very powerful and effective at the national level in controlling employment levels and pursuing solidaristic wage policies. At the same time, it left little room for local bargaining, since wage issues were settled at the national level. The rate of exploitation was steadily increasing as local employers were able to afford higher wages than those stipulated by law, and often made larger profits than those tolerated by public standards. Increased dissatisfaction among workers was inevitable. A new ideology began slowly to take shape. Given that unions were less powerful at the workplace than at the national level, something had to be done for nonwage issues, if unions were to retain their members' support. The emerging New Left ideology reinforced the public discourse on those issues by questioning the existing authority structures and by supporting citizen participation in industry and in all institutions.

Third, as mentioned above, the aim to increase economic growth through structural changes and technological innovations intensified the pace of work, dehumanized working conditions, and endangered worklife. Increasing turnover rates, absenteeism, and recruiting difficulties all pointed to one explanation: Workers had become dissatisfied.[15] Increasing numbers of workers had a hard time adapting to the new rationalization procedures, and the prospect of losing their jobs in case of further change became very real and stressful. Older and disabled workers, who had been displaced by change, had a particularly difficult time getting the newly created, more demanding jobs, despite retraining and relocation assistance programs. Undoubtedly, dissatisfaction among workers was growing to a point that LO and other unions began to document its existence and sources. What is difficult to determine is whether the growing dissatisfaction was the result of absolutely deteriorating and stressful working conditions or of people's decreasing tolerance for those conditions. Some suggest, for instance, that welfare state provisions and social security benefits had made people less tolerant and unwilling to accept working conditions that might in actuality have been no worse than those in the past.

Fourth, the increasing educational levels compounded the problem. For young, better educated people in particular, who had been brought up in less rigid schools and who had not experienced unemployment as the previous generations had, the prospect of boring, monotonous, dangerous jobs was not appealing (Åsard, 1986: 209; Cole, 1985: 577; IDE, 1981b: 51; Martin, 1977: 65, 66–67, 1979: 11; Stephens, 1980: 59).

Finally, all these ideological positions and concerns should be understood within the broader context of the rising awareness of existing social and economic inequalities not only within the country but also abroad. The anti-Vietnam War movement, the Paris revolt of 1968, and the rise of the critical ideology of the New Left had a strong impact on virtually every aspect of society. As community groups sprang up all over the country, as people started questioning authority relationships and the traditional distribution of power and wealth, and as demands to realize equality on the basis of not only distributive, but also participatory rights, began to be articulated, major institutions and established relations came under attack (Albrecht, 1980; IDE, 1981b; Martin, 1979). Within the sphere of industrial relations in particular, it became apparent that the subordinate position of workers in authoritarian control relations at the workplace had to be changed, that technological innovations and other changes had to be adapted to the workers' needs, and, therefore, workers and their representatives had to have more access to business information and greater power in managing the company's affairs. This implied that basic managerial prerogatives had to be curtailed.

The Legislative Approach to Participation

In 1971, LO under its umbrella policy of industrial democracy responded to the concerns of the period not merely for ideological reasons but for organiza-tional survival as well. It actively began to take measures to appeal to rank-and-file concerns in order to maintain its legitimacy. First, it demanded the reduction in managerial prerogatives, and second, it began to address ways the democ-ratization process of work could start, by supporting the expansion of works councils and by introducing legislation that would facilitate such a process. At that point the strength of the labor movement as a sociopolitical force proved very crucial. There had been union infighting over the priorities which the various suggested forms of participation would assume (Cole, 1987: 56), and there were signs of union erosion. Nonetheless, the labor movement was still strong and had the organizational capacity and resources to transform its ideological position into concrete legislation enactment that could reduce managerial prerogatives (Bouvin, 1977; Stephens and Stephens, 1982). Both the LO and TCO were unified on their position, and thus the issue of industrial democracy was gaining political momentum. Such a stance made it difficult for the SAP to resist a legislative solution. At the same time, it provided an opportunity to be exploited politically, since the party could claim its support for both blue- and white-collar interests, and thus expand its constituency (Martin, 1977, 1979).

The issue of industrial democracy enjoyed the support of the labor movement, the SAP, and, to a certain extent, nonsocialist parties.[16] Consequently, the 1970s witnessed a series of legislative acts that went far beyond the joint-consultation schemes and the reorganization plans based on sociotechnical planning, which management for the most part initiated and unions approved. Between 1972 and 1978, a series of legislative acts were introduced, including the Security of Employment and Promotion Acts (1974), the Act on the Status of the Shop Stewards (1974), the Worker Protection Act (1974), the Work Environment Act (1976), the Act on Employee Representation on Boards (provisional in 1972, definite in 1977), and, finally, the Law on Joint Determination (MBL) (1976) (Albrecht, 1981: 307; Albrecht and Deustch, 1983: 289; Åsard, 1986: 209–210; IDE, 1981b: 56–58; Lind, 1979: 23–27; Long, 1986: 376–377).

Through these legislative acts, the labor movement sought to establish industrial democracy at different levels by reorganizing the workplace and by reducing managerial authority over issues that decisively affected the work environment and working life (Albrecht, 1980). In 1972, the Swedish Work Environment Fund was established whose goal was to promote the improvement of the work environment by conducting research and distributing information on codetermination. The 1974 Act on the Union Officials' Status at the Workplace considerably strengthened the position of safety stewards and committees and expanded the scope of health and safety regulations to include all kinds of employment. Based on the provisions of the act, safety stewards were granted the power to stop work considered to be dangerous. The law further guaranteed the security of their jobs and salary while they were performing their duties and acquiring the necessary training during regular work hours. Moreover, for health and safety reasons, employers were obliged to provide stewards with all relevant information when planning to introduce any changes regarding new work methods, purchase of machinery, plant layout, and the like. Other acts restricted the right of employers to hire and fire, enhanced job security, and reinforced the position of union officials in the workplace (Comisso, 1980: 50; Long, 1986: 376; Martin, 1977: 51, 1979: 12–13).

The Employee Representation on Boards Act, first enacted in 1972,[17] required that all Swedish companies with at least 100 workers (except insurance companies and banks), grant their workers minority representation on their board of directors. Unions had to request the representation, and if more than four-fifths of the workers in a given company belonged to the same local union, that union reserved the right to appoint the two worker representatives and their two deputies, who could participate in the board meetings but could not vote. Otherwise, the workers' representatives were chosen by the two largest local unions. To avoid coaptation and the dilemma of double loyalty, worker representatives were not allowed to participate in deliberations regarding labor-management disputes or in negotiations that could lead to collective agreements.[18] The right of worker representation expanded in 1976 to cover firms with more than twenty-five employees as well as bank and insurance companies. The 1976 act more than quadrupled the number of companies eligible for board representation and made coverage possible for companies with less than twenty-five employees, given that the shareholders approved such representation (Bouvin, 1977: 134; IDE, 1981b: 50; ILO, 1981: 97–99; Long, 1986: 376; Stephens, 1980: 50, 60).

Worker representation on the board of directors would normally contradict the unions' classic adversarial role within the context of capitalist antagonistic labor-management relations. The Swedish unions were not an exception to that rule. Unions in Sweden had not particularly supported the idea of worker representation on the board of directors, fearing potential worker integration and worker coaptation. The right of minority board representation obtained did not necessarily reflect the labor movement's goal to move toward Germany's co-determination model. The labor movement's position had been consistent with its past practices—that is, exercise of influence mainly through collective bargaining. In the 1970s, the unions merely attempted to expand, through legislation, the scope of collective bargaining beyond pay and employment conditions (Martin, 1977). Board representation in Sweden, therefore, was never meant to be the appropriate means to effectively influence policy, and the union leadership was aware of its limitations.

An extensive survey and evaluation of the first results of board representation undertaken by the National Industrial Board in 1975 highlighted some of those limitations as well as some possibilities. For instance, the survey pointed out the different stages of decision making and the fact that board members could participate in one or several of these stages but with varying degrees of influence; that in some companies and on some matters participation meant merely receiving information while on others (e.g., changes in the production), decisions were made without consulting the board or that the board merely approved decisions that had been taken by management.

There were some positive signs as well that encouraged the National Industrial Board to conclude that in the majority of the companies the reform had produced encouraging results and that the board representation was a useful measure, along with other strategies, to facilitate democracy in work life. There were indications, for instance, that because of union participation the board meetings had become more lively and that the board participants had paid more attention to personnel problems. Although workers' representatives admitted that in many cases participation on the board was not real, they did acknowledge that their participation gave them access to interesting information (ILO, 1981: 97–99). This was what unions were basically aiming for all along. Board representation was perceived as one way to gain access to top-level information. Such information could be used at the bargaining table to influence decision making at the various levels of the company.

In 1975, the SAF signed an important collective agreement with LO and TCO. Under that agreement joint economic committees were established with three worker and three management representatives at the plant level, giving workers for the first time the right to extensive company information and the right to examine management financial matters. Under the same agreement unions also gained the right to hire their own economic adviser who was paid with company funds to check the company's books and accounts (Bellace and Gospel, 1983: 67; Foy and Gadon, 1976: 74; Garson, 1977: 15). The significance of that agreement lies in the fact that workers' representatives on the board of directors could obtain through those committees timely, accurate, and detailed information regarding company matters. One of the criticisms of board representation was that although workers' representatives had access to the same documentary information as shareholders, such information was often incomplete and delayed. Besides, in some cases, as in family business and particularly in subsidiaries of foreign companies, decisions were taken by management and not by the board of directors (ILO, 1981: 98). Unions were hoping to compensate for such drawbacks through economic committees and economic consultants. But the 1976 negotiations came to a halt, and the two parties canceled the agreement and awaited legislation. Unions at that point were optimistic and expected favorable legislation inasmuch as the Social Democrats were in power. The 1976 legislation act on employee participation in decision making proved them right.

The Joint Regulation of Working Life Act (also known as the Joint Determination Act or the Law on Codetermination in Work—MBL), enacted in June 1976, went into effect in January 1977. This important piece of legislation enlarged union power considerably by basically nullifying Paragraph 32 of SAF's rules and thus restricting managerial prerogatives considerably. The law was to apply to the whole Swedish labor market, including government and public services, with some exceptions including religious, scientific, trade union, political, and similar activities (Lind, 1979: 23–24). The law guaranteed unions the right to negotiate collective agreements for codetermination in a whole range of issues regarding company management, labor-management relations, and the work environment, on which matters management used to have unilateral decision-making powers.[19] Specifically, matters such as hiring, firing, work organization, and management of the firm, once considered under Paragraph 32, managerial prerogatives, in 1977 fell within the scope of collective bargaining. An employee or local union member could take up any of those issues for negotiation with the local employer. In case negotiations failed, workers could strike. By giving the union the right to use conflict tactics, the legislators were attempting to make employers more interested in codetermination agreements. The assumption was that employers would give up some of their prerogatives rather than suffer the costly consequences of a strike (Albrecht, 1980; Bouvin, 1977; IDE, 1981b; Lind, 1979; Long, 1986).

Another significant article of the law stipulated that employers had the primary obligation to initiate negotiations before they introduced any important changes, including reorganization of production methods, expansion, changing the business direction or working conditions and individual tasks, personnel transfer, and the like. In order to safeguard their members' interests, the law also gave unions the right of access to information with regard to the running of the business. This included the right to examine company books and other relevant documents, or to make reasonable requests for help, in case assistance was needed to analyze and interpret provided information. The law did not make any exceptions regarding confidential information. It did, however, give the employers the opportunity to initiate negotiations regarding the confidentiality of information (Bellace and Gospel, 1983; Lind, 1979; Martin, 1979, 1987).

Another fundamental provision of the law relates to the right of interpretation of agreements. The law shifted the priority of interpretation of collective agreements concerning work organization and codetermination from the employers to the unions. This meant that in case of disagreement, and while a resolution to a given dispute was pending, the union's interpretation prevailed. To maintain their interpretation, employers had to initiate negotiations at the local and national levels. If the outcome was not satisfactory for both parties, the matter had to be brought up to the labor court to be resolved. In sharp contrast to past practices, and also in contrast to what is taking place in other countries, especially the United States, where mostly "management acts and the union grieves," the series of legislative acts enacted in Sweden in the 1970s indicates a considerable shift of power in favor of the unions and their constituents (Bellace and Gospel, 1983: 69; Lind, 1979: 26; Martin, 1977: 137–138).

Through all the legislative enactments, the limited shopfloor participation of the 1960s has been expanded. Labor's potential in influencing issues such as employment, security, health, and safety has been increased considerably. Furthermore, worker representatives appointed by unions can sit on the board of directors and have access to important information and the opportunity, albeit limited, to exercise some influence over long-term company goals. Finally, the most critical managerial prerogative, that of unilateral decision-making power, has been substantially eroded. All these legislative acts have opened up possibilities for direct and indirect worker participation. Such a legislative approach departed substantially from the previous joint-consultation approach, where management had the prerogative to initiate changes and the ultimate authority to make decisions, and has strengthened the union's position in its ability to challenge exclusive managerial prerogatives. The possibilities opened up by the new legislation are important for symbolic reasons as well, since they convey the message that not only management, but also labor, could be responsible in making decisions affecting business. Therefore, such an approach has greater potential for redistributing power within the workplace than all the previous participation experiments and joint labor-management projects had. Whether such a potential can be realized in practice depends on a number of factors.

First, it requires a strong, united labor movement, which can exploit the opportunities opened up by the law. Already in 1976, the labor movement in Sweden had acknowledged the fact that legislation was not entirely satisfactory, but it was the first step for a better work environment (Martin, 1987: 108). For the labor movement to be effective in its pursuit of greater workplace democratization, it is imperative that workers and their representatives acquire a broad range of knowledge, training, and skills in order to have a reasonable understanding of the problems to be solved and thus effectively fulfill their new role. To that end, the labor movement has established an elaborate educational network to educate thousands of members of codetermination committees, shop stewards, and work environment representatives on the new laws, labor policies, workers' rights and responsibilities, and financial and organizational aspects of business. The establishment of educational programs on industrial democracy is under union control, despite SAF's objections that they should be a joint effort (Eiger, 1986: 106–107). This, once again, indicates the strength of the labor movement and its determination to accomplish its goals.

Second, it is equally important that the government support efforts to diffuse alternative forms of work organization, so that the provisions of the law do not become a dead issue. The fact that the Social Democratic government in Sweden had been in power continuously for forty-four years since 1932, and then again after 1982, proved to be crucial, not only because it helped to pass legislation on industrial democracy, but also because it offered financial and organizational support toward that end. Financial support, for instance, was given to both trade union and employer organizations for courses and training activities that would help familiarize workers with the new laws and the new ways of work organization (Eiger, 1986; Lind, 1979). It is difficult to determine the extent and effectiveness of such assistance to the unions, given the lack of specific information on the point, and given the fact that overall in Sweden, as in Norway, there is competition for allocating resources among different union activities such as codetermination at the plant level and small-group activities (Sirianni, 1987: 15).

Steps Toward Economic Democracy

Strong and committed labor unions and a favorable political context are not always sufficient to accomplish participatory goals, if the economic conditions don't help. In Sweden, the favorable economic situation and low unemployment rates, which were so prevalent in the 1960s and early 1970s, came to an end by the late 1970s. Worsening economic conditions (e.g., rising inflation, unemployment, low levels of investment) forced the LO leadership to even greater awareness of the limitations of its past policies, including industrial democracy. They helped the formulation of its new position, that is, greater union involvement in the macroeconomic aspects of business, including capital distribution and control, technological research, and development. Demands for full employment and equal distribution of income could not possibly be accomplished by merely expanding the scope of collective bargaining, unless investment decisions and the capitalist economy in general became subject to public democratic control. Only then could a fairer distribution of wealth and power be accomplished.

The gradual and multilevel development of industrial democracy since the

1960s facilitated the overall debates and formulations over issues of economic democracy during the late 1970s and 1980s. The accomplishments and limitations of shopfloor involvement, collective bargaining practices, and legislative reforms made obvious the connection between workplace and economic democracy. If worker participation on the shopfloor was to be effective, if legislation was to effect real changes, if labor representatives sitting on the boards of directors were to influence decisions about production, investment, or technology, greater labor control over capital generation, management, and distribution seemed inevitable. Consequently, whereas industrial democracy focused on distribution of control within the work environment, economic democracy centered on distribution of control within the economic sphere. In pursuing its goal of democratic transformation of the Swedish society, the labor movement sought not only to increase worker and union participation in the running of the enterprise, but also to introduce economic democracy by linking workplace participation with participation in the economy (Albrecht and Deutsch, 1983; Esping-Andersen, 1981; IDE, 1981b; Martin, 1977, 1978). On the basis of these assumptions and convictions, the 1976 LO Congress supported the wage-earners investment fund plan submitted by the Meidner committee at its request.

The Meidner plan addressed the problems inherent in the solidaristic wage policy approach advocated by the LO and pursued over the years by the SAP. As mentioned above, over the years the solidaristic wage policy approach promoted a wage structure based on the kind of work performed rather than the profitability of different firms and industries. The same strategy imposed wage restraints on better paid groups regardless of their employers' ability to pay more. This policy, along with other structural reforms (e.g., allocation of investment capital to expanding areas to maintain competitiveness), helped narrow wage differentials, maintain to a large extent full employment, and moderate inflation rates. It also contributed to the political cohesion of the labor movement by eliminating interunion fighting over wages. However, it produced some negative results in that it encouraged the concentration of excess profits within the strongest and most profitable sectors of industry, and thereby contributed to the already high concentration of wealth in Sweden (Åsard, 1986; Esping-Andersen, 1981; Martin, 1977).

The growing labor discontent regarding those effects, compounded by LO's policy of centralized wage negotiations which didn't allow for local bargaining, pressed the LO leadership seriously to confront the unequal distribution consequences of its long-standing economic policy. LO began to consider collective ownership in order to protect employee power in the workplace and to maintain the equal distribution of wealth. The Meidner plan was perceived as a first step in that direction by proposing that 20 percent of the company profits be transferred to a central, union-controlled investment fund. The so-called wage-earner investment funds would be owned and controlled collectively by all employees and their unions and would be used for investment. Dividends from those funds would be used to improve the collective welfare of the workers (e.g., recreation, housing, and education), and to support unions in exercising their decision-making rights. As stock funds were to accumulate, unions would gradually gain control over most of the Swedish capital. It was predicted that within a 20- to 30-year period the most profitable companies could accomplish labor majority ownership (Albrecht, 1980: 310; Albrecht and Deutsch, 1983: 291–292; IDE, 1981b: 58; Kesselman, 1982: 415; Meidner, 1981: 310–311; Mydral, 1981: 321).

If the above provisions were to materialize, and unions gained shareholder voting rights, their already strong bargaining position could be enhanced considerably. In that respect the pursuit of the Meidner plan was compatible with the labor movement's industrial democracy goals, since it could further increase workers' influence over the whole economic process through the collective ownership of the generated wealth. Along these lines the 1978 SAP Congress pointed out that the wage-earner funds were to accomplish four basic goals: (1) to solve the problem of excess profits as a result of the solidaristic wage policy; (2) to counterbalance the concentration of wealth and power in industry; (3) to increase through co-ownership the wage-earner influence with regard to reforms initiated by legislation; and (4) to increase collective savings for productive investments and job creation (Albrecht and Deutsch, 1983: 306, 314).

In contrast with the previous codetermination reforms and employee board representation schemes, the changes proposed in the Meidner plan were far reaching, threatening to change the whole economic system. Therefore, it is not surprising that the Meidner proposal provoked hostile reactions from SAF and the nonsocialist parties. The plan was opposed on many grounds, the most important of which were as follows. Such an approach would create a European type of state socialist economy and thus Swedish socialism would be hurt; freedom would be threatened by the concentration of power; incentives for technological innovations would decline and thus the industry's competitiveness would weaken; and union bureaucratization would replace flexibility guaranteed by the free market (Esping-Andersen, 1981: 118).

Both the TCO and the LO agreed on the major provisions of the Meidner plan, and this forced SAF to compromise by submitting its own version of the plan that entailed individual instead of collective shares ownership. The LO eventually rejected that counterproposal. But the LO and the Social Democrats started very late to inform and mobilize public support on the issue of economic democracy. The heated public debate over the Meidner plan eventually hurt the Social Democrats, who lost the elections in 1976 (IDE, 1981b). The labor movement's delayed mobilization and the fact that the Meidner plan involved radical changes made the public skeptical as well. Meanwhile, radicals within the SAP as well as workers themselves raised objections. The projected concentration of power within the hands of the union leadership could result in oligarchic tendencies by replacing manager and employer bureaucrats with union bureaucrats, without benefiting the rank and file. As an alternative, it was suggested that the wage-earner funds be managed by the rank and file, and not by union representatives (Esping-Andersen, 1981).

The debate over the wage-earner funds continued over the years and helped accelerate the capital-labor contention that had begun in the early 1970s in Sweden. During the pre-election campaign in 1982, issues of industrial and economic democracy were used to mobilize support and to capitalize tactfully on the left-wing tendencies of the time. The Social Democrats won the elections and came back to power in 1982. The bill on wage-earner funds finally passed in late 1983, despite opposition from the business community and some segments of the white-collar workforce, and despite confusion within the general public (Åsard, 1986; Eiger, 1986; Long, 1986). However, the original proposal was modified as a result of the pressure applied by employers, the business community, and the nonsocialist parties. On the basis of the new proposal, the profit-sharing formula was modified, and the fund trustees were to be appointed by government, not the unions. Regardless of legislative provisions, the government moved very slowly in establishing the funds and appointing trustees while the labor movement's interest in the issue waned substantially over the years (Long, 1986).

The failure of the Meidner plan to be implemented can be better understood if we consider that its proposed changes divided the political establishment and the overall public along traditional socialist/nonsocialist lines. The nonsocialist parties and employers became increasingly threatened by the union drive for democratization, culminating in the wage-earner fund proposals. Collective ownership, rather than an individual profit-sharing scheme, became the focus of this prolonged, controversial debate. The bourgeois parties in the pre-1976 election period and long thereafter presented their own interpretation of the Meidner plan to the public and fiercely opposed the concentration of labor power and the confiscation of property that in their eyes the proposal called for. This was despite the assurances of the Social Democrats that all proposed changes would take place within the context of the market economy, that the intention was not to abolish the market economy, but rather to place some constraints on it along the social democratic tradition for a more prosperous and egalitarian society. Olof Palme himself had stated that the goal was to "change the distribution of wealth and influence within the market economy" (as quoted in Albrecht and Deutsch, 1983: 304). Finally, in addition to these forces of opposition, the Meidner proposal generated a considerable amount of debate and even opposition within the LO, TCO, and SAP themselves, although a general agreement among all parties did exist. For instance, the TCO in its 1982 National Congress adopted a neutral position on the debate, given that many of its member unions chose not to support any change that would transform the economy.

SACO, the Swedish confederation for professionals, also opposed the collective wage-earner funds proposal, favoring instead the development of citizen funds. Within the LO and SAP the degree of consistency, support, and enthusiasm varied throughout the different stages of the debate, the biggest differences drawn along the more moderate and more radical elements within those organizations. The Social Democrats were not particularly effective in their attempt to convince the public that the proposed changes could reverse the economic crisis, which the bourgeois parties were blamed for. They could also help to revitalize and democratize the economy, maintain welfare policies, and improve quality of life (Albrecht and Deutsch, 1986; Long, 1986). The proposed changes threatened to harm long-lasting interests and transform the society in new and unfamiliar ways that the public and especially the capital in Sweden were not yet ready to accept. It is easy then to understand why Meidner's proposal provoked such a controversial debate, opposition, and divisions, why proposals like that would be extremely difficult to work out as practical, workable solutions accepted by all concerned parties, especially within the context of increasing labor-capital antagonism of that period. Under those circumstances, the forces of opposition and to some extent the labor movement's own inability to face such opposition in united, consistent ways proved crucial in determining the way the initial Meidner proposals were finally implemented in real life.

Labor Participation in the Development of Technology

The worsening economic conditions of the 1970s and 1980s, and the introduction of new and more flexible technologies in response to rapidly shifting global market demands to which the Swedish economy is tightly linked,[20] have contributed to the shift of interest from indirect participation to workplace reform and worker participation in the development and utilization of new technology (Cole, 1985; Long, 1986). Regardless of the economic and technological changes and demands, some other conditions prompted this renewed interest in workplace participation. First, union disillusionment with the policy of democratization at upper organizational levels partly contributed to this shift. As mentioned above, the labor movement was aware of the limitations of the board representation, and its goal was not to pursue the German style of codetermination. The realization was growing slowly that legislation was not as effective as had been expected and that unions had to find other ways, including union involvement in research and development, to increase labor influence in the workplace. Some empirical evidence seemed to confirm those inclinations: Laws didn't seem to stimulate further democratization, and indirect participation didn't seem to increase workers' influence, commitment, and satisfaction, as direct participation did (Long, 1986: 378).

Second, the introduction of new technologies caused labor realignment, as jobs were increasingly changing from blue to white collar, requiring more of the workers' input and involvement. The new technology also made more clear the limitations of labor's past strategies. If the impact of the new technology as it relates to workers' safety, health, and mental state had to be controlled, legislative and bargaining approaches, or any limited influence which labor might have through board representation, were not perceived to be sufficient, as long as new technology had been developed and adopted before these processes took place (Long, 1986: 378; Martin, 1987).

Finally, although management was opposing the legislative union approach to enforce changes, especially the idea of wage-earner funds, it had been more supportive of a micro-kind of reform than in any other Western country. It perceived these reforms to be beneficial for both management and workers, and, to a certain degree, management could have more control over those reforms. The fact that Social Democrats came back to power in late 1982 again facilitated the collaborative relations between labor and management.

A main argument of this book has been that worker participation is a dynamic process toward democratizing the workplace and worklife. All the seeming setbacks and shifts in orientations and strategies described so far in regard to the Swedish case seem to confirm such a position. The growth and development of participation schemes in Sweden were strongly affected by ideological positions, conflicts over interests, accumulated experience, as well as economic, political, and technological changes. Throughout this process of growth and development, and regardless of opposition, the labor movement's commitment to the issues of QWL and democratization of the workplace has been very strong. In the late 1970s and 1980s, changing economic conditions and new technological developments prompted the labor movement to reevaluate its past strategies and approach the whole issue of workers' participation from a different angle (Albrecht and Deutsch, 1983; Long, 1986).

In 1982, after long and heated negotiations, the Agreement on Efficiency and Participation, known as the Development Agreement, was signed by SAF, LO, and PTK, the federation for private-sector white-collar unions. The purpose of that agreement was to determine the specific ways the broad guidelines provided by the 1977 codetermination would be carried out in practice. The agreement reflects a significant compromise between labor and management, as unions decreased their initial demands and management agreed to sign the agreement in anticipation of the Social Democrats' return to power. The agreement also reflects the need to promote efficiency, profitability, and competitiveness. Both sides seemed to agree that employee influence on these matters was essential for the realization of those goals. That agreement adopted language that confirmed the employers' conviction that utilizing and developing workers' abilities served as an instrument of effectiveness. In contrast, unions could only participate in organizational and technological changes as observers, not as equal actors, although their rights under the codetermination law were confirmed and their right to bring outside consultants and researchers in was also granted (Martin, 1987: 118–119).

The agreement helped to renew activities related to workplace reform, with special emphasis on introducing new technology that could benefit both labor and capital (Cole, 1985: 379; Long, 1986: 377–378). Management needed worker cooperation and commitment in the changing production strategies because of the introduction of new technologies, especially computers, in order to successfully compete in the international market. Unions, on the other hand, were gradually becoming aware that their ideological commitment to worker autonomy, work satisfaction, and general improvement of the quality of work could not be effectively realized through the policies pursued up to that point (e.g., collective bargaining, board representation, workplace participation), unless unions had a decisive voice in developing the new technology. Computers, for instance, could be used both to enhance and diminish the quality of worklife, depending on the values and goals of those who designed and managed their application. The choice of technology is not a value-free issue but one that entails social choices, with tremendous consequences for worklife and human life in general.

During the same time, unions also enlarged the scope of their health and safety objectives. For example, they expanded the definition of safety to include not only physical injury, but also psychological health. This modified definition not only implies protection against stress and isolation, but also allows for conditions that facilitate personal development through participation, competence, and the like. Therefore, although the unions still considered technological development and advancement as an indispensable element of an industrial policy, which a small and open economy like the Swedish one had to pursue in order to successfully compete in the international market, a strong emphasis was placed "on union influence on the development of new technology that determines the scope for choice concerning the characteristics of jobs resulting from structural and technological change" (Martin, 1987: 100). The realization of such an objective implied that the unions themselves had to engage in autonomous research and development, to counterbalance technology's negative impact, which stemmed mostly from employers' interest in productivity and efficiency. On the contrary, independent union research would enable unions to design technologically alternative solutions on the basis of the QWL considerations, such as secure and meaningful jobs, as well as healthy, secure, and democratic working environments. (These, and similar positions were presented to the 1981 LO Congress by the committee called LOFO, which was set up to prepare a research policy program.)

Along with those convictions came the realization that unions lacked the resources and skills needed to perform the new roles which the new vision about technology called for. Unions had to have access to public funding in order to develop the necessary capacity to define problems and the needed expertise to administer research. The labor movement's stance on the issue was that, unless work quality objectives became part of a national policy similar, for instance, to health and education policies, such public funding wouldn't be readily available to unions. Such a national policy that would enable unions to play an independent role in technological development has yet to be developed, although certain projects, among them the very well-known UTOPIA project, have been financed by the STU, the major governmental funding agency for research and development.[21]

The Prospects for Industrial Democracy in Sweden

The radicalization of labor in the late 1960s and early 1970s, the legislative provisions, the broad-scale experimentation with worker participation and experience, and the public debates and education programs on issues related to industrial democracy—all have helped to build the notion that employee participation could be beneficial for both capital and labor. However, regardless of long collaborative relations between capital and labor in Sweden, the scope and degree of that participation has always been the subject of contention between the two parties. The labor movement in Sweden has been in a more advantageous position than that in most industrialized countries, because it has to a large extent managed to be ideologically and organizationally united in pursuing its industrial democracy goals. The fact that during most of the period under consideration the labor movement in Sweden had had political support at the national level further facilitated its goals in that it helped unions to mobilize support and escalate their demands. It also allowed them more flexibility to respond to labor market, socioeconomic, and technological changes, as well as to be consistent in their approach toward industrial democracy and the ways it could most effectively be realized.

Unions in all the other countries examined in this part of the book, with the possible exception of Norway, lack the ideological commitment or the organizational strength and political capacity necessary to effectively pursue participative goals, although socioeconomic and technological factors conducive to participative reforms might be present there as well. In the United States, for instance, because of the rapidly changing technologies and increased international competition, management and unions had to face similar concerns regarding technology as their Swedish counterparts. Worker participation has also been considered as a way of dealing with the economic problems and changing markets of the 1980s. However, workers' involvement and participation in the United States have been used by management primarily to increase productivity and as a mechanism to keep unions out and to coapt workers. This has made unions very hesitant to adopt participatory schemes. Unions in the United States are weak, at least at the national level, and the political prerequisites for industrial democracy in that country are missing. Therefore, the extent of participation schemes and workers' influence within them is very limited. Unions in Sweden, on the other hand, because of their strong alliance with the Social Democratic government and having been helped by the overall unity of the political parties, were able to build on their past experiences, to advance participatory demands at the higher company levels, and to adopt the legislative path in demanding their codetermination rights.

The labor movement's approach during the 1970s and 1980s opened up some possibilities for increased worker participation. Whether, and to what extent, those possibilities will be realized remains to be seen and in light of the new economic, technological, and organizational challenges unions face in light of capital's opposition. For instance, in an era of rapid technological changes, labor market composition is changing rapidly as blue-collar jobs are phased out and white-collar jobs increase substantially, thus resulting in stronger white-collar federations. The Metal Workers Union, for instance, which is the biggest individual union in Sweden, has recently lost thousands of its members (Long, 1986: 378). In many industries affected by technological change, workers are competing against each other for the remaining jobs and unions are fighting over changing occupational categories for membership.

Technological changes have dictated the blurring of occupational lines, but the unions that represent the various occupational groups do not have the same political affiliations. Groups like machinists, for instance, are represented by the metal workers' union, while designers and programmers are represented by the private-sector salaried workers' union. But although the metal workers are supportive of Social Democrats, the salaried workers are not (Martin, 1987: 136). There has also been a new trend toward bargaining at the regional instead of the national level, and this undoubtedly will have an impact on the labor movement's organizational capacity to effect changes because of its strong centralized nature. Recently, for instance, engineering employers concluded an agreement with the metal workers (Long, 1986: 378).

Among all these challenges unions also have to face the growing power of management since the late 1970s and 1980s and its opposition when long-entrenched managerial interests are at stake as a result of the labor movement's efforts to increase workers' and unions' power at different levels and through different ways. With the introduction of new technologies, the power struggle within the workplace and the broader industrial arena have again been pushed to the forefront. In the past it was basically management, especially in the large industrial firms and in collaboration with universities and technical institutes, that had the power and resources to influence technological research and development choices, as well as the applicability of that research. As unions pressured the government to change the national research policy and incorporate in it union concerns about safe and satisfying work environments and to support the development of alternative technological solutions under union influence, management fought back.

Some cases have been documented wherein management is threatened by developments in the autonomous work groups and workers can acquire multiple skills and be very effective in their performance. The concern is that dependence on workers' skills makes management vulnerable in the event workers leave and apply their knowledge and skills elsewhere. Such a move also weakens management's position at the bargaining table. As a result, management is using techniques that have been inherent to mechanisms of bureaucratic control in the industrial world: the provision of incentive schemes and buildup of skills that are company specific in an attempt to increase workers' identification with the company. All these changes and developments will undermine the unions' power and have a strong impact on the future development of worker participation schemes, as the labor movement's unity, its political clout, and its organizational survival seem to be threatened by economic and technological changes.

The foregoing analysis has also shown that the labor movement has a strong commitment to industrial democracy and a strong capacity to adjust its strategies when faced with various challenges. Furthermore, the legitimated workplace reforms, the long tradition of welfare policies in that country, and the overall cultural and political commitment to democratic and egalitarian ideals could also justify a slightly more optimistic approach. Such an approach envisions the labor movement as effectively utilizing the new possibilities opened up by the recent laws and thus successfully overcoming the emerging challenges in its effort to maintain past gains and advance new demands toward industrial democracy.

THE CASE OF NORWAY

Over the years, Norway has followed a similar path to Sweden's in its road to industrial democracy. Major participation forms in Norway, as in Sweden, include joint-consultation and information schemes, practices institutionalized by national collective agreements between management and labor, legal provisions for workers' board representation, and a number of legal stipulations. The objective of these stipulations is to reform the work environment through workers' input in decision making, much as the 1977 Swedish legislation attempted to do.

Before World War I, the formation of unions and the establishment of basic workers' rights, such as job security, working conditions, and the right to bargain, characterized the industrial relations system in Norway. The issue of workers' control and demands in regard to establishing works' councils did not arise in Norway until after World War I. Norway—as Sweden and the rest of Europe—was swept by the revolutionary enthusiasm of the early 1920s. The events of the Russian Revolution radicalized the labor movement. This radicalization was reinforced by the socialist theoretician Martin Tranmael, who espoused the idea that revolution was the only way the working class could gain power and control. Within that climate some efforts were undertaken to democratize the workplace. To that end a proposal was initially developed suggesting the introduction of workers' councils with rights and functions similar to those of the Soviets in the USSR. That proposal was never implemented, however. Instead, the law that was eventually passed introduced councils as joint-information bodies, with responsibilities and rights similar to those performed by the Swedish councils during the same period. The law was not effective in strengthening the workers' position in the workplace, and it was eventually abolished. The councils were basically preoccupied with issues such as time and wage questions that the unions traditionally handled. This overlap of responsibilities often caused competition and conflicts, and it also contributed to the abolition of the councils (Gustavsen and Hunnius, 1981; IDE, 1981b).

The fate of works' councils, the emphasis on welfare policies, as well as labor-management cooperation starting in the late 1920s, can be better understood by examining the socioeconomic and political circumstances prevalent in the country during that time. First, the labor movement was divided along various ideological lines (e.g., the pro-Moscow section; the Tranmael group and the reformist Social Democrats). Second, radicalism remained mostly ideological and did not translate into any practical reality. Third, unemployment was high at the time, and up to the early 1930s the country had gone through three recessions. Therefore, economic conditions were not favorable for strengthening the power of the labor movement (Gustavsen and Hunnius, 1981: 17–19). The parliamentary strength of the Labor party was steadily increasing, and the "possibility of gaining political power via electoral politics may well have had a moderating impact on the labor movement" (Gustavsen and Hunnius, 1981: 19). Therefore, if we exclude the period of the 1920s, from the Great Depression on, Norway's labor-management relations are marked mostly by compromise and cooperation between the two parties (Gustavsen, 1986; Schiller, 1977).

Early Labor-Management Cooperation

The Congress of Trade Unions (LO) and the Labor party, which has been in power during most of the postwar period, have strong ties, and their close relationship has facilitated cooperation between labor and management. As in Sweden, this relationship meant that the labor movement could more effectively translate its goals into reality with the support of the national policies instituted by the Labor party. At the same time, the Labor party could count on the labor movement's electorate support to remain in power. Employers' organizations on their side have traditionally held the position that conflicts could be better resolved through cooperation and compromise and not through confrontation. This is reflected in the overall low rates of industrial action in Norway, with the exception of the period between the two world wars. The adoption of policies since the 1915 Labour Disputes Act also helped to maintain industrial peace by prohibiting an official strike and lockouts as long as a collective agreement lasts. The highly centralized bargaining structures of worker and employer federations kept conflict between capital and labor at low levels as well (IDE, 1981: 23–24; Qvale, 1976: 455). The cooperative labor-management relations reflect the overall consensus of values among different social groups: In industry this was reinforced by the strong commitment of the Labor party and the LO to transform society slowly, through reforms (Gustavsen and Hunnius, 1981; IDE, 1981b; Lafferty, 1984; Qvale, 1976).

In 1935, the Labor party in Norway won the elections and formed a government, three years after the Social Democrats had come to power in Sweden. As happened in Sweden in 1938, in 1935 the Norwegian Confederation of Employers (NAF) and the LO signed their first Basic Agreement denoting the new spirit of cooperation between labor and capital.[22] Low unemployment rates and small wage differentials between white-collar and the blue-collar occupations pursued consistently over the years by both the Labor party and the LO reflect that cooperation and the traditional egalitarian ideology that characterizes the country. The rationale behind the strategy of cooperation lies in the claim that one gains more by sharing information, by cooperating and by consulting with the other party, than by assuming a confrontational stance (IDE, 1981b: 17; Lafferty, 1984: 123–132; Qvale, 1976: 456).

In the spirit of that cooperation, unions never seriously opposed technological development or other measures utilized by management to increase productivity by proclaiming their exploitative character. In contrast, technological advancement was considered an indispensable part of the government's policy toward economic growth, which in turn was perceived as a prerequisite of developing a more democratic society. Within industry, this cooperative spirit found expression in the labor movement's positive response to the national call for reconstruction and economic development. During the postwar reconstruction period, unions became strongly committed to increasing productivity on both local and national levels. The German occupation of Norway and the postwar reconstruction spirit also helped to increase solidarity, cohesion, and cooperation within the overall population.

As a result, during the 1950s and 1960s production committees emerged with parity representation and limited consultation and information rights regarding shopfloor issues. Meanwhile, with strong U.S. ideological guidance and financial support under the auspices of the Marshall Plan, several collective agreements between the NAF and the LO incorporated in their provisions a number of scientific management principles regarding production (Gustavsen and Hunnius, 1981: 24; 39; IDE, 1981b: 19). Eventually, by revising and supplementing the Basic Agreement, an extensive system of joint-consultation provisions was established (IDE, 1981b; Qvale, 1976).

Collective agreements also strengthened the position of shop stewards and granted employees the right to exert influence, sometimes equal to that of management, on personnel, welfare, and safety matters. Shop stewards and workers were also protected against any arbitrary employer dismissals (IDE, 1981b: 19; Schiller, 1977: 65–66). At that point of time the goal of the labor movement was not to increase worker participation in decision-making processes per se. Instead, the emphasis was on economic development and on welfare policies. As a result, most of the labor movement's achievements were accomplished through labor-management collective agreements, not through legislation, and interest in industrial democracy did not grow until the 1960s. The reasons for such a shift will be considered in the next section.

A Growing Interest in Industrial Democracy

The 1950s in Norway were marked by rapid economic growth and intensive use of scientific management techniques in the production process and in the management of work. The application of scientific management techniques required a detailed and specialized division of labor, a high degree of supervision, heavily controlled work roles, and, finally, very limited possibilities for worker development and social interaction within the workplace. But as in the rest of Scandinavia and Europe, the technological and structural changes that accompanied the industrial development and expansion of the 1950s had negative results for the economy and for the physical and psychological well-being of the workers. Rising levels of regional unemployment, plant closures, relocations, and increased symptoms of dissatisfaction and alienation, as well as high levels of absenteeism and low productivity, were the result of the rigid, authoritarian production processes. The LO and the NAF leadership, alarmed by these negative results, began to take action.

Demands for greater worker control over working conditions soon emerged in Norway, as in the rest of Europe (Gustavsen and Hunnius, 1981; Qvale, 1976; Schiller, 1977). A survey of 1,128 employees from seventeen large companies in the Oslo area at the time indicates that 56 percent of the blue-collar and 67 percent of the white-collar workers expressed interest in participating in decisions that affected their work and work conditions. The same survey showed that 78 percent of the blue-collar and 59 percent of the white-collar workers thought they were not sufficiently involved in decisions. Finally, 47 percent of the blue-collar and 54 percent of the white-collar workers thought they were capable of performing more difficult tasks than those they were assigned to (Emery and Thorsrud, 1969: 107).

During the same period, the compulsory free education system—pursued since the 1930s as part of the government's social reform policy—became standardized in an attempt to offer quality education to all young people regardless of socioeconomic and regional differences. Moreover, strategies such as keeping unemployment rates low,[23] the compulsory public pension, the social security system, progressive taxation (e.g., tax deductions based on economic needs), and similar welfare policies sought to equalize the distribution of income and wealth and thereby create a more democratic and egalitarian society (IDE, 1981b).

Conditions in industry did not reflect these democratic intentions. With few exceptions (e.g., private control of prices, restraint of competition), public intervention in the production and marketing processes was minimal (Gustavsen and Hunnius, 1981). Furthermore, bureaucratic and authoritarian work structures severely limited the democratic participation of workers within industry. Paradoxically, the welfare policies that facilitated the rise in living standards and created a relatively egalitarian society also helped to increase people's awareness of working conditions. They also helped cultivate a new set of values and expectations regarding work. Because industry was hurting and demands for control over one's own working life were gradually increasing, the need to reorganize work to correspond to those expectations became compelling.[24]

In addition, the wave of critical and revolutionary thinking and unrest that swept Europe in the 1960s impacted Norway as well by shaking its institutions and undermining its prevailing values. Individual rights became subject to reevaluation, while authority structures and the overall legitimacy of institutions came under attack. The growing dissatisfaction and criticism among the rank and file and local unionists in regard to the rigid, centrally organized labor movement reflected the critical spirit of the period. Under those circumstances, the debate about industrial democracy began in Norway in the early 1960s. The notion of industrial democracy that emerged at the time entailed the distribution of power to be shared by all those who were engaged in industry, rather than being concentrated in the hands of a minority (Qvale, 1976: 454).

The LO and the Labor party leaders realized that the extensive system of joint consultation and information, as well as the minority representation of labor directors on the boards of state-owned industries—an institution that was effective since 1948—was not sufficient to ensure a fair distribution of power in industry (IDE, 1981b; Qvale, 1976). The centralized nature of the LO—one of the most centralized among the Western industrialized countries (IDE, 1981b: 22–23)—was not helping either. Trade union and Labor party leaders sensed that information and consultation schemes and board representation, though important means to democratize the workplace, could not be as effective without more direct forms of worker participation. The growing alienation among workers required that other, more effective mechanisms be established to ensure that workers voice their opinion and have more input in the decision-making process; these mechanisms would increase workers' knowledge, influence, and self-development. The organizational challenges made that need even more pressing for the LO to seriously consider worker participation. The welfare state was well established and effective. Union legitimacy was dangerously eroding, however, and in order for the labor movement to be able to influence socioeconomic and political developments new goals had to be established (Qvale, 1976: 456). As noted above, at about the same time the Social Democrats and the labor movement in Sweden adopted industrial democracy in their effort to solve similar problems, including worker alienation and eroding union legitimacy.

Some political developments in Norway accelerated the process of industrial democracy. The new Socialist party[25] included industrial democracy in its 1961 election campaign. Meanwhile, the bourgeois parties had also shown some interest in the issue. Until the LO and the Labor party developed their own agendas on the issue, their political legitimacy was at risk (Schiller, 1977). Concerned about all these developments and about the growing problems in the workplace, NAF had no other option but to accept demands for more democracy at the workplace. Besides, the idea of using human resources more effectively was a welcome opportunity for some employers. Norway's natural resources, such as minerals and hydroelectric power, had been almost exhausted, and the notion of using human resources to compensate for such a loss seemed appealing to employers. "Democratization" was merely a way to attract and sustain more committed employees (Qvale, 1976: 456).

All these developments also have to be understood within the context of the international environment within which the Norwegian economy operates. Norway is a small country whose economy, like Sweden's, depends heavily on international trade. Foreign trade, for instance, constitutes between 40 and 50 percent of the GNP (IDE, 1981b: 17). Norway, as Sweden, had been under strong pressure to be flexible, innovative, and ready to adjust to the emerging demands of the international market. By using human resources such as skills, knowledge, and education in flexible and innovative ways, the nation could effectively respond to the challenges of the international market. To some extent this precarious position in the international market, as well as the long liberal tradition, explain why Sweden and Norway started so early to reform the organization of the workplace and utilize their human capital at work more effectively and democratically. Another consideration is that at the time the debate about industrial democracy started, Norway was preparing to enter the Common Market, and employers were strongly interested in increasing productivity. Workers' participation was perceived as instrumental in facilitating that goal.

First Steps Toward Industrial Democracy

Under those circumstances, the leaders of the labor movement and the employers' confederation, as well as representatives of the Institute of Industrial Social Research, established an alliance in 1962 that resulted in the formation of a joint committee whose goal was to finance and support the Industrial Democracy Program (IDP). Briefly, the goals of the program were to study and analyze the experiences of Norway and other countries in terms of worker board-level representation; to initiate alternative forms of work organization in selected enterprises; and to analyze the diffusion results of those efforts (Gustavsen and Hunnius, 1981: 46).

In view of the history of the Norwegian industrial relations, it was not surprising that labor and management cooperated to achieve those goals. In contrast to other countries, where the feudalist system had caused much rigidity and sharp differences among social classes, and thus made democratization of work extremely difficult to achieve, Norway had had a tradition of independent fishermen and farmers and industrialization had taken place late. Class conflict and animosity were not as high there as in the countries where industrialization had started earlier. Besides, the LO and the Labor party were established soon, and their similar ideologies and goals helped to maintain industrial peace and cultivate even further the collaborative relationship between labor and capital. When the political debate on industrial democracy started, cooperation and trust among the leaders of the industrial relations system had already been well established owing to the productive relationship between labor and capital during the war and immediately after, and to the political stability, steady economic growth, and achievement of full employment (Thorsrud, 1972).

What was unique in the 1960s, however, was that, for the first time, social scientists were brought in to share responsibility in designing experiments to solve specific workplace problems. The experiments were to function under specific guidelines: Without hurting the economic growth of the companies involved, and without decreasing wage levels, better conditions for participation in decision making had to be established. Changes were to take place without altering the existing power structure in any major way, which meant that from the start there were limits in producing any fundamental changes in the industrial relations system (Gustavsen and Hunnius, 1981; Jenkins, 1973; Qvale, 1976).

In accordance with the first goal of the IDP program, Thorsrud and Emery evaluated the worker board representation experience in Norwegian (state-owned), West German, and British companies. In their report, however, both opposed the notion that board-level worker representation could help increase the workers' influence within the firm. Their position was not that different from that held in Sweden and other industrial countries, and it was verified by some empirical evidence. Their objections were based on the following grounds. First, board representation didn't seem to have a great impact on the average worker; second, structural changes in the work environment and in the ownership of business made management rather than board decisions more important for the workers; and, third, board membership created a role-conflict problem for the worker representatives.

Thorsrud and Emery opposed not only employee board-level representation, but also the conventional, hierarchical way the companies were organized. The scientific management approach applied in industry since the 1950s had resulted in specialized and heavily controlled work roles that left little room for learning, skill maintenance, autonomy, and communication among workers. Thorsrud and Emery suggested an alternative approach that was greatly influenced by the ideas generated at the Tavistock Institute of Human Relations in England. Industrial democracy could succeed only if its starting point was the workplace (Emery and Thorsrud, 1969). As they stated, their aim was to investigate "under what conditions can more rights and responsibilities be achieved for the individual at the workplace" (Emery and Thorsrud, 1969: 95). Their overall approach was strongly influenced by the principles of the sociotechnical perspective.

One basic assumption of that perspective is that neither technology nor tasks, and the task interdependencies that technology generates, have to be accepted as given. A given technology often lends itself to different definitions of tasks and task relationships, and thus to a variety of organizational choices. Furthermore, systems can be changed to accommodate socially defined needs, such as freedom and competence at work. This suggests that tasks can be restructured to encompass broader work roles and thus allow workers to grow, learn, assume responsibility, and develop social contacts with their fellow workers (Trist et al., 1963). The joint committee approved the suggestions informed by the sociotechnical perspective. Thus, when the second phase of the IDP began, a number of firms were selected which between 1965 and 1969 began experiments along those lines.[26] By making the appropriate changes, such as offering training and restructuring work tasks and rules, the reformers were striving to better utilize the human potential and thereby encourage workers to participate more and thus learn, grow, develop, and progressively gain more control over their work environment. These changes were expected to have spillover effects at higher labor and management levels as well as outside the workplace (e.g., in communities and schools). In a way those changes were perceived as the ground-work for an effective board representation on which the labor movement was already preparing legislation in promoting workers' interests.

In 1969, the joint committee reviewed the first experiments and found the results to be very promising. As a result, a new phase of diffusion in the industry began. On the basis of its findings, the committee also suggested relinquishing managerial decision-making power to semiautonomous work groups in the company. The experiments spread throughout Norway, and as was noted above, they also influenced similar developments in Sweden and in other countries (Qvale, 1976; Schiller, 1977). The diffusion process took place, and some institutions became involved. Resources became available in promoting worker participation goals. For instance, the Work Research Institute, which initiated the Cooperation Project in late 1969, launched other projects as well. The joint committee, which was set up in 1962 by employer, government, and union representatives to assist researchers in planning, carrying out, and evaluating research on the issue, also provided resources. Employers' and union organizations prepared seminars, and literature was prepared and sent out. Employers' organizations also initiated and financed projects (Emery and Thorsrud, 1969; Qvale, 1976; Schiller, 1977).

As noted above, similar institutions were also established in Sweden in the 1960s, when the whole process of democratizing the workplace began. It seems, however, that in Sweden the whole diffusion process was more systematic and better organized among employers and production engineers to communicate experience and lessons from one company to another, whereas in Norway, despite participation from other parties, union organs were expected to carry out most of the work (Qvale, 1976: 468). Since the unions generally have only limited resources to have an impact, it is not surprising that the overall diffusion process in Norway was not as extensive as had been hoped. Nevertheless, efforts to democratize the workplace continued although they were not always effective in producing that democratization. In 1966, for instance, the Basic Agreement was revised providing for a Cooperation Council, while a 1970 agreement be-tween the LO and the NAF established an Education and Research program that sought to help workers to participate in decision-making processes. In addition, the LO designed and supported a number of informative courses for shop stewards (Schiller, 1977).

As in the case of Sweden, the labor movement in Norway has not only been ideologically committed, but it also had the political support to carry out its commitment in its pursuit of increased worker participation. With the exception of Sweden, what distinguishes the Norwegian effort for workplace democrati-zation from similar attempts in other countries is, first, the strong position of its labor movement. Second, the employers' motives to increase productivity that underlay the joint labor-management efforts for workplace democratization might not have the same significance as in other countries (e.g., the United States, England, and France).

As noted above, unions did not perceive efforts to increase productivity as exploitative. The unions supported productivity goals since in the long run economic growth was perceived as a means to accomplish national welfare and in that respect workers could benefit from such growth. Besides, labor was a strong partner in those efforts, and managerial intentions and movements could always be checked by unions. Theoretically at least, this was theoretically true, since one of the challenges unions face everywhere is lack of knowledge and technical expertise to substantially effect changes (Gustavsen and Hunnius, 1981; IDE, 1981b). Moreover, employers in Norway, as in Sweden, and in contrast to other countries, such as England, Germany, and the United States, had strong incentives to innovate, and their diffusion efforts are somewhat noteworthy. Therefore, given the political climate, the strength of the labor movement, and the cooperative nature of industrial relations in Norway, as in Sweden, both labor and management attempted to restructure the workplace in the 1960s. The motives to increase productivity and efficiency soon took concrete dimensions as both management and labor tried to create the infrastructure and to provide the necessary resources for the introduction and diffusion of the new work arrangements.

Legislative Acts and Worker Board Representation

During the 1960s the labor movement in Norway placed more emphasis on direct than indirect forms of worker participation. As mentioned earlier, during the years of the IDP, the labor movement was also preparing legislation to introduce worker representation at the board level. The issue had not been forgotten; it had just receded temporarily. The labor movement was organizationally and politically strong and in 1973 succeeded in getting legislation passed for board representation. Without any extensive empirical evidence, it would be difficult to determine the degree to which the goals of the IDP were accomplished in increasing workers' influence in the decision-making process at the workplace so that board representation could be applied more effectively. Some empirical evidence, however, seems to indicate that reorganization efforts (e.g., autonomous work groups, decentralization of shopfloor activities, more worker participation at the shopfloor) helped to produce some moderate economic, social, and political improvements. For instance, not only did productivity increase substantially in many cases, but also workers' knowledge and skills improved, which meant their bargaining position within the company and the labor market also improved.

The overall diffusion of work reorganization projects was not very successful in Norway because top management was unwilling or unable to carry out changes, and, in addition, union bureaucracy, to some degree, became an obstacle. The centralized nature of the labor movement was not particularly suitable for a decentralized, democratic process through which workers could become empowered. Strong ideological support for the IDP program clearly came from the top of the union movement, but at the local level the whole reorganization process threatened to undermine the union leaders' control, and their involvement in the whole process was very weak (Qvale, 1976).

Nonetheless, union interest and involvement, public discourse on the issue, educational programs, and projects and experiments had planted the first seeds of awareness and consciousness in regard to participation issues. Workers' expectations to expand their field of influence were also raised, as they got involved in more challenging jobs, and became more knowledgeable and competent. Thus, despite objections regarding board-level representation raised by critical elements within the left wing of the labor movement, the emphasis in the early 1970s was on employee board representation and, later, as in Sweden, on improving the working environment.

Historically, worker participation in Norway had been the subject of national collective agreements. The 1970s marked a shift in that tradition when legislation was passed to institute workers' participation. The position of the LO at that time, as expressed by its influential chairman Tom Aspengren, was that the "bottom up" policy of the IDP and the board representation strategy should be seen as supportive of each other, and in order to be effective, they should be developed together. To study the issue further, the Eckhoff Committee was established, which consisted of management and labor leaders, as well as neutral members. In its *White Book* published in the late 1960s the Eckhoff Committee recommended worker board representation, basing its supportive arguments on the balance-of-interest model (Gustavsen and Hunnius, 1981). Briefly, this model supports the notion that the enterprise is a place where a number of groups with diverse interests come together to perform a variety of agreed-upon tasks. The enterprise should not be the battleground where divergent interests are played out; instead, it should be a place where the various interests are equally represented. Management and employer interests are well represented, and so should be the interests of workers. Being part of the broader democratic theory called the *elite theory*, the balance-of-interest model further suggests that it is the elite who can best represent and pursue the interests of the nonparticipating members of the various groups in the enterprise (Gustavsen and Hunnius, 1981: 88–90; Tomlinson, 1983: 594–595).

The balance-of-interest model was never implemented in its theoretical/ideal form. Regardless of overall cooperative labor-capital relations in Norway, conflict does exist over the goals and interests that the various social groups bring to the workplace. The long-standing practices and habits of working and managing in Norway, as in other industrialized countries, have been dictated primarily by managerial interests. To incorporate workers as equal partners in that process would not come easily and without a fight. The cooperative relations simply encouraged and facilitated negotiation over those conflicting interests. The balance-of-interest model, like similar theories and debates, contributed to that process by preparing the ground for the introduction of board-level representation, which only somewhat approximated the provisions of the ideal, equal interest representation model. Consequently, as in the rest of Scandinavia, starting in the early 1970s the labor movement in Norway pressed for legislation that would ensure worker representation on the board. At the same time it retained its overall position that the scope of worker participation should be expanded and industrial democracy should be promoted at various other levels within the company.

To that end the Company Act, applicable to certain industrial sectors, was signed in May 1972 and became effective in 1973. The act was applied to mining and manufacturing in 1974 and to the construction, transportation, and service sectors in 1975. The act provides for one-third employee representation on the board of directors in companies with more than fifty employees. Smaller companies could apply a similar system, given that both labor and management agreed on it. Obviously, such minority worker representation could not upset the balance of power within companies or allow for any fundamental worker influence in the decision-making process, especially if we consider that in reality major decisions are often taken by management. Besides, as critics of such representation have always argued, workers run the risk of being hostages of managerial intentions, since managerial expertise, skills, and organizational arrangements favor managerial domination.

Any changes in the industrial relations system advocated by unions in Norway were not easily achieved, especially if their goal was to challenge interests long ingrained in the system values. Worker participation in Norway, as everywhere, is a process that slows and advances, depending on the outcome of the political struggle involved. In Norway, an employee board representation such as the one described above could only be used for access, albeit limited, to company information, and it could only be useful if participation at the lower levels was effective. Such a strategy was consistent with the overall union orientation of representing workers' interests through different ways and at different levels. Unions were aware of the limitations of such representation, some of which they attempted to address by introducing the company assembly.

The company assembly is an organizational body unique to Norway. Originally, it was to be established in companies with more than 200 employees. It was to be composed of at least twelve members, one-third of whom had to be elected by the company's employees and the rest by the shareholders. The employee representatives had to be elected among all employees through a secret ballot on the basis of simple majority vote, unless at least two-thirds of the employees requested proportional representation. The duty of the company assembly was to appoint the board of directors, which is more of a supervisory body than a management board. The supervisory board assumes responsibilities, which in other countries are usually undertaken by the shareholders (e.g., investment policies, transfers, and the like). Therefore, this system of representation differs substantially from the German two-tier system. The reasons why the assembly was introduced are not very clear (Gustavsen and Hunnius, 1981: 86; Harrison, 1976: 66–67; IDE, 1981b: 28; Lafferty, 1984: 127; Schiller, 1977: 68). Gustavsen and Hunnius speculate that avoiding the hostage problem associated with the representation system could be one reason for the introduction of the corporate assembly, since "members of the company assembly would be less closely tied to the managerial structure and decisions of the company and could therefore maintain a higher degree of independence" (1981: 86).

The Company Act further provided for the establishment of works and department councils in firms with more than 100 and 400 employees, respectively. In firms with under 100 employees such councils could be established on a voluntary basis. Both bodies were to consist of 50 percent management and 50 percent employee representatives. Since the councils had rights only of information and consultation, they lacked any fundamental decision-making powers. Their "main task shall be through co-operation to work for the most efficient production possible and for the well being of everybody working in the undertaking" (as quoted in Harrison, 1976: 65). Based on the provisions of the 1974 Basic Agreement, the status of the councils was further strengthened to allow for more responsibility and authority at the departmental level on issues decided by the members of the council (Harrison, 1976: 65).

Management was required to supply the councils with confidential financial information, and only under exceptional circumstances could it demand confidentiality. Moreover, management was to provide the councils the same information that they supplied the shareholders every year. The councils were entitled to be kept informed on all company activities, including future production plans, and were to be consulted on issues regarding welfare schemes, vocational plans, and training. Management was obliged to discuss with the works councils all issues affecting employees and their working conditions, such as methods and changes in production plans, quality and development of new products, expansion or contraction, and the like. Finally, the councils had the right to suggest new approaches for improving safety and health. The department councils dealt with the same issues as the works councils, but at the department level, and their focus was on budgets, plans, reports, and ways to improve production. They only had advisory powers, unless management decided otherwise (Harrison, 1976: 66; IDE, 1981b: 28; Lafferty, 1984: 128).

The 1973 Company Act, as well as the 1977 Work Environment Act, were products of the new union policy pursued through the 1970s. Employers, however, strongly opposed such a policy. Specifically, they rejected the idea of giving employees legal representation in decision making, their position being that board representation should be the subject of management-labor negotiations. Their demands were doomed to fail, given the strong position of the labor movement and since the Labor party was back in office. By gaining board-level representation, employees achieved a new position, which was both practically and symbolically very important, by denoting that labor was an interest group at the same level as management. This new position could allow employees to have access to more information, gain more insight on the company business, and thus potentially strengthen their bargaining position. However, the unions achieved only minority representation on the boards of directors. Within the context of the employers' right to control because of ownership, such board representation was limited. Their only hope of fulfilling the possibilities opened up to workers through that route and of avoiding becoming hostages to managerial intentions was that board representation was merely one of several parallel developments and mechanisms that would ensure workers' input in the decision-making process. Indeed, unions became very demanding in their requests for more participatory rights for their members (Gustavsen and Hunnius, 1981: 87).

The Work Environment Reform enacted in 1977 is one more manifestation of the unions' determination: it is indicative of a new union policy that began to emerge in both Sweden and Norway in the late 1960s. The new policy entailed the integration of traditional health and safety considerations with notions of worker participation, and thus should be perceived as part of the Industrial Democracy Program pursued up to that point in Norway (Gustavsen and Hunnius, 1981; Kalleberg, 1985). Paragraph 12 of the 1977 Work Environment Act expanded the concept of work environment to cover technology and the premises of its development, the way work is arranged, working hours, wage systems, and the like. The act stipulates that all these factors should be taken into account, "so that employees are not exposed to undesirable physical or mental strain and so that their possibilities of displaying caution and observing safety measures are not impaired" (as quoted in Gustavsen and Hunnius, 1981: 197).

The act provided that employees and their representatives had to be informed about the systems used to plan and carry out the work, as well as about intended changes in those systems. In addition, they were entitled to training that would enable them to learn these systems, and thus participate in their design and planning. Furthermore, the right to self-determination and professional responsibility had to be taken into account before planning and arranging work tasks (Gustavsen and Hunnius, 1981; Kalleberg, 1985; Lafferty, 1984). The act applied to all enterprises with more than 50 employees, with the exception of sectors such as shipping, hunting, and agriculture, where special acts or arrangements applied in regard to employee participation. Participation in implementing the act was mandatory, which is a new element in the tradition of industrial relations in Norway (IDE, 1981b: 27; Schiller, 1977: 72–73).

The Work Environment Act has to be understood as a strategy to increase workplace democracy, since it provides workers and their representatives with a legal basis and administrative channels, as well as resources to influence control and planning systems, arrangements, and hours of work. More specifically, the act guarantees the employers' right to control because of ownership, but it also holds them responsible for maintaining a satisfactory working environment, since the work environment influences workers' well-being and affects them mentally and physically as individuals or as a social group (see Chapter II, paragraph 7: 1 in Gustavsen and Hunnius, 1981: 195).

One basic assumption of the act was that employees are potentially the most appropriate and the most capable individuals to solve their workplace problems, since they are most immediately affected by those problems (Kalleberg, 1985). This could be accomplished provided that the employees' influence over their working environment increased. The act stipulated that certain arrangements had to be made, and resources had to be available to employees, in order for their potential to be fully and effectively utilized. In that respect, the assumptions of the Work Environment Act are in line with the philosophy behind the IDP developed during the 1960s (Gustavsen, 1986; Gustavsen and Hunnius, 1981). The act stipulated that in enterprises with more than fifty employees, work environment committees had to be established. Workers could elect half of the committee's members, while employers could appoint the rest. Employee and employer representatives would alternate the chairmanship of the committee. According to the act, the duty of the work environment committee was to establish a "fully satisfactory working environment." To that end the committee was to participate in planning safety and environmental work and follow any developments related to workers' safety, health, and welfare (Paragraph 24: 1). We should emphasize, however, that the environment committees are mostly advisory bodies; therefore, their power is limited. Nonetheless, they have the potential to effect changes since they can influence employers to take measures to improve the working environment. They also have the authority to ask the employer to have the working environment examined or tested (Paragraph 24: 4).

Furthermore, the act provides for safety delegates, who have the authority to halt work they consider dangerous, without the risk of losing their wages or jobs. The act clearly states that "if the safety delegate considers that the life or health of employees is in immediate danger . . . work may be halted" (Paragraph 27). Employers cannot, based on their control rights, reverse such a decision, unless their position is upheld by the Directorate of Labor Inspection (Kalleberg, 1985: 25).

An extensive educational program, ranging from long-term university-based education programs to short courses of a few hours stressing the importance of employee participation, took place. The aim of those courses and programs was to provide knowledge and training on environmental matters. Education was essential to supplement the act and to ensure its effective application, given that new skills and tools were required, before workers and their representatives assumed their new roles and responsibilities. According to some estimates, between 1980 and 1985 approximately one out of ten employees in Norway had attended a course on the work environment (Kalleberg, 1985: 21). By the end of 1983, a total of 185,000 out of a workforce of less than 2 million had participated in the overall training program (Gustavsen, 1986: 125).

Let us briefly consider the factors that brought about the concerns addressed by the act and helped to mobilize such large numbers of people, so that the act would not become just another paper regulation. First, the environmental debate raised questions regarding the impact of chemical substances on health and in so doing proved very effective in increasing public awareness with regard to environmental issues at work. Gradually, as in Sweden, the debate was broadened to include issues such as stress, other psychosocial hazards, early detection, and preventive measures of diseases. Traditionally, these issues had never been raised within the work environment context, nor had they been covered by legislation. Moreover, health and safety concerns took on a special dimension in Norway in that health and safety risks were not merely linked to human mistakes, as management had traditionally claimed, but were associated with the lack of power and control. They were explained by the lack of interesting and flexible jobs in which workers could use their initiative and judgment and thus grow personally and professionally (Sirianni, 1987b: 20). The increased concern about health and safety issues related to the work environment was also reflected in an increasing number of projects, studies, and reports about working-life conditions during the same period (Gustavsen, 1986; Gustavsen and Hunnius, 1981).

Second, a number of illegal strikes which were triggered by the strike in the Swedish mining company, the LKAB, also raised health, safety, and general work environment concerns. These illegal strikes put unions in a strained position, since unions were obliged to restrain their members from striking while labor contracts were in effect. On the other hand, they helped clarify the weaknesses of the existing centralized system of negotiations that was unable to grasp the reality of local conditions and thus solve problems experienced by workers at their immediate workplace (Gustavsen and Hunnius, 1981).

Third, the split which the European Economic Community issue had caused within the Labor party and the trade union movement had to be addressed and a solution had to be found. The Labor party leadership supported Norway's entrance into the community, while the grass-roots members of the party tended to disagree. Issues of worker participation were once more caught within the political struggle, and to a large extent worker board-level representation and the Work Environment campaign were attempts to help restore faith and legitimacy within the labor movement (Gustavsen and Hunnius, 1981). The first official initiative emerged when the Labor party and the LO drafted a program for Work Environment Reform, just before the 1973 parliamentary elections. The work environment reform attracted a considerable amount of interest within the labor movement, where more than three thousand members within the LO voluntarily reviewed and commented on the proposal for the act. The Work Research Institute also became very instrumental in developing a strategy for reform by linking work environment issues with the notion of industrial democracy. Ultimately, the institute was responsible in formulating Paragraph 12 of the act (Gustavsen, 1986).

Employers, on the other hand, opposed certain provisions of the act, including the use of legislation to enforce it, and the training of workers at the expense of employers during work hours. Nearly 10 percent of the entire workforce had completed a forty-hour training program in learning how to analyze and improve their work environment (Howard and Schneider, 1987: 82–83). Since the reform had the support of the labor movement, the Labor and Socialist People's party, and also some center-to-right parties, the employers did not strongly oppose it. It was apparent that the parliament was to approve the act unanimously and that any efforts to oppose it would have been unsuccessful. By emphasizing the importance of employee involvement in the work environment and by providing mechanisms to influence decisions on environment matters, the act to a certain extent was based on the same principles as the IDP of the 1960s, which many employers and managers had supported.

Worker Participation and Technological Change

In Norway as in Sweden, there has also been a proliferation of efforts and legal and organizational mechanisms to expand workers' participation in technological change. Beginning in the mid-1970s, a number of national and local Technology Agreements were signed establishing rights for workers and their unions in the areas of the design, introduction, and use of new technology, beyond the general guidelines provided by the Work Environment Act. Some of the rights established by those agreements include the right of information, bargaining, participation, education, and training on technological matters. The fundamental premise of those agreements is quite similar to that of the Work Environment Act: The people who are affected by technology and technological change should also be provided with the resources and mechanisms to regulate them (Schneider, 1983). Unions were once again instrumental in introducing such changes.

By the late 1960s, unions had became very dissatisfied with the limits of workplace projects, especially with issues pertaining to technological change over which the interests of labor and management often conflicted. As a result, it became very difficult to maintain the cooperative relations of the earlier years. Gradually, unions began to develop their own strategies to address technological change in the workplace, often with the cooperation of some very influential technical experts who were sympathetic to union goals. In working in a number of projects with those experts, unions were aiming to build their own expertise on technology. This in turn stimulated union activism and resulted in a number of Technology Agreements, the first of which was the national Framework Agreement signed between the LO and NAF in 1975. Similar agreements were signed over the next several years in the public sector, while some provisions of the Technology Agreements were incorporated in the 1977 Work Environment Act (Howard and Schneider, 1987: 81–82).

One of the basic principles of the Technology Agreements was that unions should be given information regarding the new technical systems, something that is also true for Sweden. Unions also have the right to negotiate over company plans with respect to technological changes. In an attempt to evaluate the impact of technology, as well as to prepare for collective bargaining over technology issues, unions in Norway, as in Sweden, can hire outside consultants paid by the company. Unlike Sweden, however, they have the right to elect a permanent data shop steward to supervise and negotiate technological developments. Workers are guaranteed job-related training as well as education on computers and their design.

As unions and workers became more familiar with the technical aspects of organizations and more knowledgeable about technology issues, they realized the limitations of the rights which the Technology Agreements gave them. It became apparent that those rights were not sufficient to increase their influence over technological change. Up to that point, the unions' role had been to negotiate the application of new technical systems after those systems had been designed and introduced. Gradually, however, and more extensively than in Sweden, unions began to develop what Howard and Schneider call a before-the-fact approach that aimed to extend union and worker participation in the designing stages of the new technology. This approach, which has been applied systematically and quite extensively from banks to business to postal services in Norway, entails taking into consideration broader social criteria regarding the organization of work and incorporating worker influence into the early planning stages of the development of new technologies.

One example that demonstrates the incorporation of union broad social goals in trying to accomplish efficiency while improving workers' jobs and quality service is the project that took place in the late 1970s in the Norwegian post office. Very briefly, the goal in developing such a large project was to automate the accounting process in about 450 local post offices. The postal workers union was able to achieve the representation of two experienced union members in the formal steering committee that was formed to oversee the development of the system responsible for such automation. Workers gave their advice about various technical issues, and their knowledge proved valuable in developing the new automatic procedures. Soon, however, the unions realized the limitations of their participation, since no mechanism was available to them in determining the impact of the application of the new system on workers and their work environment. Consequently, and under the supervision of the unions, informal worker research groups were established in an attempt not only to study the potential consequences of the new system, but also to develop alternative social, organizational, and technical criteria in designing it. Although the members in those research groups did not participate in the designing process itself, they were able to influence that process considerably because of their close ties with union representatives in the formal design team and because of the expertise they themselves had accumulated through their participation in the whole project. Those informal ties and contacts have been cultivated and proven quite effective in making the rights provided by the legislation or collective agreements effective in similar projects and situations as well (Della Rocca, 1987: 160–161; Howard and Schneider, 1987: 82–85).

Concluding Remarks

The new Technological Agreements and the laws regarding industrial democracy have opened up new possibilities for a substantial union and worker influence in the Norwegian work environment. The Norwegian experience with worker participation indicates a long process of workplace changes toward democratization, changes that have been introduced and reinforced by a strong labor movement. As the experience and knowledge accumulated throughout the years, new questions were raised and new demands formulated, which then led to more radical goals. As the goals became progressively more advanced and radical, and as new socioeconomic, political, and technological conditions emerged, new means were sought to accomplish them. The labor movement, being strong ideologically, organizationally, and politically, was able to respond to emerging circumstances and its members' demands by successfully enacting legislation to further expand participatory rights.

As the foregoing analysis indicates, both Norway and Sweden show similar patterns in regard to the development of workers' participation schemes, although Norway did not experience Sweden's tight labor market conditions in the 1960s. But alienation and productivity problems were similar, and the cooperative nature of the industrial relations system facilitated the emergence of workers' participation schemes in Norway as well. In both countries we note an evolutionary development of workers' participation schemes corresponding to structural and value changes, rather than a cyclical one.

Such an evolution was not simply unilinear but multiphasic. Participation schemes did not evolve simply because of benevolent and perceptive employers and managers, or because cooperation in those countries produced a harmonious balance of interests between labor and capital. Rather, regardless of cooperative relations, labor and capital still have their own values, interests, and goals, which very often became the source of conflict between labor and capital in both countries. Participation schemes were merely the result of a power struggle over all of these. Consider, for instance, the fact that Braverman's book was studied extensively as a tool in that struggle. His thesis on deskilling had a considerable impact in sensitizing the labor movements of Sweden and Norway in the development of technology agreements in both countries.

Participation schemes in these two countries were not introduced only when the managerial position was challenged or as a coaptive mechanism to achieve labor's compliance and thus advance capital's interests. Such a position, advanced by Braverman and some cyclical theorists such as Ramsay, ignores the instrumental role workers and their strong unions played in those countries in advancing participatory goals. Although the employers in both countries, in protecting their long-standing interests, resisted certain changes and fought the expansion of democratic rights at work, they themselves had strong interests in supporting certain participative schemes. But participation in both Sweden and Norway was not entirely directed by management, and in contrast with other countries examined in this part of the book, workers and unions managed to some extent not to become hostages of managerial intentions and goals. Legislative measures and board representation in both Sweden and Norway opened up possibilities for increased worker influence on the work life and the work environment. Along with the political and organizational strength of the labor movement, the unique supportive political context (which other countries lack) has facilitated the development of formal institutions in both countries to represent workers' interests. This seems to indicate that workers' participative rights have better chances to be materialized there.

These countries, as others, face several basic economic and technological barriers in this era of economic uncertainty, globalized competition, and rapid technological change. For instance, technological systems designed on the basis of broad social criteria as suggested by the labor movements in these countries can be expensive, at least in the short run, for some companies to adopt. In addition, new technologies in Scandinavian countries are mostly transferred from the United States. Transferred system packages can be very inflexible, and they can seriously challenge the unions' attempts to participate in the designing of the new technology in those countries. It remains to be seen how these challenges will affect the ongoing process of workers' participation in these countries.

The Scandinavian model of participation as exemplified here in the cases of Sweden and Norway constitutes a classic example of this ongoing, dynamic process. What distinguishes this model of worker participation from experiences in other countries examined in this book is principally its extensive character which goes beyond piecemeal changes, isolated projects, and experiments. Regardless of limitations, problems, and barriers to workplace democratization, the Scandinavian model has some important theoretical implications for other contexts by illustrating mainly the importance of the extensive institutional support which workers' participation has attracted owing to the unique social, political, economic, and labor relations climate prevalent in these countries. It also offers a vision and an example for other countries by denoting the potential of alternative ways to organize work life and the work environment in the overall process of democratization of work.

NOTES

1. For a more detailed analysis of the socioeconomic, political, labor market, and international conditions that promoted workers' demands for control over the production process, as well as the official workers' organs that emerged during the First World War and immediate postwar period, see Sirianni (1983: 254–310) and Poole (1978: Chapter 4).

2. In 1920, for instance, a parliamentary committee was set up and was assigned the task of studying the issue of industrial democracy. The committee produced a report three years later emphasizing the goals of job satisfaction and productivity. It also suggested the formation of joint labor-management consultative committees in enterprises with more than twenty-five employees. The ultimate goal was to promote cooperation between labor and management and to enable workers to gain better insight into the production process and thus promote their active involvement in it. Eventually, both the LO and the employers viewed these proposals negatively. The unions argued that employers ignored the class struggle, while the employers found such proposals very extreme. See Jenkins (1973: 253); Ryden (1978: 93).

3. The Guild Socialism movement emerged in England in the 1910s and 1920s under the leadership of the historian G.D.H. Cole demanding worker control. On the basis of its principles, workers, through craft unions or Guilds, were to control the various sectors of the nationalized industry. The representatives of craft workers were to manage production in their respective industries. These representatives were to collaborate closely with the leaders of the state (which would own the means of production), who would have ultimate control over national economic policies. See Kendall (1972: 61–62); King and van de Vall (1978: 7–8); Poole (1978: 106–109).

4. Work reorganization started at the Saab-Scania plant in 1972. This was the first plant within the automobile industry where the assembly line was abolished. Instead, the plant was divided into three separate construction areas, where workers could control the pace of work and divide the tasks among themselves. Also at Volvo, Sweden's largest company, a new experiment started in the mid-1970s. The line on which the cars were assembled was abolished. Instead, the work was organized among small, autonomous groups of fifteen to twenty workers. These groups were responsible for a particular section of the car (e.g., electrical system, brakes) and were in control of the pace of work. It is estimated that 300 to 500 companies adopted similar measures. For more details on these and similar experiments, see Cole (1987: 43–44); Jenkins (1973: 264–273); Long (1986: 376–377); Poole (1978: 67); Qvale (1976: 461).

5. See Cole (1987: 43). He suggests that Sweden's welfare policies such as legislated unemployment and benefits have facilitated high turnover and absenteeism rates among employees, since such behavior has low costs to them.

6. The first strategy (e.g., recruitment of women), which was reinforced by governmental policies, proved more or less successful. The second one (e.g., increase of migrant workers, especially in the mining, quarrying, and manufacturing sectors) proved inadequate in solving the problem since, first, employers continued to have problems finding workers to do the least desirable jobs; and, second, the steady influx of aliens (from 121,747 in 1962 to 221,925 in 1973) was perceived as a threatening social problem. Furthermore, absenteeism and turnover rates (50 percent in 1970) were continually increasing. See Cole (1984: 28, 1987: 43); Tsiganou (1982: Chapter 2).

7. In the early 1960s, the young psychologist Einar Thorsrud from the Institute for Research in Industrial Environments in Tondheim became interested in the work done at the Tavistock Institute in London regarding work organization. The Tavistock Institute became well known for the development of the concept of the sociotechnical system, that is, the integration of social and technical aspects in the organization of the workplace. The goal at the institute was to increase the power and responsibility of workers on the shopfloor in order to manage their work under minimum managerial supervision. The work was to be divided among workers who belonged to small, cohesive, autonomous

work groups. This in turn would increase productivity. Thorsrud, in collaboration with people from the Tavistock Institute, started a number of experiments in Norway applying the above concepts and later introduced the idea of autonomous groups and related concepts in Sweden. See Cole (1987: 49–50); Jenkins (1973: 247–258); Poole (1978: 66–67).

8. In 1906, an agreement, the so-called December Compromise, was reached between the LO and SAF. According to that agreement, LO accepted the employers' right to enclose Paragraph 23 (later known as Paragraph 32) in every contract signed from that time on. "Paragraph 32 provides that management has the right to freely hire and fire workers, to manage and assign their work, and to use workers from any union or worker outside unions" (as quoted in Jenkins, 1973: 260); see also Albrecht (1980: 307); Martin (1977: 55–56).

9. The 1938 Basic Agreement basically prescribed the rules and regulations of collective bargaining. These included, among other things, the use of strikes and lockouts during periods of dispute over new contracts; the "peace obligation" during the contract period; employers' obligation to give one week's notice and to consult with the unions in case of disputed dismissals; the dismissal of employees with the least seniority among equally qualified ones; and so on. Although the employers' prerogatives to hire and organize work remained intact, their right to fire was restricted somewhat. See Geijer (1974: 268); IDE (1981b: 46); Martin (1977: 60–61).

10. For instance, in cases of shutdowns and layoffs, the National Labor Market Board and local branches, comprised of governmental and labor representatives, would offer workers assistance regarding relocation and retraining. Companies facing difficulties would be subsidized for a period of time, so that workers could adjust more smoothly to the new conditions. Finally, the government started programs for employment opportunities. See Stephens (1980: 57).

11. Sweden has one of the highest standards of living in the world. The GNP per capita is among the highest in Europe. Measures to equalize income distribution have been taken, and unemployment has been kept low in most of the postwar period. The increase in educational levels has been one of the central elements of Sweden's welfare state policies. See IDE (1981b: 38–39); Jenkins (1973: 262); Stephens (1980: 63–64).

12. Councils were established in firms with more than fifty employees. They are joint, labor-management bodies, with one-third of their members appointed by the employers, and two-thirds by the local unions. The worker representatives could remain in office at least two years, but no more than four. Councils are consulted and receive information on the following issues: Principles and methods of recruitment, selection and promotion, overall planning of recruitment and training; production matters such as techniques, organization, and planning. Management must disclose its investment and marketing plans, unless it perceives that such information could hurt the company's competitive position. Finally, the councils cannot deal with disputes regarding collective wage agreements and regulation of employment terms, areas that fall within the union jurisdiction. See Harrison (1976: 72); Jain and Jain (1980: 66–67).

13. Educational levels had risen, and so, young people were unwilling to accept routine, dull jobs. Furthermore, most of the Swedish young people were graduating from the nine-year Comprehensive School (ages seven to sixteen), and by 1968 some 80 percent of the sixteen year olds were going on to further education. See Cole (1984: 19–20).

14. One such failed attempt was the lengthy, almost three-year negotiation—from

1969 to mid-1972—to revise the 1948 work study agreement with only information and suggestion exchange results. See Martin (1977: 69).

15. See Note 6 above.

16. In most of the postwar period, the Social Democrats have been the largest party in Sweden by winning the majority of the parliamentary seats. The nonsocialist parties include the Conservatives, the Centre party, and the Liberals. All these parties, except the communists, supported the laws in regard to industrial democracy. Communists were especially opposed to worker representation on the board of directors, claiming that it was an unacceptable class collaboration. See Åsard (1986: 210); IDE (1981b: 41).

17. An English version of the law can be found in *Board Representation of Employees in Industry*, the National Swedish Industrial Board, 1976.

18. In 1975, an official agency in collaboration with the Ministries of Industry and Labor, and employers' and workers' organizations carried out an extensive survey to evaluate the first results of this participation. They found that workers had not exercised their right to board representation in only 9 percent of the companies covered by the legislation. For a summary of the survey, see National Swedish Industrial Board: *Board Representation of Employees in Sweden, A Summary of a Survey*, Stockholm, Liber Forlag, 1976.

19. There are exceptions to this rule. Under pressing circumstances, employers can make a decision without negotiating with the union. But employers always run the risk of being held liable by the Labor Court and therefore of paying damages to the union, if their reasons for not negotiating are not proven sufficient. See Lind (1979: 25).

20. In the late 1970s, over 40 percent of the overall domestic industrial production was going into foreign markets. Also, the rate of overseas capital investment by Swedish firms was increasing far more than the domestic rate of increase. This heavy involvement and dependence of the Swedish economy is further compounded by the fact that Swedish companies invest more in foreign markets than foreign companies invest inside Sweden. For more about the Swedish economy, its development, and international character, see Albrecht and Deutsch (1983: 300–303).

21. The UTOPIA project is a joint effort of the Nordic Graphics Union and the Swedish Center for Working Life. The acronym stands for Swedish words meaning Training, Technology, and Products from a Quality of Work Perspective. The project started in 1980, and its goal was to reverse the tendency of poor work content and elimination of work among graphics workers because of the introduction of computers. In pursuing such a goal, the UTOPIA project developed alternative technology to be used as a tool for skilled printing workers and in accordance with the union considerations of work quality. For more information, see Martin (1987: 121–137).

22. The Basic Agreement in force since 1935 comprises the first part of every collective agreement. It recognizes the right of employees to organize; it includes provisions referring to the duties and rights of shop stewards; it limits the use of conflict measures while the collective agreement is in force; but it recognizes the right of strike over disputes of interests, and so on. See Gustavsen and Hunnius (1981: 29–30).

23. The state took some decisive measures to control unemployment. For instance, in the late 1940s in an attempt to create employment and promote economic activity, the government built a state-owned steel works and an aluminum smelter. These policies were relaxed later on, and private and international enterprises were allowed to create hydroelectric plants. Since the 1970s, however, in order to secure national control over

important resources, such as energy and oil, the state bought back a number of these plants. See IDE (1981b: 19–20).

24. The realization of such a contradiction and the need for industrial democracy are clearly reflected in the following extract from a publication of the Iron and Metal Workers' Union published in 1962: "We have talked about it [industrial democracy], and something has been achieved. But the main task remains to be done, that is, the transfer of power and responsibility within the individual enterprise from the private owner to the organized unity of all employees. We cherish democracy in political elections, in organizational life, in social politics, in cultural politics. Why should democracy stop at the workplace where people spend one-third of their working life. It was Franklin D. Roosevelt who formulated the well-known slogan that we cannot live half-free and half-slave. It can be said with the same justification that a society cannot, in the long run, cherish democracy as a leading principle and then deny the introduction of this principle in industry, which is the foundation of that society." (As quoted in Emery and Thorsrud, 1969: 9). For similar views of political leaders, trade unionists, and business leaders, see Emery and Thorsrud (1969: Chapter 2).

25. The new party was supported by the intellectuals, youth organizations, local union-ists, and workers, and it was mainly against NATO membership and nuclear weapons, as well as against the pragmatic productivity-oriented policies that dominated Norwegian politics after the war. See IDE (1981b: 14).

26. One of the many companies to experiment with the new organizational structure was Norsk Hydro, among the biggest companies of Norway (8,000 employees). The company was producing power, chemicals, oil, metals, and so on. Labor-management relations were very poor owing to the bureaucratic nature of the organization. Problems became even worse because of the competitive conditions on the world market for fer-tilizers, which was one of Norway's major products. As a solution, the management considered employee participation in the decision-making process and better utilization of human resources. Toward that goal autonomous groups were formed, training was introduced, and rotation and flexibility became part of the system. Because of employee suggestions, staff reductions took place. This resulted in a 30 percent reduction of the cost of every ton of fertilizer produced. Workers' satisfaction levels increased, and soon similar reform projects started in a cabinet plant and in another one producing magnesium. For more details on this experiment and similar ones, see Jenkins (1973: 246–258).

3

The European Experience with Workers' Participation

THE CASE OF ENGLAND

Following the First World War, workers in England, as in other European countries, experienced a considerable decline in their working and living standards. Labor in England, as in other countries, cooperated with management during the war. But the notion that this cooperation would have some implications for work reform was not well founded. The sacrifices labor made during the war, the realization of existing inequalities and class tensions, the increasing labor shortages in conjunction with the demands for more war production—all increased the potential for labor protest and opposition (Sirianni, 1983). However, because of political and strategic considerations, the workers' demands and the official union policy did not coincide. Therefore, most of the workers' radical demands, including the demand for more worker control over the production process, were suppressed in the name of uninterrupted war production (Brannen, 1983a; Sirianni, 1983).

Meanwhile, the radical shop steward movement that emerged during the war and the various experiments for more worker control in the immediate postwar period, influenced by Syndicalist and Guild Socialist ideas, did not last long. The syndicalist movement collapsed owing mostly to the changed economic and industrial conditions. In response to the radical shop steward movement, whose goal was to increase the informal and direct influence of workers at the shopfloor level, the government, following the recommendations of the Whitley committees, sponsored labor-management committees. These were consultation committees established to contain workers' aspirations and to avoid fundamental changes that would correspond to the emerging demands of workers' control (Jones, 1977). Even if the government had failed to suppress the radical demands of the period, the economic conditions would have done just that. By 1922, high rates of unemployment put an end to workers' demands for control. Meanwhile, the Whitley committees began to dissolve, and by the 1930s, lacking the support of the employers, they ceased to have any substantial influence (Shenfield, 1978).

During the interwar period the political debate focused on nationalization. Socialists turned mostly to corporatist models of industrial participation. Unions, which earlier had opposed involvement in management, were then perceived as the only means to carry out worker participation. Industrial democracy became a mechanism to protect workers' economic interests rather than a way of defending democracy in the workplace. The affluence of the 1950s and the extensive nationalization facilitated the advancement of such a position, which was sustained until the early 1960s (Street, 1983: 521). Provisions for some worker control were introduced, while legislation on nationalization in the post–World War II ensured the placement of some union representation on the board of directors (Thomson, 1977: 33). During the Second World War labor and management again cooperated to increase war production. The result of that cooperation was the establishment of joint labor-management committees (Garson, 1977).

With the exception of producer cooperatives, which are beyond the scope of this book, England's experience with worker participation is limited primarily to plant-level joint-consultation schemes, as well as a very small number of worker directors sitting on the boards of some nationalized companies (Jones, 1977). In general, efforts to introduce participative schemes fall within the human relations tradition. In the name of better industrial relations, participatory schemes have been introduced mostly by management with the intent to increase productivity. Unlike its Scandinavian and continental counterparts, England has not undertaken any major legalistic measures to provide for worker participation. The features that typify the British industrial relations system are, first, decentralized bargaining. All encountered problems and disputes are solved by collective bargaining through the union apparatus at the company rather than the national level, although national negotiations provide a framework in many industries. The second feature is occupational segmentation. Unions and collective bargaining are organized on the basis of occupation, and as a result multiunionism at the company level prevails. Third is voluntarism. England has traditionally had a high degree of informality in regards to rights and procedures (Della Rocca, 1987: 142). Reliance on the law and administrative procedures is minimal, whereas involvement in enterprise affairs is generally avoided. As a result, collective bargaining via the formal union apparatus and plant-level negotiations through an informal, but very powerful, shop-steward movement have traditionally been the primary forms of industrial democracy practiced in England. Instead of cooperative roles of participation, the British industrial system has adopted adversary roles of collective bargaining. This system of collective bargaining reflects oppositional interests between labor and management and is rooted in the long tradition of class struggle and conflict of the British society.

Workers' Participation as a Response to New Challenges

The Trade Union Congress (TUC), which represents the collective interests of unions, has historically been a strong advocate of the position that through negotiation, and not through participation, unions should better be able to defend their members' interests against those of capital. This position is rationalized on the grounds that unions would only be able to defend workers' interests by negotiating wages and conditions of work, and not by participating in a system to which they were fundamentally opposed (Ogden, 1982). It is also rooted in the ideology of British socialism which equates workers' control with the socialist state. This explains to a large extent why England, in comparison with other European countries, and with the possible exception of the work at the Institute of Workers' Control[1] seems to lag behind in industrial democracy. Thus, TUC has long been opposed to the idea of workers' participation. However, during the immediate postwar period and especially during the 1960s, this traditional collective bargaining approach to industrial relations seemed inadequate in responding to the needs of the new era. Consequently, interest in worker participation increased as segments of the labor movement demanded codetermination rights on the supervisory boards through legislation (Sorge, 1976: 279). What explains this upsurge of interest in worker participation and the change of attitude within the labor movement?

First, the postwar increase in wealth, higher levels of education, and increased worker gains through the growth of the welfare state contributed to rising expectations in regards to the standards of worklife and the standard of living in general. In the work environment, the increasingly well-educated workers tended to become more alienated and expressed an increasing interest for more control. This, together with the impact of the *New Left* ideology of the 1960s, led to the challenge of authority structures and the questioning of institutions; to increasing demands for more say over one's destiny, including more control over one's immediate job. Union leaders were demanding that the great reserve of intelligence, knowledge, and enthusiasm which workers possess be utilized at the shopfloor and at the board level (Brannen, 1983: 49–51; Coates and Topham, 1970: 417; IDE, 1981b: 115; Foy and Gadon, 1976: 71; Jenkins, 1973: 186–187). As discussed above, the circumstances were similar in Sweden and Norway, and to a great degree facilitated the emergence of workers' participation schemes in the countries examined in this part of the book, by forcing greater political attention on the issue of workers' participation in the decision-making process.

Second, by the early 1960s the whole industrial relations system based on collective bargaining was facing a major crisis. The number of unofficial strikes had increased substantially, as had the number of shop stewards and the unofficial plant-level agreements. These were indications that the formal trade union structure was losing control over bargaining and that the legitimacy of the formal union structure was dangerously eroding, especially because of the increase in informal plant-level bargaining (Brannen, 1983a: 53; Thomson, 1977: 34).

Third, although plant-level bargaining agreements were localized and were concentrated on economic issues, they nonetheless helped frustrate the economic objectives of both management and government (Brannen, 1983a). Not only trade union leaders, but also government officials and employers' associations began to give special consideration to all these factors in an attempt to overcome the crisis.

The Donovan Commission, which was formed to thoroughly examine the British industrial relations system in its 1968 report, made some policy recommendations without, however, challenging the ultimate managerial responsibility to run the enterprise. Constrained by the considerable increase of the shop stewards' shopfloor power over the previous years, it instead sought to institutionalize conflict through collective bargaining by strengthening formal procedures (Brannen, 1983a: 55). Its analysis was based on a pluralist notion of interest groups that needed to collaborate with each other. Their differences were to be settled through collective bargaining, a position articulated in the late 1950s by Hugh Clegg. This position entailed that unions refrain from participating in managing and sharing the responsibilities for management policies, since such a strategy would undermine their ability to defend their members' interests. Instead, industrial democracy could be accomplished through collective bargaining by an oppositional trade union movement. Up to that point the official TUC ideology largely reflected that position (Brannen, 1983a: 56; Thomson, 1977: 34).

In an attempt to defend its interests from the new developments that threatened its vitality, the TUC gradually began to articulate a different position. In presenting its position to the Donovan Commission, the TUC argued that trade unions would not run the risk of being undermined, if trade unionists participated in management affairs up to the point when these affairs became subject to negotiation. This interest in new forms of industrial democracy was accelerated as the government produced the white paper "In place of Strife" and threatened to legislate and restrict the unions' collective bargaining powers (Brannen, 1983a: 54). By the early 1970s, the TUC had further developed its position on participation in management. Instead of a voluntary mode of industrial relations, a legal mode was advocated so that unions could establish a better influence over the economic direction of the enterprise. The TUC also made a number of recommendations to improve industrial democracy by widening the scope of collective bargaining. It supported statutory obligations on companies regarding disclosure of a wide range of information to the unions (Ogden, 1982). This shift in union policy can be best understood within the context of occupational and technological changes and the escalating economic problems of the 1960s and early 1970s.

The traditional industries such as textiles were declining, while takeovers and mergers were increasing. Consequently, unemployment rates began to rise, and occupational and employment patterns began to change (Guest, 1986). For example, in 1911 manual workers comprised 80 percent of the working population; by 1971 they comprised only 50 percent. White-collar occupations, on the other hand, gained more members. They increased from 13.4 percent in 1911 to 43.3 percent in 1971 (Brannen, 1983a: 50). And although half of the labor force is unionized, less than half of these workers belong to TUC affiliated unions. Therefore, the labor movement is not particularly strong or unified as a socio-political force to successfully push for its goals, as is the case in Sweden and Norway. Besides, unionization is high in manufacturing and rather low in service categories (IDE, 1981b: 110). The service categories, however, were precisely the sectors that experienced considerable increases in membership in the late 1960s. Again, structural changes like these deeply affected the strength of trade unions, since traditional sectors, where unions were strongly represented, began to decline.

The serious economic problems such as inflation, unemployment, and the increase in the number of strikes which accompanied these structural changes urgently required solutions. At the national level, this led to the establishment of a social contract between the TUC and the Labor government, which won the 1974 elections. On the basis of that contract, unions accepted some voluntary wage controls, while the government promised to address some of the economic and industrial relations problems. As a result of that compromise, a number of legislative acts took place during the 1970s. For instance, section 17 of the 1975 Employment Protection Act guaranteed workers protection against unfair dismissal. Under the same act, and upon union request, employers were obliged to disclose certain information for the purpose of collective bargaining (Guest, 1986: 686; Shenfield, 1978: 30). Therefore, labor consultation became statutory. Moreover, under the 1974 Health and Safety at Work Act, if two or more union-appointed safety representatives so requested, employers were obliged to establish safety committees that would include employee representatives in them (Brannen, 1983a: 55; Guest, 1986: 686–687; Ogden, 1982: 550).

Regardless of the legal provisions and of the extension of the scope of collective bargaining, the managerial prerogative to control the flow of information regarding company affairs remained intact. Unions became increasingly disillusioned with the limitations of legal provisions in lessening substantial managerial prerogatives, since disclosure of information on profits, plant relocation, and the like was not required by law. In addition, employers exploited a number of exceptions and ambiguous points regarding disclosure of information to their advantage. For instance, employers had the right to withhold certain information on the grounds that such information was potentially harmful for their business (Bellace and Gospel, 1983: 65). Moreover, although the scope of collective bargaining had been enlarged, strategic decisions, including takeovers, mergers, investment policies, and closures, which critically affect people's work lives, were excluded from collective bargaining (Bellace and Gospel, 1983).

Board-Level Representation

The limitations of the introduced changes helped develop a new union position; new forms of union control needed to be developed to include these crucial areas. Increasingly, the notion of worker directors gained support and by the mid-1970s became the major TUC strategy toward industrial democracy, although the TUC acknowledged the inherent conflict of interests if workers' representatives were placed on the board of directors (Bellace and Gospel, 1983; Ogden, 1982). The TUC advocated worker representation on the supervisory boards of a two-tier board system to be initially applied to about 600 enterprises with more than 2,000 workers each. The placement of worker directors on the boards was seen as a new form of control that would enable workers and their unions to exert influence over strategically important matters, which up to that point were beyond the scope of collective bargaining, such as investment, product policy, and relocation issues. Half the members of the supervisory boards would be elected through the trade union (Thomson, 1977: 36).

In addition to the reasons mentioned above, other outside factors contributed to the increased interest in industrial democracy through board representation as well. First, the German experience with boardroom representation and similar developments in other Scandinavian countries had an impact on developments in England. Second, England was about to become a member of the Common Market in 1973, and pressures to take into consideration EEC developments toward workers' participation were increasing (Brannen, 1983a; Schuller, 1985; Thomson, 1977; Ursell, 1983). The above recommendations of the TUC were clearly influenced by developments and practices in other European countries. However, the TUC strongly rejected the European practice of the works council on the grounds that it would undermine established trade union interests within the enterprise. The TUC was afraid that the introduction of the works councils would either duplicate existing structures at the plant level or displace existing union arrangements (Thomson, 1977: 36).

To search for ways to achieve boardroom representation, a committee under Lord Bullock was formed. According to the Bullock report, companies with more than 2,000 employees would be obliged to have equal numbers of worker and management directors on their supervisory boards, as well as a quota of outside directors to keep the balance. This is known as the $2X + Y$ formula. The Majority Bullock report, however, was not accepted. Instead, the white paper on industrial Democracy, presented to the parliament in 1978, modified the above provisions by recommending that companies with more than 500 employees should be obliged by law, before taking any decisions, to discuss them with their employees. This would be accomplished through joint representation committees. In companies with more than 2,000 employees, employee representation would be established, provided that two conditions were met. First, before employees could be represented on the supervisory board, joint representation committees had to be in operation for at least four years; and second, such representation had to be supported by the overall workforce of the company and not just by union members. Up to 1979, however, when the Labor government lost the elections, legislation had not been introduced. The Conservatives who won the elections strongly opposed boardroom representation. Instead, they encouraged employee involvement through consultation, communication, and financial participation (Brannen, 1983a: 60).

This outcome is not surprising considering that the proposal by the Bullock report of parity single-channel representation based on trade union organization would considerably hurt employer and management interests. It was thought that worker directors interfered with the managerial prerogative to manage and were in violation of ownership rights. For instance, the employers' organizations and the Confederation of British Industry strongly opposed the Bullock provisions, claiming that, owing to the conflicting interests, the institution of worker directors would jeopardize efficiency and discourage investors. In a way employers feared that parity representation was just another way for unions to achieve nationalization, and they did not like it (Brannen, 1983a; Ogden, 1982; Shenfield, 1978). In their Minority Report, they instead proposed a two-tier board system, less than parity worker representation, and representation for all employees, including management (Brannen, 1983a: 101; Shenfield, 1978: 38–39). On the basis of those provisions, management would still be in control to safeguard its interests. Consequently, because worker boardroom representation met a lot of strong opposition, it was only introduced in a few private firms, in the nationalized Steel Corporation, and in the Post Office (Batstone et al., 1983; Brannen, 1983b; IDE, 1981b; Ogden, 1982).

The poor diffusion process can best be explained if we consider that management and owners were not the only parties who opposed worker boardroom representation. In sharp contrast to Sweden and Norway, the labor movement in England was divided on the issue, and therefore it could not provide a united and strong front. Those in favor of worker boardroom representation argued that such a position would enable workers and their unions to exert influence over critical decisions that up to that point were beyond the scope of collective bargaining. They further argued that such a position would enable workers to take part in the initial stages of policy formation and planning. As a result, workers would have the opportunity to dispute and debate policies and decisions, instead of reacting to them after they had been finalized (Ogden, 1982). Parity representation was perceived as essential for the institution of workers' directors to be effective, since it was doubtful that workers' directors would be willing to become involved and thus share responsibility in policy formulation unless such a condition was met first. On the other hand, it became apparent that if their constituents knew that their representatives could always be outvoted by the representatives of shareholders, their credibility could be easily undermined. Parity representation thus became imperative.

Some parts of the labor movement strongly opposed the idea of worker representation on the boards of directors. This is not surprising since such a notion runs counter to the long tradition of collective bargaining in England. As in other countries, in England, too, the typical concern with regard to worker representation on the board of directors has been worker coaptation. It was argued that the incorporation of trade unions into the management structure through boardroom participation would undermine their independence. This in turn would weaken their oppositional power and their effectiveness in representing their members' interests. It was also maintained that the institution of workers' directors would reinforce the legitimation of the existing industrial power and wealth structure, which workers and their unions so strongly disapproved. In place of worker boardroom representation, they favored extending the scope of collective bargaining to include issues such as planning, investment, takeover issues, and closures (Ogden, 1982; Schuller, 1985).

Limited Efforts of Worker Participation in Technological Change and Concluding Remarks

The 1975 Industry Act and the so-called Technology Agreements are manifestations of the efforts to penetrate into areas previously considered exclusively under managerial control. The 1975 act, however, failed to provide the unions with the right to enter into extended collective bargaining with companies. Such a prerogative belongs to the enterprises and the government, and the unions' involvement falls within the jurisdiction of the minister. As for the Technology Agreements, only a few have been signed and the amount of control exercised by unions with regard to technology implementation varies (Ogden, 1982: 555). These agreements are negotiated at the production unit and/or the company; in that respect they do not modify the decentralized structure of the industrial relations system. But this decentralized structure presents barriers in the implementation and diffusion of those agreements.

The subjects of those agreements include job security issues, training, physical and psychological impact of new technologies on workers, and the like. The unions' overall intent in those agreements is to acquire and exercise rights of consultation and information at the initial stages of technology introduction. Such efforts have not been particularly successful, however, and in very few cases unions have been involved in the initial critical stages of the development of new technology. In most of these agreements, unions were able to establish rights during the implementation stage and just before the final decisions regarding instruments and working methods were made. Since the introduction of new technology often poses serious threats of unemployment for a large number of workers, unions in England, as in most of the countries examined here, are particularly concerned with the impact of technology in that respect. To avoid such serious consequences, unions in England had demanded the reduction of working hours so that the overall working force would remain the same, but without success. Another area in which unions were not particularly successful was their ability to incorporate the physical and psychological impact of the new technologies, especially computers, in the overall quality of work, although some provisions for ergonomic improvements at the workplace have been made (Della Rocca, 1987: 156–157).

Such developments, though less extensive and successful than those in Norway and Sweden, indicate that unions, faced with the challenges of new technology for their organizational survival, have modified their traditional approaches. As a result, they have considered utilizing collective bargaining to enter into areas where managerial discretion was undeniable before. As expected, however, there has been strong employer and management opposition to extending the scope of bargaining. Furthermore, since enforcement of the existing legal provisions is rather loose, it is doubtful whether employers would agree to negotiate on such strategically important matters and would disclose relevant information to unions. Unions face another serious difficulty in their effort to control the impact of the new technology. Not only the conflict of interests between labor and capital has to be resolved, but also that among the unions themselves, which tends to compound the problem. New technologies often cause changes in tasks, skills, and occupations as a whole. Thus, unions are put in the strained position of fighting with each other in an effort to protect their occupational members' interests as they relate to the distribution of costs and benefits which the new technology brings about (Della Rocca, 1987: 157–158).

Employers, on the other hand, use offensive mechanisms that seek to make workers identify with company goals by introducing some "cosmetic" changes, which in itself presents another challenge for the unions. Faced with multiple challenges such as growing pressure to provide unions with more information, mounting economic problems, and the threat of legislation that would introduce worker boardroom representation, both employers and management, in an attempt to counterbalance such challenges, have encouraged a less threatening "bottom-up" participation that involves the introduction of a number of joint-consultation schemes (a strategy adopted by employers in most countries). The expectation was that joint-consultation and information schemes would ease some of the differences between management and labor by uniting them to face the adverse economic situation.

These schemes, however, allow management to retain its control over decision-making processes. They therefore offer workers limited opportunities to influence such processes and effect changes (Brannen, 1983a; Ogden, 1982). We should also stress that management in England could get away with such consultation plans more easily than management in Sweden or Norway. Given the specific structure of the industrial relations system, union division, and weak ideological commitment to worker participatory goals, management in England did not face strong pressures at the political or labor market levels in order to introduce participation schemes that would undermine its prerogatives. When it was forced to take a position on the issue, it initiated joint-consultation and information schemes that did not provide workers with any real decision-making powers.

The labor movement, on the other hand, was largely committed to an oppositional stance toward industrial democracy by relying primarily on collective bargaining to protect its members' economic rights as well as work conditions. Periods of economic growth strengthened labor's position, and the distributive gains of workers increased. Meanwhile, a strong steward movement enhanced labor control at the plant level. In late 1966 and early 1967, the TUC officially acknowledged the need to explore participatory devices, but their policy statements indicate that they were more influenced by the problems of rationalization than by the growing demand for control at the grass-roots level (Coates and Topham, 1970: 438). When the issue of board-level representation surfaced, the highly decentralized, and at the national level weak, labor movement proved crucial in determining the fate of the issue. Since unions within the TUC vary in regard to their commitment to the TUC as a central institution, and since the link between the TUC and its members is relatively weak, polarization on the issue was inevitable. Declining unionization rates, and the fierce managerial attack of the shop steward movement compounded the problem, as the already organizationally weak TUC was unable to present a strong united front and push for changes and legislation. It became apparent that minority representation on the board of directors would jeopardize the unions' independent and oppositional stance, that it would further weaken direct shopfloor control, and that the system could not protect workers as long as mechanisms to make worker directors formally accountable to their members that voted for them were lacking. Given the history of labor relations, the request among union and Labor party leaders to extend the scope of collective bargaining and introduce statutory protection was very appropriate as a first step before broader aspects of economic planning at the board level were considered.

In contrast, participatory arrangements at the company level in Sweden and Norway are regulated and strengthened through legislation and through national agreements with the support of a pro-labor government. To a large extent, the same is true for worker board-level representation. In contrast to its Scandinavian counterparts, in England the labor movement is not particularly strong or united. It lacks not only strength and organizational capacity, but also a firm ideological commitment to participative goals. As a result, it is not a sufficiently powerful sociopolitical force to push for strong legislation and changes at the national level. Also in contrast to the almost continuous incumbency of Social Democratic parties in Scandinavia, the Labor party in England was not very successful during most of the postwar period. We could also argue that the strong presence of unions at the shopfloor level in England, in contrast to Sweden and Norway, might have preempted the need for participation schemes at that level. When we consider all these factors, we can understand why participation schemes in England are less extensive, and the degree of power exercised by workers more limited, than their Scandinavian counterparts.

THE CASE OF GERMANY

Worker participation has a long tradition in Germany. The German model of worker participation, the so-called codetermination model, has been extensively debated in Germany with possibilities of expansion in more industries. It has also received attention outside the country, serving as a basic European model for the legislative road to industrial democracy. Germany has apparently found a middle course between unlimited capitalism and bureaucratic communism by having workers participate in the decision-making process as well as in capital sharing. It has also been argued that because of its system of cooperation and participation, Germany has avoided extreme confrontations between labor and capital and, therefore, has come out of recessions in better shape than other countries (Rosenthal, 1977). In Germany we observe two types of codetermination. One, a basically consultative model, operates in the overall industry and in public administration through works councils and one-third representation on the supervisory boards of companies. The other goes beyond consultation and provides workers with a higher degree of control over management. It is called *Qualifizierte Mitbestimmung*, or "special" codetermination. It operates in the iron, steel, and mining industries, where workers are entitled to equal representation on the management boards (King and Van de Vall, 1978: 11, 74).

As in most countries in Europe, in Germany, too, the First World War facilitated the development of a strong labor movement. The political crisis of the last months of the war took on revolutionary dimensions, as it gradually became apparent that the defeat was inevitable and that the political reforms were minor and unsatisfactory. This resulted in the formation of the workers' councils which assumed workplace control. With the councils' approval, factory committees sprang up all over the country (Sirianni, 1983). The 1919 Constitution of Weimar explicitly incorporated the concept of codetermination in its regulations by calling the workforce to cooperate with entrepreneurs and to promote equal rights in regulating wage and working conditions (Monissen, 1978: 61). The 1922 Act on the Delegation of Works Council Members into the Supervisory Council further reinforced codetermination by stipulating the delegation of one or two members of the works council to the supervisory councils of the respective enterprises (Monissen, 1978). During the Nazi period every form of democracy was suppressed, as were unions and works councils.

Codetermination and the Conditions That Facilitated Its Emergence

After World War II, the labor movement's goal was to reinstate some of Weimar's best traditions and to improve the system of industrial democracy. In contrast to the oppositional and confrontational approach that characterizes the English industrial relations system, the German system is best known for its application of a more cooperative approach. Such an approach provides employees with information, consultation, and codetermination rights, though always within the context of the capitalist economy. That there is a conflict of interest between capital and labor is accepted, but it is also assumed that, through institutional arrangements, both unions and managers can share decision-making powers in running the enterprises and thus conflict will decrease (Carroll and

Mayer, 1985). Regardless of their beliefs or actions, unions recognize that they will always be held accountable for the economic performance of the enterprise. If through codetermination unions are fully informed about company problems and activities, as well as economic and technological conditions and changes, first they will be able to influence changes, and second, they will be held accountable on more objective grounds. On the basis of those assumptions, the labor movement has been supportive of joint decision making and thus the share of responsibility (Sturmthal, 1977: 16).

Two critical historical developments influenced the emergence of the German codetermination system: (1) divisions within the trade union movement, which weakened its resistance against Nazism and thus contributed to the tragic end of the Weimar Republic; and (2) the collaboration of big business with Hitler (Poole, 1978: 145–146; Stephens, 1980: 48). Having learned how destructive divisiveness could be, unions in the immediate postwar period strove for unity. The formerly separate socialist and Christian unions joined forces in pursuing their common goal, which also included worker participation in the management of the enterprise (Sturmthal, 1977). Codetermination was perceived as the labor movement's best strategy to unite its politically diverse membership and secure industrial democracy.

The idea was not new, and there was a tradition behind it since industrial democracy through works councils and worker representation on supervisory boards had been the labor movement's main strategies during the 1920s (Schregle, 1978). The political conditions also facilitated this development since the two leading political parties, the Social Democratic party (SPD) and the Christian Democratic Union (CDU), were committed to reforms and were supportive of legislation that would give formal participation rights to employees at the board level (Poole, 1978: 146). On the other side, business leaders and managers, especially in the coal, steel, and iron industries, had been highly discredited because of their support for Hitler. The fact that workers in those industries had begun to make demands for nationalization and self-management (which threatened to place the management of the enterprise entirely in the hands of workers) explains why conditions after the war were conducive to labor gains in the direction of industrial democracy (Diamant, 1977: 30). Thus, the dismantling of the labor movement during the war, and capital's compliance with Hitler not only undermined the credibility of employers, but also helped to increase the unions' legitimacy and political leverage. Since it had become apparent that political democracy was not enough to secure a free and democratic society, unions pushed for additional gains in industrial democracy.

The Practice of Codetermination in German Industry

In the immediate postwar period, the German labor movement pursued two goals. First, it became interested in securing labor's influence in macroeconomic matters through legislation; and second, it aimed to counterbalance employers' power at the workplace through workers' participation (Allen, 1987: 182). Meanwhile, the Social Democrats reevaluated their political and economic goals. As a result, they renounced their support for nationalization and workers' control plans, and instead adopted the codetermination road (King and Van de Vall, 1978: 11). Thus, in 1947, 50 percent of the representatives on the supervisory boards in the steel companies in the Ruhr were given to labor representatives, while the rest were occupied by shareholder representatives.

In 1951, under the threat of nationwide strikes in the Montan industry, the most notable piece of legislation was passed, the Act on Codetermination. That act extended codetermination rights to employees in the coal and iron mining industries (Harrison, 1976; Jenkins, 1973; Monissen, 1978; Poole, 1978; Stephens, 1980). In these years after the war when Europe was in the process of reconstructing, the demand for coal, iron, and steel was huge. This put the unions in the Ruhr industries in a stronger bargaining position to demand higher level participation for their workers. This union victory should be understood within the context that, overall, unions at that time were not very strong; they were just reemerging, and they were still too weak a sociopolitical force to be able to extend their demands for parity representation to the rest of industry, as they were planning to.

As capitalists, through rapid economic growth, began to regain their credibility and political strength (e.g., the conservative Christian Democratic Union and the Christian Social Union became politically dominant), and as the immediate postwar militancy started to fade away, union demands for codetermination became difficult to achieve. The Works Constitution Act of 1962, for instance, gave the works councils in enterprises with more than five employees only limited consultation rights (Scholl, 1986). The works council is elected through a secret ballot by blue- and white-collar workers separately, unless otherwise demanded. Candidates for representation are nominated by the unions. Its functions include matters such as concluding plant agreements, supervising the implementation of laws and decrees, regulating working hours and breaks, leave, and holiday schedules, participating in accident prevention measures, and so on. Although the works councils have mostly consultative powers, those powers are far more extensive than those that the joint-consultative committees enjoy in England (Poole, 1978: 140). The same act also provided for one-third employee representation on the supervisory board of companies with more than 500 employees. This is a minority representation, since shareholders outnumber employees, and their will could always prevail against that of the workers (Allen, 1987: 183–184; Diamant, 1977: 29; Poole, 1978: 147; Stephens, 1980: 49). This right did not satisfy the trade unions, and it is doubtful whether it had any significant impact on industrial relations.

As we try to understand and evaluate the importance of these participative schemes, we should keep in mind that, in sharp contrast to the labor movements of Sweden and Norway, the German labor movement is not very strong. Only 30 percent of the labor force is organized. The labor movement is not weakened by competition among unions with different political ideologies or creeds, since 80 percent of the unions belong to the German Confederation of Unions (DGB). Overall, the labor movement in Germany is committed to industrial democracy in contrast to the English union movement. Still it lacks a strong ideological as well as an organizational base to successfully mobilize its members in accomplishing its objectives. Moreover, during the 1950s and early 1960s it was economic growth and increase in distributive gains, and not worker participation goals, that unions were pursuing (Stephens and Stephens, 1982: 231). During the same period, the Swedish and Norwegian labor movements were striving for similar goals. But owing to the strength and ideological commitment of those movements, they satisfied more of their demands for extension of worker participation rights than the labor movement in Germany did.

We should also emphasize that the dark period of fascism not only broke the socialist tradition within the working class, especially among younger workers, but also instilled distrust into the working class regarding the merits of mobilization and collective action. It was extremely difficult, therefore, for the DGB to have an impact on the rather apathetic and demoralized working class, especially through its initially radical visions of nationalization and codetermination in managerial decisions, and in the overall design of the economy. As a result, as well as because of the government's pro-business orientation and the public's preoccupation with order, union action became the subject of a highly restrictive legal system. In addition, union leaders themselves adopted a highly legalistic approach in order to safeguard their interests (Stephens, 1980: 51).

Thus, regardless of union goals and visions, codetermination rights did not expand to cover all industries, and the participation rights of the works councils at the workplace level were limited. Still, unions had won substantial gains, and the continued economic growth of the 1950s in conjunction with the unions' agitation for higher wages and low unemployment rates helped to keep the working class satisfied (Sturmthal, 1977). However, collective bargaining for wage and general working conditions takes place on the regional level, and so the impact of the local unions is limited (IDE, 1981b: 130). By 1969, it had become evident that the accepted moderate wage increases in the name of national reconstruction were falling behind increases in the corporate profits and that the promised social policies had not taken place.

The Radicalization of the 1960s and Its Impact on Participatory Reform

Such conditions contributed to increased worker unrest and to a number of wildcat strikes over wages. The same period also witnessed the resurgence of political activism within the ranks of the SPD and the labor movement itself, owing to the infiltration of the movement by the young leftists of the 1960s. As in the rest of Europe, in Germany too, New Left ideas, increasing affluence, and increasing levels of education had a strong impact on rising expectations as regards quality of work life issues. We should also observe the structural changes in the German economy, including high capital intensity, emerging disparities among social groups and sectors, and the large numbers of *Gastarbeiter* (guest-workers) who entered the country in an effort to overcome the country's labor shortage (Allen, 1987; Tsiganou, 1982). The conditions were, therefore, conducive to mobilizing activities for increased participation at the factory level, as happened in the late 1960s and early 1970s.

The radicalism of the period contributed to the radicalization of the works councils as well. In the 1972 works councils elections, for instance, old established members were replaced by new, more militant ones. Also, during the same year the Works Constitution Act was revised; the revised act extended the influence of works councils by giving them codetermination rights on certain issues (Stephens, 1980). Furthermore, unions became more persistent in demanding redistribution of control and income rights. Since the beginning of the 1970s, the DGB had fought persistently for the extension of parity worker representation on supervisory boards (Stephens, 1980). At the political level, the SPD was also supportive of worker participation and since the late 1960s had requested the formation of a commission to study the issue and make recommendations (Diamant, 1977). After the late 1960s the SPD-led liberal coalition increased the unions' hopes that through the government's support and legislative measures its micro- and macro-participative goals could be accomplished.

The German Confederation of Employers Association rigorously opposed demands for parity representation as advanced by the labor movement. The labor movement was not strong enough to win parity representation either. Unionization did not keep up with the rapidly expanding white-collar sector. In 1977, only 29 percent of the labor force was unionized, the same proportion as in 1950 (Stephens, 1980: 47). Furthermore, despite the DGB's close relationship with the SDP, the labor movement was not able to give the party the needed political support that would enable SPD to win sovereignty in government. In order to stay in power, the SPD had to form a coalition government with the Free Democratic party. But the Free Democrats were concerned with increased union power, and as a result they did not support the unions' demands to expand worker power.

The Codetermination Act that was signed in 1976 was merely a reflection of the political balance and a compromise among various interests of that period. It also reflected the overall union orientation of the 1970s: that is, pressing for parity representation via a legalistic channel rather than trying to empower and mobilize its membership at the workplace. Together with the labor movement's commitment to increase the distributive gains for workers by relying on statist measures, such an approach ignored other realities at the workplace level: The growing dissatisfaction with boring, mass-production jobs; the growing concern with health and safety issues; the questioning of technological developments as well as the growing participatory demands that had begun to be heard in the early 1970s (Allen, 1987: 186–187).

The new codetermination scheme did not give workers the same decision-making rights as it did management. Two important provisions safeguarded management's ultimate decision-making right, despite numerical parity between employer and employee representatives on the supervisory board of the firms with more than 2,000 employees (Allen, 1987; Furstenberg, 1977; IDE, 1981b; ILO, 1981; Monissen, 1978; Poole, 1978; Scholl, 1986; Stephens and Stephens, 1982). On the basis of the first provision, at least one employee representative had to be designated by a group of employees exercising managerial functions. In general, however, such a person was expected to vote in favor of employer interests. The second provision indicated that, in case of stalemate, the chairman, nominated by shareholders, was to cast a double vote. Such provisions indicate that employee interests could always be outvoted by employer interests (Furstenberg, 1977: 51; Scholl, 1986: 163). As a whole, the law was disappointing and contrary to the unions' belief that only parity representation could ensure the effective representation of workers' interests. The labor movement did not achieve its goals in extending codetermination rights (similar to those held in the iron, steel, and coal industry) to the rest of the industry.

The weak labor movement, the lack of political support, and the strong position of employers on the issue contributed to that outcome. Employers strongly opposed parity representation and the overall efforts to increase workers' power. Employers' organizations, for instance, contended that such participation would hinder flexible and economic decision making and could possibly bring it to a deadlock. These same arguments have been raised in most European countries. Even a year after the law had passed, a number of employers' organizations challenged its legality before the Federal Constitution Court (Rosenthal, 1977). They challenged the law on two grounds: First, full parity would interfere with the protection of private property and thus the right of employers to dispose of their property as they would wish; and second, equal numbers of capital and labor representatives would violate the right of freedom of association and collective bargaining between equal parties independent of each other (IDE, 1981b: 134). Because of strong employer opposition, the 1976 law did not become constitutional until 1979 (Allen, 1987).

The Practical Implications of Codetermination

The foregoing analysis indicates that in Germany as in other countries worker participation is a hotly debated political issue. Since an ongoing opposition between labor and management is not particularly welcome in Germany, it is inevitable that any institutional scheme designed to bring together opposing forces in order to resolve differences will be strongly influenced by the ideology and strength of those forces. The labor movement is weaker than other forces in German society, owing mostly to the stagnation of unionization rates, to the lack of a strong ideological base to mobilize constituents in pursuing alternatives to the capitalist free enterprise system, and to internal structural deficiencies, such as restrictive legal regulations and a general bureaucratization of industrial relations (Sorge, 1976; Stephens, 1980).

Codetermination implies that equal numbers of partners decide on a whole range of company matters.[2] In practice, however, codetermination is limited by the design of the scheme and by the number of legal restrictions that are in force (IDE, 1981b). Employee representatives are theoretically part of the company structure inasmuch as they participate in managerial decisions on an equal basis. In the practical order, however, this cannot be accomplished, since in companies with only one-third worker representation on the supervisory boards, the scheme is one of joint consultation and information, not codetermination. As a rule, the decisions of the employee representatives cannot prevail over those of shareholder representatives, but even in companies with more than 2,000 workers, the principle of parity can be undermined by the decisive vote of the chairman. The issue of dual loyalty should not be underestimated either. Workers' representatives who have access to information regarding company affairs run the risk of viewing the situation not from the workers' point of view, but from that of the shareholders', and are therefore inclined to compromise (ILO, 1981).

Employee representatives sit on the supervisory and not the management board, which it appoints and supervises. Granted, the supervisory board decides on important matters such as closures, relocations, and investment (Schregle, 1978: 88), but it convenes only three to four times a year and its activities are rather remote from day-to-day management operations. The supervisory board usually endorses plans that have already been discussed in more detail at the management board level. Consequently, under this system of representation, the authority of the management board, which decides about important technical, economic, and social aspects of the firms, has not been seriously challenged (Allen, 1987; Furstenberg, 1977).

Only the mining, iron, and steel industries seem to be exempt from these limitations. Under the provisions of the 1951 Codetermination Act, labor directors have been introduced at the management board level in those industries (IDE, 1981b: 129; Monissen, 1978: 68; Poole, 1978: 147; Rosenthal, 1977: 9; Stephens, 1980: 48). The labor directors are responsible for the personnel and labor relations policies of the enterprise and participate in deciding the major policies of the company. They cannot be appointed against the will of the employee representatives on the supervisory board. The 1976 law on codetermination, however, removed such a requirement, and the labor director, as all the other members of the management board, is appointed by the majority of the supervisory board (Furstenberg, 1977: 50–52; Rosenthal, 1977: 10; Schregle, 1978: 83). This means that beyond the mining, iron, and steel industries, workers' interests are not directly represented on the management boards. Even in these industries, however, the effectiveness of labor directors in representing worker interests is questionable, considering their minority status and the fact that labor directors are highly qualified intellectuals or technical experts, and not union or works councils' members. Besides, their role runs a dual loyalty risk as they try to develop a social or labor policy compatible with the company's economic goals.

The risk of coaptation becomes problematic not only at the board level but also at the plant level, where workers' interests are represented primarily by works councils. Following the national legalistic tradition, works councils in West Germany are instituted by laws, such as the 1951 Codetermination Act and the 1972 Works Constitution Act. The legal rights of the councils in Germany, compared to similar institutions in other countries, are very extensive and impressive. Some of their duties in countries like Britain and the United States are undertaken by unions; others coincide with the duties of a personnel department. Still others relate to the councils' major function of a consultative communications channel between employers and employees. To that effect Article 49 of the Works Constitution Act clearly states that the goal of the works council is to cooperate with unions and the employers' associations for "the well-being of the establishment and its employees with due consideration for the general welfare" (as quoted in King and Van de Vall, 1978: 89). Their rights and responsibilities cover areas such as social matters (e.g., operation of the enterprise, hours of work, leave arrangements, prevention of accidents, welfare services, jobs, and bonus rights); the organization of jobs, staff, and personnel policy, vocational training, and extraordinary firings; and finally, individual hirings and ordinary firings, as well as major economic and technical changes affecting the company. In the first two categories, works councils have co-determination rights; management cannot decide on these matters unless it has the approval of the works council. In case of disagreement, an independent body or the court has to decide on the disputed issue. With regard to the last category, their rights are confined to information and consultation before any of those changes are introduced (Furstenberg, 1977: 47; Harrison, 1973: 40–41; IDE, 1981b: 128; King and Van de Vall, 1978: 88–89; Monissen, 1978: 71; Rosenthal, 1977: 13–15; Schregle, 1978: 86).

One advantage of the works councils is that they can defend workers' interests not by reacting to managerial decisions, but by having the chance to influence them. This sometimes means that works councils can cooperate with management and avoid solutions such as layoffs that would hurt employees. In other cases, however, being influenced by managerial criteria and objectives, works councils cannot always support workers' interests (e.g., they might themselves prepare the lists for layoffs). The same problem might also arise when works councils, driven by company interests or compelled by the limited choices arising from structural changes, come into conflict with overall union policies affecting, for instance, a whole industrial sector. The 1972 Works Constitution Act gave unions more workplace power at the expense of the works councils (e.g., the outgoing council prepares the list of the works councils candidates in consultation with the unions). Often the memberships of the representatives of the two groups overlap. Moreover, disputes over areas of jurisdictions between the two bodies create resentment and splits among members of the labor movement. For instance, the union-backed list usually wins in the works councils elections, and the council members are often identical with union shop stewards. Being part of the works councils structures, however, these members cannot initiate or take part in strikes. On the contrary, in their capacity as shop stewards they can do so and also try to influence disputes within the firm. Furthermore, they can use information provided by the union to put pressure on management. Finally, the works councils relate to workers at the workplace in more direct and personal ways since they handle matters such as wage negotiations and worker grievances. Under these circumstances the grass-roots segment becomes more indebted to the works councils than the unions, while the council members have more leverage in their interactions with the union leadership. All these factors weaken the labor movement's position especially in its impact on the shopfloor. Its influence on that level has always been weak; even weaker is its ability to effectively advance and support workers' participatory rights, owing to the role of the works councils (IDE, 1981: 130–131; King and Van de Vall, 1978: 92–93).

In large companies, there is another barrier to workers' participation at the workplace level. In these large companies it is difficult to reflect the complexity and variety of groups and interests in the composition of works councils, and thus underrepresentation of certain groups is always possible.[3] Moreover, in large companies where works councils members are full time, the tendency of bureaucratization and thus loss of contact between council members and the rank and file is strong. This tendency is strengthened as the leaders of works councils strive to match management qualifications in negotiating and thus become increasingly professionalized (Furstenberg, 1977; ILO, 1981). We might also add that works councils in profitable firms can conclude local agreements for higher wages than those concluded at the regional or national level by unions. Although these agreements can be revoked, still the works councils are not allowed to go on strike. Finally, as mentioned above, the works councils are not allowed to disclose confidential company information, and their overall role is primarily to maintain a good relationship between labor and management.

Concluding Remarks

The labor movement in Germany has largely followed a defensive position by working within the contextual parameters set by corporatist interests. In sharp contrast to the Scandinavian countries, the labor movement in Germany has not won the government's support in pursuing its objectives. This explains, in part, why the German model of participation, whether we refer to codetermination at the plant or board level, became more or less a way to integrate workers and to institutionalize conflict, rather than an instrument to extend workers' decision-making power (Allen, 1987; IDE, 1981b; Stephens, 1980). If unions were ideologically strong and active organizationally to mobilize workers for participation goals, as was the case in Scandinavia, then participation demands might have been expanded and codetermination would not have had such a limited impact. As another critic of the unions' stance has put it, the unions "did not fully realize . . . that effective influence and control depended not on the passage of a law but on the active mobilization and participation of their membership" (Allen, 1987: 189).

The growing worker dissatisfaction with repetitive work, rising concerns about workplace health, safety, and technological changes, as well as major structural and technological changes in the society, prompted unions in Germany, as in the other countries examined here, to consider worker participation over those issues at the workplace level. The overall union policy, however, had long concentrated on quantitative gains (e.g., wage increase and fringe benefits) rather than on challenging employers' prerogative to control the labor process. Therefore, when the period of economic growth ended and when employers began to attack workers' past gains, unions had a difficult time mobilizing their members toward participation goals.

An additional drawback was that union policies did not include in their agendas long-term strategic considerations such as investment policy, technological changes, and their impact on workers as well as workers' roles in implementing such changes at the workplace level (although more critical elements within the labor movement throughout the 1970s and 1980s have been raising those issues). As a result, when deep structural and technological developments began to transform whole industrial sectors and unemployment levels increased considerably, ranging from 4 and 5 percent in the late 1970s to 8 percent by the early 1980s, the labor movement's approach was neither aggressive nor offensive. The unions generally responded much as they had responded for years: They did not challenge the premises of an economic and industrial structure that had created the problems to begin with, and they did not make any serious efforts to influence the long-term economic and technological transformation of the German economy. For instance, the unions sometimes demanded subsidies to protect the disadvantaged sectors such as steel, and they pressed (not always successfully) for reduction in the workweek hours to avoid high unemployment rates (Allen, 1987: 189–191).

In contrast, the labor movement in Scandinavia, and to a certain extent in England, seriously considered the impact of those changes and pushed for workers' participation in those crucial matters. Similar strategies were pursued on health and safety issues as well as technological design and implementation. In Germany existing institutional arrangements and structures, did not lend themselves to such issues. For example, in Germany safety committees are to be established according to the Labor Safety Act of 1973. In practice, such committees were not always established, and even when they were, they were not very active. Since those committees were to be subordinated to works councils, the works councils were not effective in dealing with issues such as health, safety, and technology. Health and safety issues seldom get the attention they deserve because works councils are preoccupied with so many tasks and responsibilities and because of lack of knowledge and experience (Gevers, 1983: 418; Sirianni, 1987: 19).

Thus far, unions in Germany seem to have missed the opportunity which the existing systems of participation provide to challenge the basic managerial pre-rogative of controlling the production process. Participation schemes in Germany became instruments of integration and accommodation rather than a means of extending workers' power because of the unique historical conditions that gave birth to codetermination, the employers' strong opposition to the union demands for codetermination, as well as the unions' ideological and organizational weak-ness and inability to mobilize workers' and government's support to combine codetermination with workplace democracy.

THE CASE OF FRANCE

In contrast to Germany, in most of its recent history the French leftist discourse has focused on nonstatist definitions of workers' control, although in most recent years statist definitions have also developed. Both approaches have been the focus of debate between the two major leftist groups in France, the socialists and the communists, but there have not been any impressive results regarding policies in either direction. Since its formation in 1895, and especially during the first decade of the twentieth century, notions of decentralization and workers' control have motivated the largest union federation of France, the Confédération Générale du Travail (CGT). The year 1906 symbolically marked the culmination of CGT's syndicalist militancy, when in its famous Charter of Amiens, the CGT called for self-liberation and direct control of production by workers. During the First World War, for reasons similar to those in other countries, militancy and syndicalist ideas resurfaced. This radicalism did not last long, however, and from that time on, especially in the 1960s, the CGT developed a more statist definition of workers' control. Specifically, it advocated an increase of workers' power through national political reforms, such as nationalization and worker boardroom representation, and not through direct workers' control as the syn-dicalists envisioned.

Significant structural changes in the society such as widespread mechanization, decline of craft-based industries, and economic rationalization were instrumental in that philosophical shift. CGT's basic goal was to improve working conditions and standards of living, as well as to prepare workers to assume control over production. But the CGT's commitment to the war, its support of Taylorism, and increased productivity alienated much of its rank and file. CGT was even-tually forced to broaden its base by cooperating with engineers and progressive bourgeois groups and accepting them in its ranks.

In general, the 1920–1921 period was characterized by the split and divisions within the labor movement and in the French left generally. The labor movement, lacking the support of workers in the newly emerging sectors of industry and ineffectively responding to its members' problems and demands, was weak and divided. The major demands of the period relate to sharing the benefits of increased productivity, such as decreased working hours and increased wages, both of which were seen as resulting from support of the Taylorist reorganization of work. Thus, its demands for worker control had receded, to be replaced by more distributional reformist ones (Cross, 1983). At another level, the social democrats were pursuing similar reformist demands by emphasizing nationalization, increasing influence of workers over economic decisions, and economic growth through state marcoeconomic and social policies. The communists, on the other hand, following the Soviet model, were theorizing about the abolishment of property, the elimination of capitalism, and the achievement of workers' control through the centralized political establishment, but without any concrete results. This division of the labor movement meant that "France resisted powerful trends elsewhere toward the unification and reformist homogenization of working-class politics" (Ross, 1987: 200). This subsequently allowed anarcho-syndicalist and other radical visions to survive during the first half of the twentieth century.

In the 1930s, various reformist groups as well as the Program of the National Council of Resistance raised demands for more worker control. In the Popular Front of the 1930s and during the resistance-liberation period with the left in power, the focus was on nationalization and welfare state services, such as schooling, health care, and pensions.

Participatory Reforms after the War

After liberation, some measures were taken to achieve worker control but without any significant results. For instance, union representatives could sit on the board of the nationalized industries, but their power was limited since they had little access to key information. Thus, they had small impact on decisions. The only organs that sought to give workers more decentralized control were the works committees (Comités d'Enterprise). The enterprise committees were first established by the Ordinance of February 1945. Their goal was to regulate the workers' production committees, which had taken over production in enterprises that had been abandoned by their owners at the time of the liberation. The law was passed the following year, and it was amended in 1966. The committees were equivalent to the works councils established in other European countries during the same period. Beyond the limited amounts of funds they were provided for social activities, the committees had little control over the running of the enterprise, since they were granted limited economic information (Bornstein and Fine, 1977; IDE, 1981b; Jain and Jain, 1980; Ross, 1987; Stephens, 1980).

As in other European countries, the committees were introduced within the context of the postwar reformist atmosphere, when labor unions and the leftist parties enjoyed a temporary period of strength. Unions had played an important role during the resistance years, while the country's elites had been discredited because of their collaboration with the German occupying forces (Stephens, 1980). Again, as in other countries, the war in France had created the necessary conditions for increased labor power. The law's objective in introducing the committees was to foster cooperation between management and labor and to develop a form of worker participation in management.

The committees were mostly advisory bodies that had information and consultation rights on issues such as the organization of work, management, employment conditions, and financial aspects of the enterprise. The committees, along with management, were also responsible for improving the workers' working and living conditions, and were in charge of the social welfare schemes within the firm (Harrison, 1976; IDE, 1981b; Ross, 1987; Stephens and Stephens, 1982). But despite the strength which the unions and leftist parties enjoyed during that period, the committees did not have any real decision-making power, although worker representatives in the committees were elected from the lists of members submitted by the unions, and therefore unions could have a real impact in turning these committees into decision-making bodies. However, unions at that time were not particularly interested in participation issues. Instead, they emphasized issues of economic reconstruction, nationalization, and participation in political decision-making processes (Stephens, 1980: 230). Moreover, because of their overall revolutionary tradition, unions were reluctant to accept any labor-management scheme that implied cooperation (Jain and Jain, 1980; Jenkins, 1973).

Because unions were not particularly interested in the works committees, they did not undertake any serious efforts to mobilize workers or inform them as to their legal rights. Workers' apathy contributed to the ineffectiveness of the committees, but that was not the only reason. Management supplied the committees with limited information, and important decisions were not announced until it was too late for any action (Jain and Jain, 1980). A new law in 1976 attempted to remedy this problem by establishing time limits within which consultation had to take place (Harrison, 1976). Since pressure from organized labor to introduce committees was lacking, not all firms bothered to introduce them either. In 1964, for instance, out of the 15,000 enterprises affected by the law, only 10,000 committees were established (Jain and Jain, 1980: 56). Where they were introduced, management succeeded in preventing them from becoming organs that would increase workers' control over the firms' activities. Instead, the committees had some influence on some minor social and recreational programs. In the end, the enterprise committees became ineffective in challenging the power distribution not only at the plant but also the board level. In a limited number of companies, the enterprise committee had the right to appoint two of its members to attend all meetings on the supervisory board (Harrison, 1976), but those representatives on the board level lacked any real decision-making powers. At the board level as well as the plant level, important issues were decided informally, before the formal meeting took place and without the participation of the trade unions. Management in most of the countries examined in this part of the book had used this practice (Bornstein and Fine, 1977; IDE, 1981b; Stephens, 1980). Such outcomes can be best understood if we consider the fact that neither employers nor major unions supported worker representation at the board level either.

The French Leftist Discourse and Conditions That Facilitated *Autogestion*

After the mid-1960s, beyond the spontaneous manifestations of the workers' desire for more control over their working lives, the issue of workers' control became the subject of numerous ideological debates and programs of the major unions and parties of the left. The government also introduced some legislative measures to increase the workers' influence within the firm, while industrialists themselves initiated some experiments to humanize working life. In general, participation schemes in France have been introduced mostly in response to increased labor militancy. Generally, workers in quasi-revolutionary situations, such as in 1968, have employed work-ins and factory takeovers, in challenging the legitimacy of the existing patterns of control and in demonstrating their ability to run the firms themselves.

The radical climate of the 1960s had a tremendous impact on every aspect of life throughout Europe. In comparison with other countries, however, the extent and the scope of participation schemes in France remain very limited. Unions are organizationally very weak and ideologically divided. In fact, the French labor movement is considered the weakest in Europe. French unions are well known for their militancy in regards to strike behavior,[4] but they are not strong either economically or politically (Stephens and Stephens, 1982). Only 20 to 25 percent of the total labor force is organized (IDE, 1981b: 86; Kesselman, 1982: 420). Low membership is not the only weakness of the labor movement. Multiple unionism, weak collective bargaining that operates mostly at the regional level, and fragmentation of trade unions on ideological and political grounds have weakened the labor movement even more (IDE, 1981b; Kesselman, 1982; Stephens and Stephens, 1982). Not only does the labor movement lack the power of a strong sociopolitical force in the society; it is also not united on the issue of participation.

The CGT is the oldest and largest labor confederation in France.[5] Most of its members are manual workers, and some of its leaders are members of the Communist party. Its basic philosophy is that the exploitation of the working class will end only if workers gain collective control of the means of production. Along the Marxist line, any kind of enterprise reforms to increase workers' participation within the capitalist system is considered illusory, as a way to coopt workers by integrating them within the system (Bornstein and Fine, 1977; Stephens, 1980). In 1968 and the early 1970s, the CGT espoused what came to be known as *Gestion Democratique*. This policy included nationalization, workers' representation on the board of directors, empowerment of unions, as well as the management of society and industry by the people through national level reforms guided by the party.

The second largest labor confederation is the Confédération Française Democratique du Travail (French Democratic Workers' Confederation—CFDT), which does not accept capitalism either. It rejects the capitalistic system on the grounds that it exploits workers, alienates them from their work and their co-workers, and dominates every aspect of their lives through its hierarchical institutions. Unlike the CGT, however, it does not support collective and bureaucratic models based on the top-down authority structures, such as the one exemplified by the centralized Soviet model (Bornstein and Fine, 1977). Instead, CFDT has been supportive of democratic planning, *autogestion*, and decentralization in order to overcome the evils of capitalism (Ross, 1987). Its position on participation has been influenced by the systems of worker control developed in Algeria and Yugoslavia. As a result, CFDT has supported the development of a decentralized, socialist society, which would be based on small, autonomous, self-managed units. This notion of participation, or autogestion as it came to be known, entails direct intervention, increased responsibility, and the autonomy of individuals and groups in every aspect of society and not just in production units. According to the guidelines of that model, the unions' very critical role is to safeguard the rights of ordinary people within society (Bornstein and Fine, 1977).

In contrast to other countries such as Sweden, Norway, or Japan, French management in general has not had to face any serious labor market conditions that would force it to initiate participation schemes. Only under certain circumstances, such as increased militancy, and mostly in order to protect productivity objectives, has management had an interest in pacifying workers, and thus it introduced participatory experiments. For the most part, however, management has strongly resisted efforts that challenge the authoritarian structure of power and authority within the firm. Conditions during the 1960s challenged such managerial position. In sharp contrast to prewar economic stagnation, the postwar French economy experienced a rapid and continuous economic growth. Between 1960 and 1972, the average growth rate of the GNP in volume had been 5.8 percent, the highest among the OECD countries (IDE, 1981b: 182). Rapid postwar economic growth brought some deep social changes in the society. France was rapidly becoming transformed from an agrarian and less industrialized country into a modern, urbanized, consumer society, a society whose industry was changing rapidly owing to technological change; a society whose service sector was rising rapidly, while the working class that had provided most of the support for the political left was weakening, only to be replaced by new middle strata with new ideas and new goals in life (Ross, 1987).

Increased levels of education, higher standards of living, as well as the radicalism of the 1960s, together with the emergence of new expectations and ideals, created a growing interest in quality of work life issues and workers' control. Reinforcing those trends was the French society's extreme reliance on bureaucratic, centralized, and almost autocratic social structures and institutions. "Almost alone among Western European countries, France has stubbornly clung to a nineteenth-century system of precisely patterned, unyielding institutions, which determine the direction and extent of social development" (Jenkins, 1973: 137).

This "bureaucratic phenomenon," as Michel Crozier calls it, transcended all spheres of French society from industry to government to education. Bureaucratization also characterized labor-management relations. Management was ruling in archaic, almost dictatorial ways, and workers were rarely appreciated for their contribution and were treated like second-class citizens. The state's interference in the company business, which was strongly resented by management, and the family-controlled company that characterizes the French industry reinforced these anachronistic modes of managing. Those conditions became the focus of increasing radicalism among workers and students and the very themes around which the 1968 movement evolved (Jenkins, 1973: 135–139).

Strikes, factory occupations, direct production by workers, and the revival of traditional trade union structures such as the strike and shop committees—all reflected increased rank-and-file radicalism and militancy.[6] Under the circumstances and under the banner of autogestion, CFDT strategically exploited the opportunities which the situation had offered by supporting local strike activities, as well as decentralized and anarchosyndicalist union tactics, in an attempt to gain the support of the dissatisfied new working class (Ross, 1987). Its goal was to strengthen the position of workers and unions at the enterprise level. That goal was satisfied to some extent, since unions gained recognition through a new established institution, the union steward (Delamotte, 1977: 56). The workers' increased militancy had a great impact on three levels: the government level, among the reformist managerial groups, and within center to left parties and unions.

The need for new forms of work organization became pressing when increasingly scientific management approaches came under attack and strong emphasis was placed on quality of working life. The government and some reformist elements among owners and managers advocated and initiated a number of reforms to accomplish industrial peace and higher productivity rates. As a result, job enrichment schemes and semiautonomous work teams similar to those in Sweden and the United States were established under the initiative of some innovative managerial circles. De Gaulle himself, in the midst of the 1968 crisis, advocated worker participation in the firm, as a third road between capitalism and socialism and as a remedy for all of society's ills (Bornstein and Fine, 1977; Jain and Jain, 1980; Jenkins, 1973). This more favorable managerial stance toward workplace reforms, especially enterprise committees, has to be understood within the overall climate of the critical spirit and reform that permeated the society at that time. In contrast to the autocratic environment described above, where secrecy prevailed and where even providing employees or the public with minimal information was perceived as radical (Jenkins, 1973: 139), in the late 1960s and early 1970s communication and information sharing came to be seen as essential features of labor-management cooperation and as prerequisites of workers' involvement in the firm.

Consequently, during the late 1960s and early 1970s, a number of laws were introduced which expanded the rights of enterprise committees. For instance, in 1969, a national collective agreement on job security provided that employers should consult the enterprise committees before they initiated any dismissals. A 1971 law expanded the committees' jurisdiction to include their involvement in vocational training as well (Jain and Jain, 1980: 60). Since the composition of the committees depends on the plant-level elections among all employees and, therefore, was less susceptible to outside influence, management, of course, preferred enterprise committees to union stewards.

The unions gradually realized that the committees could function as an important source of information for them since the unions had themselves been recognized and accepted at the plant level. Increasingly, the unions came to recognize the importance of enterprise committees for their own survival and effective functioning. Moreover, although employees could exercise some influence over managerial decisions, they still would not get directly involved in or be held accountable for managerial functions. Such a position was in accordance with the confrontational stance of the two major trade unions, the CGT and CFDT (Delamotte, 1977). The same adversarial notion has also informed the reaction of the major unions against the profit-sharing schemes introduced by the Gaulist government in the mid-1960s. A law under his administration provided for profit-sharing rights (as opposed to the promised decision-making rights) to employees in firms with more than 100 employees (Harrison, 1976). This scheme was strongly opposed by the labor movement on the grounds that it was a mechanism to increase productivity and integrate workers into the capitalist firm without increasing their power.

Not only some managerial groups, but also the government was influenced by the reformist spirit of the 1960s, and began to initiate the humanization of work projects and experiments. Committees were set up, and study groups were formed to examine and report on experiments with semiautonomous work groups and job reorganization experience in France and other countries (Delamotte, 1976). As a result, in the 1970s a number of experiments were introduced, and under Valery Giscard d'Estaing the government attempted to initiate some comprehensive company reforms. The 1976 Sudreau Report, for instance, recommended the establishment of autonomous groups of workers, training on the job, and expansion of information given to the enterprise committees. The Sudreau Commission also suggested one-third worker representation at the supervisory boards of firms with more than 1,000 or 2,000 workers. The prospective representatives had to be in the firm at least two years.

Since workers were to assume only one-third representation, the suggested worker representation scheme was consultative in nature. In that respect, it was not similar to the parity representation of the German codetermination system. Despite this scheme of representation, the power dynamic of the enterprise would eventually remain unaltered, given that unions would not have any influence on the appointment and dismissal of the directors. Worker representation could not possibly challenge the directors' authority, since there were no provisions in those schemes for mechanisms that would allow workers to do so. Finally, we should emphasize that board representation was applicable to big companies only, and therefore, a major part of the French productive system was not affected by those changes.

These weaknesses, and the fact that basic union demands including protection from arbitrary discrimination, the right to strike, and more adequate health and safety regulations were not addressed, compelled unions to oppose the changes suggested by the Sudreau Commission. The unions perceived those changes in the same way that they viewed the profit-sharing schemes, namely, as mechanisms to integrate workers and increase their productivity. Since employers for obvious reasons did not support these measures either, and since the government did not embrace the commission's suggestion to enforce the proposed changes with legislation, both measures were doomed to failure (Bornstein and Fine, 1977; IDE, 1981b; Stephens, 1980).

The circumstances of the 1960s forced management and the government to initiate some reforms that entailed greater worker involvement in running the enterprises. These circumstances also challenged the legitimacy of unions and their customary ways of controlling and channeling worker discontent and militancy. Furthermore, the spontaneous demands among the workers themselves for more control over their working lives, and the subsequent enthusiasm generated in factory occupations and sit-ins, had a great impact on the CFDT's formulation of autogestion. Between 1969 and 1974, CFDT in the name of autogestion strongly supported and participated in workers' local struggles, in militant strikes, and in illegal tactics such as factory occupations (the Lip factory case being the most famous one) and locking in employers. At the same time, it began to formally acknowledge its commitment to autogestion, the first step being CFDT's thirty-fifth congress in 1970. In that congress for the first time the CFDT made known its belief in the class struggle and its goal of creating a socialist society based on autogestion, and socialization of the means of production, and democratic planning. Such a socialist transformation according to CFDT's vision would be possible through political means as well as through the involvement of the rank and file in the community and the workplace. Unlike CFDT, CGT rejected autogestion, although it recognized the need for a new interpretation of work conditions and social life. Following the same line of philosophy as the PCF, the CGT called for a more statist definition of control, the so-called gestion democratique that envisions major societal transformation through broad national reforms under the aegis of the party.

In the 1970s, autogestion got caught in the middle of a political struggle which not only helped refine its philosophy and goals, but also made the two principal political groups, the communists and the socialists, recognize the need for leftist unity (*union de la gauche*), if a left government were to come to power. In

1972, the Socialist party (Parti Socialiste-PS) and the Communist party (Parti Communiste-PCF) signed the Left Common Program. That movement caused dissent and disputes over the content of the common program among members of both camps. Nonetheless, it clearly reflected the fact that the main ideological groups of the French left had realized the importance of the left unity, if their political goals were to be accomplished. Eventually, the united left espoused autogestion out of the need to attract the support of the emerging intelligentsia and the middle strata of society. Their effort (for a short time at least) proved more or less successful; in the presidential elections of 1974, for example, the candidate of the united left, François Mitterrand, lost the elections by less than 1 percent.

The unity of the left did not last long. The socialists began to claim more electoral support than the communists, who had initiated the process of unity. In addition, the PS, by supporting autogestion, outdistanced many communists by winning the support of the uncommitted center and the middle strata, as well as the support of many in the working class, who had been traditionally loyal to the PCF. The communists, on the other hand, began to realize that the left unity had not worked to their advantage and began to withdraw their support for the common program. In 1977, the leftist unity ended, which led to the defeat of the left in the 1978 elections (Ross, 1987: 204, 213). At the labor movement level, the defeat, the increased politicization, as well as the end of the postwar boom, undermined the militant local struggles supported by the CFDT. Consequently, the CFDT began to reconsider its tactics, especially since the CGT had become more militant itself. Gradually, the CFDT moved away from statist solutions, began to seek less politicized strategies, withdrew its support for autogestion, and eventually moved toward more traditional trade unionism tactics by embracing collective bargaining. Beyond the social and political changes noted above, rapid economic and technological changes had a negative impact on the membership rates and the mobilizing power of both the CFDT and the CGT. Moreover, we should emphasize that "the social base for autogestion was moving on to other concerns. French new middle strata began to exchange collective political endeavors for individualistic cultural liberation" (Ross, 1987: 216). For its organizational survival CFDT had to reconsider its vision and tactics.

Forms of Workers' Participation in the 1980s

With the socialists in government in 1981, the issue of workers' participation surfaced again but without demands for radical change which autogestion had called for in the previous decade. The 1981 Auroux Report, and the subsequent Auroux Laws that were enacted in 1982, represent an effort to provide workers with citizenship at the workplace by applying autogestion. For French socialists autogestion meant that workers would take direct charge of the problems concerning them. But the Auroux Laws did not challenge the distribution of power within the firm, as the vision of autogestion implied. Under the influence of the

CFDT, the laws were an attempt to address concerns in regard to authoritarian and paternalistic relations which were so prevalent within French industry, the lack of a well-established bargaining system, and the high degree of state intervention in industrial relations. In addressing these concerns, the CFDT did not espouse autogestion but rather classic techniques of syndicalism (Ross, 1987: 215–219).

The laws, for instance, offered legal protection to local unions in firms with more than fifty employees. Shop stewards gained the same protective rights. Furthermore, the plant committees were given increased access to company information and expert economic advice. The Health and Safety Committee and the Committee for Improvement of Working Conditions, two very marginal bodies, were merged into one in order to be more effective. Other provisions of the laws allowed for extensive information and consultation rights on questions such as the organization of work, safety at work, and introduction of new technology. Workers, for instance, could refuse to work under dangerous conditions, and they could request training to learn to perform better. The laws granted two other rights, the rights of expression and the obligation of the employer to negotiate wages and work hours once a year (Goetschy, 1983). The goal behind the creation of the expression groups was to strengthen informal, company-level bargaining between management and workers.

The provisions of the Auroux Laws did not reflect the radical vision of autogestion as it was debated in the 1970s. Still they had an impact on the French industrial relations system in that first, they shifted industrial conflict from state-level politics to focus on firm-level issues. Second, they provided enterprise committees with more information, though not always adequately. In that respect, the laws could be said to have contributed to a more effective decision-making process. Because of the economic crisis and because weak labor unions did not pose a serious threat to capital, the obligation to negotiate and to sign contracts was not always fulfilled. During the first year of the application of the law, for instance, only a minority of the firms that were obliged by law to negotiate had signed a contract. In contrast, the obligation to consult with workers, which was less threatening, appealed more to management, especially in light of the publicized Japanese participative management strategies. Fearing union dominance, employers at first opposed the formation of expression groups. When they realized, however, that cooperating with workers could prove more beneficial than the old archaic and authoritarian ways, they used the expression groups to their own benefit. Eventually, the employers used the expression sessions to cut out unions and gain rank-and-file support to increase productivity—the very reason unions were opposing their establishment. The expression groups, therefore, have not become effective in extending workers' influence in the workplace.

The laws seem to have been effective in stripping management of certain responsibilities by pressuring workers and unions to assume greater responsibilities, without, however, increasing their power. Finally, the workers themselves, in light of the economic crisis and the austerity measures the government introduced, were skeptical about the effectiveness of the laws in increasing their influence and advancing their rights within the workplace. Lack of information, uncertainty about middle management's role, and excessive formality within the expression groups further reinforced the workers' doubts regarding the effectiveness of the new laws (Ross, 1987: 219).

Concluding Remarks

Although some changes have taken place in the workplace as a direct result of the application of the Auroux Laws, and although socialists were in power from 1981 to 1986, it cannot be argued that managerial prerogatives have been seriously eroded in France. As in other countries, in France, too, real changes in the workplace are rarely the result of legislative enactment. The Auroux Laws might have presented labor in France with some possibilities. At the end, however, the structure of the industrial relations system, the values and ideologies that underlay it, and the dynamic of power within it determined the laws' effectiveness in truly advancing workers' interests.

The employers' organization (CNPF) had strongly opposed the Auroux Laws. Given the paternalistic, authoritarian relations within industry, and the fact that in contrast with other countries France was lacking an institutionalized collective system, unions and workers were left without a strong means to fulfill the possibilities opened by the laws. Antagonistic labor-management relations, distrust between the two parties, and the fact that industrial conflicts were mostly regulated by the state did not help the situation. Add to all these negative aspects the fact that both the CGT and the CFDT had serious reservations about the Auroux Commission's proposed changes as well as the labor movement's division on the issue of participation and how it could be accomplished, we can then better understand the small impact the Auroux Laws had in terms of changing the dynamic of power within the workplace and in industry in general.

The radical and antagonistic nature of the French industrial system has had a tremendous impact on the development of workers' participation schemes there. Unlike the strong and united labor movement in Sweden and Norway, the labor movement in France is weak and divided. Although radical syndicalist notions had for a long time permeated the debates of the French left, for the reasons explained above, the vision of autogestion, as perceived by the CFDT, never materialized and by the early 1980s became a dead letter. Only at times of increased worker radicalism have management and governments introduced some limited participation schemes.

The Socialist party that came to power in 1981 was closer ideologically to the notion of autogestion and initiated some efforts toward participation, but without any significant results. It nationalized basic industries and introduced laws that enabled union delegates to sit on the board of directors. Restrictions regarding access to important business information made such a representation scheme ineffective, however, although unions did participate in discussions of long-term strategic company policies. Ultimately, the government used public ownership as a tool to restructure and rationalize public industry rather than as a way to advance industrial democracy goals. Finally, as the right-center, which won the elections in 1986, began to denationalize the publicly owned sector, any potential for industrial democracy that had been in place because of changes during the previous years was lost (Ross, 1987: 216–220).

The increasing conservatism of the 1980s, the serious economic problems, the great difficulties rooted in the paternalistic and authoritarian French industrial relations, the politicized nature of industrial relations, as well as the fact that unions are weak and divided, have all limited the extent and scope of worker participation schemes in France.

NOTES

1. See Ken Coates and Tony Topham, *The New Unionism. The Case for Workers' Control* (London: Penguin Books, 1974).

2. The IDE (1981b: 127) study, following the uses of German labor law, makes the distinction between participation, which refers to the rights of employees through their works councils, and codetermination, which refers both to the employee representation on the supervisory boards in large firms and on the Montan sector, as well as codetermination in comprehensive economic policy (1981b: 127).

3. This is one problem. Another serious problem is that different conditions and structural changes faced in various sectors of the economy force unions to stress different themes and not coordinate their activities in a unidirectional way. Take, for instance, the case of the IG Metal Union which was involved in two major strikes in 1978 and 1979— one in the metalworking and auto sectors and the other in the steel industry. In the first case, because the sectors were still strong but needed transformation, the unions' approach was to shape that technological transformation. On the contrary, because the steel industry was declining considerably, the unions' focus there was to control the declining jobs by reducing the hours of the workweek. For more discussion and analysis of this issue, see Allen (1987: 188–193).

4. In France the right to strike was recognized in 1864 and was legally guaranteed by the 1946 Constitution. One major characteristic of strikes in France is that they take place simultaneously at plant, industry, or even national level. For more on this and strike statistics, see IDE (1981: 188).

5. For statistics on the trade union membership of the various labor confederations, see IDE (1981: 187).

6. The strike at the LIP watch factory in Besancon from June 1973 to February 1974 was characteristic of such tactics. To avoid the sale of this old, family-owned factory, workers defied traditional union tactics and seized control of the plant. Consequently, they organized themselves in nonhierarchical ways and resumed the production and sale of the product. Although the CFDT supported all these tactics, the CGT was very critical of them, arguing that self-management on the factory level was doomed to failure within the overall capitalist environment. See Bornstein and Fine (1977: 181–183); Kesselman (1982: 209); and Ross (1987: 187).

4

Workers' Participation in Japan and the United States

THE CASE OF JAPAN

Japanese management has increasingly moved toward small-group innovations and participation of workers in small-group activities. In contrast to the other countries examined so far, the terms used to describe those activities in Japan are basically quality control circles or quality circles and decentralization of responsibility. The term *worker participation* is rarely used, indicating, as Cole (1987) has shown, that in Japan management controls the process of introducing and diffusing these small-group activities, in which workers participate but in a limited degree. These developments started in the early 1960s, accelerated in the middle of that decade, and continued throughout the 1980s (Cole, 1979, 1985; Crocker et al., 1984). According to Robert Cole (1979: 135), by the late 1970s about 50 percent of all Japanese firms were practicing some form of management policy emphasizing small groups. By 1980, 77 percent of Japanese companies with more than 10,000 employees were involved in some type of small-group activity. By 1982, one out of eight Japanese employees was participating in QCCs or some other kind of small-group activity (Crocker et al., 1984: 13–15). Participation in QCCs seems to be the most popular and most diffused of these practices. According to some estimates, about 200,000 registered circles exist in Japan (Cole, 1985: 564). William Ouchi (1981: 224) estimates the number of unregistered circles to be 1 million.

The Practice of Small Groupism in Japan

Managerial initiative is the strong force behind the expansion of small-group activities in Japan. Its goal, however, is not participation per se. At first glance, it seems that work reorganization efforts in Japan are informed by a humanitarian philosophy. Upon closer inspection, however, we realize that the main reasons for work redesign in Japan are not simply humanistic. As Cole (1985: 566) correctly points out, these efforts go beyond the liberal reformist impulse; they very much relate to some serious labor market conditions that prompted management to introduce small-group activities. In Japan as in Sweden, tight labor market conditions, along with increasing levels of education and standards of living, created the conditions that favored the restructuring of the workplace and the introduction of participation schemes.

The early postwar period in Japan was characterized by a considerable surplus of labor (Vogel, 1975: XIV). By the late 1960s and early 1970s, however, Japan experienced a considerable labor shortage, especially among young male school graduates, whom most organizations preferred to recruit, pay low salaries, and train within the firm (Cole, 1985; Vogel, 1979). Recruitment was problematic during that period, and the problems of retention were even worse. According to a 1971 survey of 1,579 establishments in the machinery and metal manufacturing industry, of the newly recruited employees in the spring of 1969, 50 percent of both the middle and high school graduate recruits gave up their jobs within a period of three years (Cole, 1979: 129). Such reactions would have been inconceivable in the years immediately after the war, when people competed for job security through employment in big corporations.

The increased educational levels of the late 1960s contributed to the rising expectations of high school graduates. Those young graduates who aspired to find white-collar jobs were less likely to accept and keep the blue-collar, boring, routinized jobs they were assigned to. Faced with this serious problem, and given the increasingly rising international competition, managers were forced to search for solutions. One of the solutions considered, but later rejected by political and economic leaders was Southeast Asian immigration (Cole, 1985). Another option was the introduction and development of small-group activities: "Small-group activities appeared to be one possible strategy to make firms more attractive to well-educated potential recruits, thereby reducing turnover and labor unrest and contributing to productivity and quality goals" (Cole, 1985: 567).

In addition, technological developments pushed Japanese management to change existing production and management practices in a more drastic way. By the late 1960s, Japanese companies were moving from labor-intensive industries, whose advantageous position in the market economy depended on low wages, to high technology fields. Business strategies, with the assistance of government policies, were directed toward modernization, rapid expansion of facilities, and rapid economic growth. Having closed the gap with the other advanced countries, the Japanese government and Japanese firms began to invest heavily in research and development (Vogel, 1975: XIV, XV). In order for business to survive the increasing world competition, special attention was paid to making better use of human capital (Cole, 1985).

Japan had emerged from the war heavily damaged and with a reputation for producing cheap, poor quality goods. The government sought ways to change that image, its goal being to rebuild the country by rapidly industrializing and by securing the country's competitive edge in international markets through the production of high-quality products (Reagan, 1985). Consequently, producing cheap, high-quality products became the driving force behind the quality control movement. In contrast to similar processes in other countries, in Japan quality control became an integral part of the management process.

As with all other small-group activities, the quality control process is carefully designed by management to mobilize ordinary workers to detect and solve quality control problems, and thus participate in the day-to-day decision-making process. For instance, employees routinely participate in QCCs. Those circles are small, relatively autonomous units, which are formed spontaneously with the goal of locating and solving problems of quality, coordination, and productivity. Members of the quality circles regularly discuss their projects, sometimes on company time and sometimes on the employees' time. They are trained in statistical methods, data gathering and analysis, problem identification, and problem solving. QCCs do not just respond to specific problems; rather, they are a continuous study process through which members scan the environment for opportunities. Therefore, QCCs continue to exist well after a problem has been located and solved. As Robert Cole has so eloquently put it, "the circle performs 'opportunistic surveillance' for the organization, which in the end helps to increase the self-control and adaptive capacity of an organization" (1979: 139).

The human aspect of organizing work is not totally lost in that process of utilizing statistical techniques and methods required for the successful operation of QCCs. There is a somewhat strong emphasis in Japan on the human aspect of the work organization. Participation in a QCC is seen as an opportunity for workers to develop as individuals and to relate to their jobs, while they receive direction, constructive criticisms, and recognition from their superiors. Of course, this underlying human aspect of organization is a tremendous help in accomplishing the company goals as management defines them. Employee involvement in small-group activities in general, and QCCs in particular, encourages the decentralization of decision making within those establishments. Employees regularly get involved in maintenance, safety, quality control, and other processes that were once the prerogatives of management. In effect, quality control has stopped being the prerogative of engineers with limited shopfloor experience and has instead become the responsibility of employees. Employees work hard to solve the problems they face, so that rework will not be necessary. Thus, interests in perpetuating its existence, as in the case of the United States, would not emerge (Cole, 1980).

This seemingly improving position of employees should be understood in its proper context. Because management orchestrates workers' involvement from the start, the workers' participation in small-group activities does not threaten managerial authority. Since foremen usually become the leaders of those activities, they do not feel threatened by workers' involvement in them. Upper management, on the other hand, is very supportive of this kind of participatory activity. At the end, the process is carefully controlled by upper management personnel, since unions, for reasons explained below, do not challenge these participatory developments. Workers become involved in primary group relationships and assume significant roles in everyday operations. As a result, they identify with organizational goals (Cole, 1979: Chap. VIII). Participation in small groups and QCCs has effectively become a means to accomplish high employee morale in order to increase productivity and high quality at low cost (Ouchi, 1981: 223).

Management as a Driving Force of the Diffusion Process

Not surprisingly, influential industrialists and management were the driving force behind the participative movement in Japan. As a result, a national, well-organized infrastructure was developed to promote different kinds of small-group activities where employees at all levels were involved. In contrast to other industrialized countries, Japanese industrial policies are characterized by a long-term business/government orientation, where not only certain changes and adjustment to those changes are planned ahead of time, but the human aspect of production is also taken into consideration for mainly productivity goals. This explains, in part, the emphasis on participation schemes in Japan. Unions in Sweden and Norway were part of the diffusion process and were able to counterbalance employers' influence and later escalate their demands. In contrast, in Japan it was the influential Japanese Union of Scientists and Engineers (JUSE), founded in 1946, that became the major organizational instrument for diffusing small-group activities and quality control practices.

JUSE is a national, nonprofit industry-financed organization that has strong affiliations with the academic and engineering community and management, as well as with practitioners from other disciplines. JUSE's multidisciplinary and influential ties with prestigious industrial organizations and universities, as well as with influential personalities, not only legitimated its initiatives but also provided the necessary resources and support to implement QCCs and small-group activities. Seminar training programs, and company exchange visits, for instance, are some of the strategies used nationwide to accomplish such goals (Cole, 1985). JUSE's efforts have proven successful: The number of QCCs registered with JUSE grew from 1,000 in 1964 to 115,254 in December 1980 (Crocker et al., 1984: 15).

The powerful and prestigious Japanese Federation of Employers' Association (Nikkeiren) has also been instrumental in publicizing and supporting small-group activities. The Japanese government, unlike its American and European counterparts (with the exception of Sweden and Norway), has also played an important role in diffusing quality control practices. In 1949, for example, the industrial standardization law was passed to encourage corporations to think seriously about quality control issues and thus be able to meet quality specifications prescribed by the Ministry of International Trade and Industry (MITI). That law also helped establish the Japanese Standards Association, a strong force for quality control. Moreover, people like J. M. Juran, a well-known and influential international consultant and lecturer, was invited to Japan. His teaching had a strong impact on Japanese companies in encouraging them to mobilize and involve ordinary workers by adopting quality control as an integral part of the managing process. Significant to the whole diffusion process was the First International Conference on Quality Control held in Tokyo in 1969, which resulted in the establishment of the Japanese Society for Quality Control. The society's major responsibility was to encourage cooperation between the industrial sector and academia (Crocker et al., 1984).

Union Role in the Reorganization of the Workplace

Unions in Japan have largely been indifferent and not very involved in the effort to reform existing shopfloor practices. Japan's industrialization process started much later than that in most industrialized European countries and the United States. As a result, throughout most of Japan's industrialization process, unions developed different strategies to pursue their interests (Reich, 1983). Because of the late Japanese industrialization, Japan skipped the early stages of handicrafts and manufacturing which developed in the other major industrial nations and entered into the modern industrial world with large-scale enterprises mostly by borrowing technology (Vogel, 1979). Because of those conditions, strong craft unions with strong job consciousness did not emerge in Japan as in the United States (Cole, 1985; Vogel, 1979). In effect, then, Japanese management was never challenged by the power and control of the craft workers. Therefore, Japanese industry did not experience the phase of intensive scientific management, with its extreme division of labor and with all its consequences in regard to job control unionism pursued in the United States. As a result, the introduction of flexible work structures and the rotation of tasks by management in the middle and late 1960s was not perceived as threatening in Japan, as in the United States (Cole, 1987).

Throughout much of its industrialization process, Japan had available reserves of cheap labor, a condition that not only weakened labor's bargaining power, but also reinforced the workers' dependence on the organization. Because of the late and rapid industrialization, firms had to obtain their workforce from the rural population, which lacked any industrial experience and consciousness. The rural workers also had to be educated and trained within the company. The result was the internalization of labor markets and eventually the institutionalization of workers' dependence on the company. Training was becoming costly for management, and thus the motivation to keep workers became stronger. Moreover, throughout this process employees grew to identify with company goals (Shimada, 1980).

Under those circumstances, the relatively weak unions realized that control of job specification and production process would not be easily attainable. Instead, unions strove to accomplish employment security (Cole, 1985; Shimada, 1980). Management's conscious effort to nurture a sense of belonging among workers, in combination with the labor movement's interests in job security, led to the development and institutionalization of a unique employment system, characterized by lifetime employment; by a wage and promotion system, called the *nenko* system, which is based on age and length of service; and by enterprise unionism (Cole, 1979; Odaka, 1975). Management's prerogatives included workers' training, deciding work assignments, restructuring job boundaries, and introducing new technology without any strong challenge from the unions. As the paternalistic attitudes and practices became gradually institutionalized, so managerial prerogatives were strengthened. Employees, being assured of having a job, participated in the everyday operations of the enterprise, and almost every aspect of their lives became dependent on the organization. Today layoffs of permanent employees are rare. Permanent employees are usually kept on the payroll even when business slows, often with monetary assistance from the state. Employees displaced by new technology are usually retrained for new jobs (Crocker et al., 1984). Workers also depend on the enterprise welfare system for housing loans, pensions, and sickness benefits because the state provides low-level insurance. This reinforces the employees' subordination and dependence on the enterprise (Burawoy, 1983; Ichiyo, 1983).

This system of life employment and the benefits attributed to it apply to only one-third of the workforce, mostly in large corporations. Of the rest, 35 percent works for small firms with less than fifty employees. Contrary to prevailing myths, most of the workers in Japan are not affected by the *nenko* system. Most Japanese workers, for instance, do not benefit from the company housing plans, and they do not have rights to recreational facilities or company welfare plans. Even in large organizations, large numbers of workers are employed on a temporary basis and so are not entitled to benefits that permanent employees enjoy. Women, for instance, are not beneficiaries of the system and are discriminated against in many ways (Bluestone and Harrison, 1982: 219–220); Briggs, 1988: 60).

Where the system applies, the characteristics attributed to it (e.g., groupism, diminished individualism, workers' participation in small-group activities, and company loyalty) are simply indicative of Japanese industrial practices that are not merely rooted in some kind of exotic and unique oriental culture.[1] Instead, they are the result of peculiar labor market conditions, conscious management strategies, and union policies. Throughout the years, these industrial practices have been successfully incorporated into the management and employment practices that both reward and compel participation (Thomas, 1985). Management wants disciplined workers who are personally motivated to reduce costs and advance productivity goals by identifying with the company. Workers also know the benefits that a permanent status and playing by the "rules" can bring, as well as the costs of being an "outsider" or attempting to defy the system. Unless employees are prepared to lose their job or to jeopardize their chances for promotion, they are better off participating (Cole, 1979).

The structure of Japanese labor unions helps to explain why the unions have not seriously challenged management initiatives and prerogatives and why participation in small-group activities and limited worker participation in the form of joint consultation have not been perceived as a threat, as in some European countries and the United States. Unions in Japan are enterprise unions. That is, unions are organized on a company basis rather than around craft or industries as in the United States, and they include both blue- and white-collar workers.

In contrast to craft and industrial unions, whose membership is only 1 percent, enterprise unions account for more than 90 percent of all unions and organized workers. Most of the organized workers work for large companies (which sheds more light on the implications of the *nenko* system in the context of the above discussion). In 1977, nearly 60 percent of workers belonging to unions worked for enterprises with more than 1,000 employees. Although large federations exist, their power is very limited. With the exception of the Seaman's Union, these organizations are comprised of the enterprise unions within a given industry. In 1976, there were about 5,394 such federations. Their role is to exchange information and mutual assistance; therefore, the unions affiliated with them are not blinded by their decisions. In Japan, the union's existence and survival are tightly linked to the enterprise. In contrast to closed shop practices in Western countries, where only union members whose union has signed an agreement with an enterprise are qualified to be hired there, in Japan, only employees of a given enterprise are qualified to be members of the union in that enterprise. In Japan being an employee is a prerequisite of becoming a union member, and so one's status as an employee is more important than participating in the labor movement. Because changing jobs is not that acceptable, and a worker's future prospects very much depends on the enterprise (e.g., wage increases, promotion, retirement, and the like), enterprise unionism becomes more appropriate in protecting the workers' interests (Hanami, 1981: 88–91).

The postwar legislative top-down formation of unions in Japan differs considerably from the militant plant-by-plant emergence of craft unions that critically affected production politics in the major industries in England and the United States. From the beginning, management dominated Japan's unions. Even when militant unions emerged, they were often replaced by second unions sponsored by management (Burawoy, 1983: 599). In order to moderate the impact of labor movement, management encourages foremen, supervisors, and white-collar workers to join the unions. Therefore, it is not unusual for union leaders to fill managerial positions later in their career. Being a union leader is a way to demonstrate one's abilities to become a competent manager. A 1981 Nikkeiren report, for instance, based on a survey of 313 corporations, revealed that one out of six Japanese executives had served at some point as a leader of a union (Crocker et al., 1984: 28).

The underlying assumption of such a practice is that managers will be in a better position to understand workers' and union's demands, since they were themselves members of the unions once. The gap between management, workers, and their unions will narrow, and thus communication will be more effective. Ultimately, a more cooperative and reciprocal union-management relationship will be established. Whether this has been the case is open to discussion, and such a claim will be addressed later in this chapter.

Managers in the United States commonly express the fear that the involvement of unionized employees in quality circles will eventually lead to unions' interference in the day-to-day operations of the circles and, therefore, will weaken managerial prerogatives. In Sweden managerial prerogatives were under attack as the politically strong unions threatened to extend their demands. However, such fears seem to be groundless in Japan, since dual loyalty or dual self-identification both to management and to unions has been part of the system for so long (Ishikawa, 1984). It is not surprising, then, that the majority of employees (77 percent) participating in quality circles in Cole's and Tachiki's sample were unionized (1983: 13).

Because of the peculiar process of industrialization with all the consequences for unionism described above, unions in Japan did not become preoccupied with aspects of work organization such as work assignments, job demarcation, or changes in technology, which were and still are perceived as managerial prerogatives. From the start, unions distanced themselves from involvement in the development and diffusion of any small-group activities, since those were perceived as managerial prerogatives. Unions did not oppose them either, as happened in the United States under similar circumstances, since participation in any form of reorganization and firm innovation was perceived as a way to advance unions' interests by encouraging economic growth and thus employment security for their constituents.

The unions' role in the industrial relations system has instead focused on collaborating with management to set up labor-management consultation committees at various levels. Consequently, joint consultation has become the most widespread form of workers' participation in Japanese industry though it is limited in effectiveness. In matters of production or management, however, joint consultation has worked primarily as a one-way communication channel from the top down. In contrast, personnel and social matters are the focus of mutual discussion and consultation, whereas working conditions and employment issues are decided jointly. Apparently, such processes have somewhat improved unions' skills in collecting and analyzing managerial information, and have facilitated labor-management communication which resulted in some benefits for workers, such as extending the retirement age from fifty-five to sixty-five. At the same time, unions in collaboration with management have been forced to restrain themselves. In the name of job security and enterprise survival, unions have also prepared voluntary retirements and have accepted wage concessions (Ishikawa, 1984: 274–275).

Concluding Remarks

Because of the peculiar aspects of Japanese industrialization and labor market conditions, managerial efforts to introduce and promote employee participation in small, innovative workplace groups have not been challenged by unions, since they could promote economic prosperity and thus secure employment for employees. From the mid-1950s to the early 1970s, the Japanese economy grew at an average rate of 10 percent per year. This tremendous postwar economic growth sustained the Japanese permanent employment system as it applied to large companies (Shimada, 1980: 12). On the negative side, the same system could become vulnerable to downturns of the economy and worldwide recessions (Thomas, 1985). How will unions and workers respond to the challenge of their basic achievements? What will happen when unions, owing to recession and computer automation, are unable to deliver employment security? Will they or the workers independently attempt to use offensive mechanisms to protect their interests? Would reductions in wages and limited opportunities for promotion be offset by the proclaimed benefits of participation encouraged by management? Some reports already contain alarming accounts of the contradictions between the ideology and practice of workers' participation in the QCCs during the phase of declining profits. According to Yamamoto, because of declining profits in some auto companies, management has put more emphasis on the *3-P* movement (productivity, participation, and prosperity) through participation in QCCs (1981: 35). QCCs are pressed to deliver in terms of cost reduction and productivity improvement. Workers' involvement, however, becomes more directed and controlled than spontaneous and voluntary, since workers' performance and chances for promotion and salary increase are closely linked with their participation in QCCs (Thomas, 1985: 181–182).

Similarly, Yamamoto's (1981) and Junkerman's (1982) studies reveal aspects of antilabor practices, including excessive requests from workers for delivery and overall labor intensive processes, with no respect for the proclaimed cooperation and egalitarian spirit, and often with health and safety risks for the workers involved. The same authors' study in Nissan further indicates the union's inability to contain workers' discontent with company practices of surveillance, the unequal reward of union stalwarts, and the overall pressure for increased productivity. As some studies indicate, the Western image of Japanese managers dressed in company overalls and eating at the same table with blue-collar workers, might not necessarily be a sign of labor-management cooperation and a humane style of management, given that workers themselves might not appreciate such a relationship. For instance, Japanese rate as very low their desire for a good working relationship with their managers. There are also indications that Japanese managers are becoming more task-centered than their Western counterparts. Because of the increased competition and in the name of productivity, managers are inclined to ignore group decisions (Briggs, 1988: 62–63).

The whole system of labor-management cooperation seems to be vulnerable not only to the downturns of the economy, but also to the introduction of new technology, such as robotics and flexible automation, since such technology might limit workers' ability to contribute to quality through QCCs (Thomas, 1985). The problem may be further compounded by the aging of the labor force. For instance, employees displaced to peripheral jobs or forced to retire can be a source of conflict. This situation has contributed to the debate about raising the retirement age. Furthermore, would young, well-educated employees with high aspirations, who cannot easily get a promotion, be expected to be highly motivated and committed to organizational goals through participation, or would they become cynical?

Already, studies contradict the popular notion of job satisfaction among Japanese workers. Stress-related illnesses, increasing rates of alcoholism, and higher suicide rates resulting from pressures at work, long twelve-hour workdays, and unused vacation time to fulfill company expectations, all contradict such an image (Briggs, 1988: 61).

In an era of rapidly changing production practices, skills must also change. Would this change reinforce the workers' integration into the firm and thus increase cooperation and participation, or would it create feelings of shock and insecurity among older workers, as some scholars have warned (Thomas, 1985)? While speculation would be interesting, only time will reveal how workers' participation practices will adjust and change, in the context of new economic needs and pressures.

Japanese managers and industrialists, as well as the state, as in Sweden and Norway, became motivated very early to restructure the workplace. Faced with labor supply problems, within the context of an increasingly educated and ambitious workforce, and in order to survive world competition, Japanese government and management committed themselves to long-term policies. As a result, they provided the needed organizational resources to accomplish long-term goals by skillfully engaging workers in small-group activities and by combining the technical and social aspects of work. Through interdisciplinary organizational ties and the hard work and commitment of the involved parties, the foundations of an organized quality control movement became solidified and an integral part of Japanese industrial life. Perhaps labor market conditions had forced management and the government to introduce workers' participation in the 1960s, as was the case in Sweden during the same period. In Sweden, however, in contrast to Japan, managerial initiatives and efforts were kept in check by the strong, united labor movement, which soon escalated its demands for more worker influence at various levels of the enterprise. Similar demands for workers' participation were raised in Norway as well.

In Japan, on the other hand, the weak and integrated labor unions, having secured the right of employment of their members, did not perceive participation to be a threat to their prerogatives. Therefore, they permitted management to be the sole initiator of participation schemes, in sharp contrast to most cases in Europe. Not only in England and France, where strong labor-management antagonistic relations prevail, but also in Germany and Scandinavia, where a more collaborative stance has been employed, unions have challenged managerial incentives. Therefore, most European countries exhibit an escalation of participation demands, as well as a trend toward workers' participation at higher hierarchical levels of the enterprise. This is clearly not the case in Japan. Although EEC developments regarding participation in general, and participation on the boards of directors in particular, have an impact on certain developments in the member countries, the role of the unions in demanding to influence long-term policies in an era of rapid technological and structural changes cannot be ignored. In Japan, because of high economic growth, the unique employment system, and long-term labor-management collaboration, a heritage of trust has been developed over the years that did not allow for such demands. Therefore, management took the initiative in workers' participation and defined it according to its own purposes.

Although workers' participation in small-group activities is widely diffused in Japan, it has been achieved not so much by increasing workers' ability to influence the decision-making process, but by utilizing workers' potential through their identification with company goals. In that respect, it is not real participation but a means to coapt workers, a way to perpetuate managerial control via the human relations' techniques of greater communication, trust, and cooperation between labor and management.

THE CASE OF THE UNITED STATES

In the United States, labor-management cooperation and limited worker participation practices have a relatively long tradition going back to the World War I period, when joint union-management committees were formed to avoid bottlenecks and to speed war production. Labor-management committees were also established during World War II, when the government, faced with labor and energy shortages, supported the committees to contain labor-management adversarial relations and increase military output. Scattered participation experiments also took place during the 1950s and 1960s. During the 1960s, theories were developed and research undertaken on issues such as worker psychology, motivation, and human nature and their relation to organizational structure and industrial relations (Simmons and Mares, 1985). These were isolated practices whose goal was not to increase workers' influence within the workplace, but rather to incorporate workers into the production process in order to increase productivity.

In the last two decades the need to innovate and humanize work has been discussed extensively in academic, management, and government circles. Theories have been developed, and strategies have been devised to improve the Quality of Work Life (QWL) to an unprecedented degree in the industrial relations, organizational, and sociological literature. A growing number of QWL experiments indicates the importance that has been attached to the notion of workers' participation.

Participative Experiences in the Late 1960s and Early 1970s

The growing economic problems of the late 1960s and early 1970s were the major force behind the renewed interest in restructuring work. Management was the primary initiator of projects and experiments to restructure work. The main motivation was to increase productivity by tapping into workers' productive capacities and human potential in general. Therefore, from the start those efforts were limited in providing workers with any real voice in company affairs. During that period, a new and enlightened image of human potential at work began to emerge. Issues such as the meaning and importance of work, the creative potential of the individual, and worker interest in productivity became the focus of debates at the local, industry, and national level.

Strikes, such as the one at General Motors' Lordstown assembly plant in 1972,[2] and most importantly the report on Work in America, published in 1973 by the Department of Health, Education and Welfare (HEW), brought to the fore the negative impact of an extreme division of labor. They also drew attention to the issue of workers' alienation that was reportedly responsible for low morale, wildcat strikes, high turnover and absenteeism rates, and low productivity among American workers. These very problems preoccupied unionists and industrialists in Europe as well. Participative systems to solve the problems were considered in the United States, as they were in Europe, but with limited success. Some of the solutions designed to meet workers' needs and to improve productivity included options such as job redesign, job enlargement, worker participation, and labor-management cooperation. All these practices reflect differences in the workers degree of decision-making power, the scope of the issues covered in those schemes, and the incentives behind these participative practices.

Selective QWL experiments were introduced in an attempt to humanize the workplace and to cure the "blue-collar blues" and the "white-collar woes" (Zwerdling, 1980). The most publicized experiments occurred in the Topeka General Foods pet food plant, the Rushton Mining Company, the General Motors Tarrytown plant, and the Bolivar plant of Harman's International (Zager and Rosow, 1982).[3] Proponents of those solutions claimed that by engaging workers more in tasks at hand and by increasing workers' responsibility and autonomy, workers' morale and satisfaction would improve. In turn, efficiency and productivity would increase. The history of these newly emerging work structures indicates, however, that the three main institutional actors (e.g., government, management, and organized labor) involved in the production process displayed very little interest in their institutionalization (Cole, 1985; Kochan, Katz, and McKersie, 1986).

Those early efforts to humanize the workplace were rightfully perceived by unions as being coaptive, as ways to undermine the role of the unions and the legitimacy of collective bargaining (Kochan, Katz, and McKersie, 1986). Because of the traditionally hostile labor-management relations, the idea was not appealing to the majority of management either, especially middle management, whose jobs were threatened by participation schemes. Although it sponsored some of the participatory experiments, the government finally continued its generally noninterventionist position (Cole, 1985). Consequently, the majority of experiments took place either in troubled plants or in new and nonunionized ones (Parker, 1985). Most of those experiments ran into several internal organizational constraints. After the initial stage of enthusiasm was over, most of them faded away, since they lacked any systematic institutionalized support (Zwerdling, 1980).

Participative Reforms in the Late 1970s and Early 1980s: How Successful Were They?

During the late 1970s and early 1980s, owing mainly to the deepening U.S. economic crisis, a significant number of new worker participation programs emerged. The increasing Japanese competition forced government, management, and unions as well to reevaluate their industrial relations positions and practices, and seriously examine Japanese management practices. Japanese practices, such as QCCs and small-group activities, began to be studied in the United States and soon thereafter became an important practice in a rapidly growing number of enterprises. In 1982, approximately 1,000 firms were experimenting with QCCs, while another 100 were engaged in autonomous group activities and another 500 had established profit-sharing projects (Kochan et al., 1984: 6). The International Association of Quality Circles (IAQC), the only national organization designed to promote small-group activities in the United States reported 7,000 members in 1982 (Cole, 1985: 571).

Through collective bargaining a number of national unions have begun to participate in union-management committees studying issues such as working conditions, introduction of new technology, and product quality (Kochan, 1985). Again, most of these schemes were introduced and developed as basically productivity mechanisms and in addition to the study of Japanese practices, the Scandinavian experience, especially the Swedish one, was studied. Although the industrial relations leaders in Sweden and Norway had productivity goals in mind when they introduced similar participatory schemes in the 1960s, by the 1970s and 1980s the radicalism of the labor movement contributed to the demand for different, higher level goals, something that never happened in the United States or in Japan.

What prompted this renewed interest in workers' participation? Although interest in and experimentation with worker participation issues has been growing in the last few years, why has the institutionalization of workers' participation processes not taken place in the United States to the same degree as in Japan, Scandinavia, and Europe? Since the mid-1960s, the almost uninterrupted prosperity of the postwar American economy began to show signs of stagnation. Declining productivity rates and increasing competition between the United States and other developed countries intensified the need for new strategies to cope with problems at home, such as poor work motivation, low job satisfaction, high turnover and absenteeism rates, and strikes (HEW, 1973: chapters XV, XVI; Reich, 1983; Zimbalist, 1975).[4]

As historical experience indicates, when organizations operate within predictable environments and under stable socioeconomic circumstances, the human aspect of organization is generally overlooked, ignored, and even controlled to fit the needs of the time (Kanter, 1983). Accordingly, scientific management theories viewed workers as being recalcitrant to organizational goals and sources of error, and from them any knowledge, initiative, and responsibility for work should be removed through deskilling. Workers were to be just another part of the production process (Braverman, 1974: 88–124; Braverman, 1984: 79–85), although there is also evidence that dehumanization, control, and manipulation met the resistance of workers, especially the skilled ones (Brecher, 1978; Edwards, 1979; Hill, 1981; Montgomery, 1979; Stark, 1980).

Such a strategy worked as long as uneducated, immigrant, or migrant rural workers were utilized to undertake simple, routinized tasks. Within the bureaucratic environment, the hierarchy of authority and inequality of power was felt strongly. High turnover rates, low productivity, shortages, and strikes during the late 1960s and early 1970s were signs that the system had backfired. Subsequently, economic strains such as the oil crises of 1973 and 1979, deeper recessions, slower growth, declining productivity, and tougher worldwide competition strongly indicated that the existing organizational structure was not working. Many analysts began to conclude that it was obsolete and had to be reevaluated and restructured.

Japan and Sweden had begun to restructure much earlier, taking the human aspect of production into consideration. Being more dependent on world market competition, they had to respond to the increasing demands for high quality and productivity (Cole, 1982). In the same way, the United States had to reconsider its strategies in order to compete during the period of what Piore and Sabel call the second industrial divide. According to Piore and Sabel (1984), economic shocks in the international economy, the saturation of markets by mass-produced products in the industrialized countries, as well as the increasing role of developing countries in the global market,[5] have encouraged the development of complex technologies requiring flexible specialization as well as highly skilled and flexible labor. In such rapidly changing times, "the number of 'exceptions' and change requirements go up, and companies must rely more and more on their people to make decisions on matters for which a routine response may not exist" (Kanter, 1983: 18).

This thesis can explain only part of the reality, however. Whereas some firms were viewing participative reforms as a way of responding to increasing competitive demands, other firms and even whole industries were totally wiped out as a result of new corporatist strategies and government policies. Since the late 1970s, the United States has been facing the terrible impact of what Bluestone and Harrison call the deindustrialization wave and the exporting of jobs through foreign investment by American corporations.[6] During the 1970s, about 32 to 38 million jobs were lost as a direct result of disinvestment, while between 1969 and 1976 investment in new industries created about 25 million new jobs. We should not be heartened by these figures of newly created jobs, since most of them require labor mobility (usually part-time service or temporary jobs) and different skills, pay lower wages, and offer less job security, if laid-off people can find them at all (Bluestone and Harrison, 1982: 9, 27, 29).

The purpose here is not to quantify how much each theory explains pertaining to the issue under consideration. Rather, each of them may shed some light and explain parts of a very complex reality. For instance, in some companies, the prospect of shifting production abroad and thus the prospect of loss of jobs meant that worker participation became less important or not important at all for all parties concerned in light of the more immediate priorities of economic survival. In others, such as Xerox, the same conditions led to the utilization of participative and innovative techniques to save jobs and avoid the shift of production.

This phenomenon is not exclusively American. Similar developments have taken place elsewhere. In Norway, for instance, the Norwegian conglomerate Viking Askim, a company that makes automobile tires and rubber boots, signed local technology agreements in the late 1960s by incorporating workers into the decision-making process concerning new technological developments and their application. But owing to increased international competition in the 1970s, the company was forced to move some of its operations to Southeast Asia. This move pressed both management and unions to concentrate on ways to restructure and save jobs rather than on participation (Howard and Schneider, 1987: 87–88).

Yet, in some industries in the United States, such as newspaper printing, insurance, and air traffic control, managerial control strategies such as deskilling, automation, and bureaucratic control were adopted. In contrast, in industries such as coal mining, automobiles, steel, construction equipment, and telecommunications, the trend has been toward increased labor-management cooperation. For instance, the United Auto Workers (UAW) and General Motors (GM) began a QWL program in 1973. In 1979, the UAW gained a seat on the board of directors of Chrysler, as well as the right to discuss outsourcing problems with management in 1984. The UAW also helped to establish a job bank in 1984, and it participates in the operation of long-term development committees. In the steel industry, the United Steelworkers, in cooperation with company representatives, established joint productivity committees in 1971 and alert committees in 1977 to avoid plant closings. In 1976, the Communication Workers of America (CWA) and AT&T lobbied without success for the passage of the Consumer Communications Act, which, if passed, would prohibit the duplication of AT&T Services by other telecommunications companies. In 1980, the CWA, the

International Brotherhood of Electrical Workers, and AT&T established labor-management committees to monitor and address issues in regards to QWL, technological change, training, and job evaluation (Cornfield, 1987: 346–347).

In order to explain the reasons for these quite opposite results, we have to thoroughly and systematically identify the conditions under which those and other industries operate, their market position both locally and internationally, their labor relations traditions, as well as the nature of their product and their relation with the government. Some studies suggest some trends to that end. For instance, in *Workers, Managers, and Technological Change*, Daniel Cornfield shows that in the fourteen industries studied the history of labor relations and the macroeconomic conditions which a particular industry/industries face explain the different results between industries that have developed formal labor-management cooperation and those that have not. For instance, the study found that external threats and the higher level of unionization were the major reasons for labor-management cooperative practices in some industries. Specifically, U.S. automobile and construction equipment manufacturing is threatened by foreign imports. In the steel industry, unionized producers are threatened by imports and nonunion domestic producers. In telecommunications, as a result of government deregulation, the Bell System is threatened by nonunion and other long-distance carriers. In regard to the second dimension (e.g., high unionization and bargaining strength), the study found that unionization gave workers the bargaining strength to request or demand cooperation. Indeed, most of the cooperative and participative practices took place under strained labor-management relations, in the wake of strikes or under the threat of a strike (Cornfield, 1987).

Similarly, rapidly shifting market demands and flexibile production technologies, by replacing predictable, mass production structures with single, standardized products, require a less rigid relationship between labor and management and thus are conducive to flexible participation practices (Piore, 1985; Piore and Sabel, 1984; Reich, 1983). As a result, many companies are trying to combine the technical with the social aspects of organization in their effort to restructure and innovate the workplace. Some are doing so with the collaboration of unions, through problem-solving groups such as QCCs, and self-management work teams or labor management steering committees, all of which denote a different degree of worker influence and differences in the scope and significance of issues they cover.

A fundamental premise of worker participation is that increasing control over the forces that affect behavior on the job will decrease worker alienation and thus most probably resolve productivity problems (Juran, 1978; Witte, 1980). As Kochan et al. (1986: 147) report, such workplace changes usually have two objectives: (1) to increase the involvement of employees in order to overcome adversarial relations and so to increase employee motivation, responsibility, and ability to solve problems, and (2) to alter the organization of work in order to simplify work, lower costs, and increase flexibility.

Other developments and changes explain the growing interest in worker participation. Social and demographic changes, as well as higher educational levels, as in Europe and Japan, have modified the composition of the workforce and have affected working-class values and aspirations. In that respect they have added further pressure for a more participative and democratic work environment. For instance, forty years ago only 5 percent of the working population had graduated from college. Today, 25 percent of the total workforce has a college degree, and this percentage continues to rise. Education is also increasing among workers who hold blue-collar jobs. Today, 20 percent of all craft workers are college graduates. Such an increasingly educated workforce is seeking work fulfillment and opportunities to use its knowledge and skills. This creates additional pressure for new management styles that allow flexibility and autonomy (Kanter, 1978: 49, 1983: 55–56).

Furthermore, the baby boom generation, with its radically different views and values, now dominates the labor force (*Business Week*, 1981: 1). Moreover, protest and radicalism during the Vietnam War generated new social movements, such as civil rights, feminist, environmental, and consumer movements, and, as in Europe and Japan, these have had an impact on participatory attitudes. The philosophical and practical concerns behind equality, self-determination, autonomy, health, consumer rights, and concerns about reviving neighborhoods and protecting the environment, have spilled over into the workplace. They have facilitated the emergence of a different value orientation, one that opposes authority, and have created expectations that affect demands for more dignity, respect, autonomy, and responsibility at work (Kanter, 1983; Kochan, 1984; Zimbalist, 1975).

Along these lines, the HEW (1973) report found that the most persistent complaint among workers interviewed was the fact that their bosses did not listen to them when they proposed better ways of doing their jobs. Another study based on 1,533 workers found that workers' first concern was that their job be interesting. Good pay ranked fifth (Zimbalist, 1975: 53). Kanter (1983: 62) also reported that employees want more rights and greater voice in decisions, while Kochan's study (1984: 106–107) revealed that the majority of workers interviewed expressed high interest in QWL issues. After having reviewed the literature on employee values and orientations, Kanter (1978: 53) came to the conclusion that two concerns predominated among workers at the time. The first concern, which she calls *expressive*, refers to work as a source of self-respect and personal fulfillment. The second, the so-called *political* concern, refers to individual rights and power, as well as to rights of justice and equity at the workplace. Both concerns are reflected in the new orientation toward issues of quality of worklife within the workplace. Fads and fashion also seem to have an impact on the movement for more participation. Hundreds of companies since the early 1980s have been redesigning jobs and workplaces by applying what was learned by forerunners, such as General Motors (*Business Week*, 1981). Indeed, as Kanter points out: "Organizations can be just as 'fashion-conscious' as individual consumers, and when a few leading ones start adopting reforms often the rest quickly follow, because they want to be modern too. Indeed, concerns about 'image' are a driving force for executives in the new more political and more public corporate environment'' (Kanter, 1983: 57). Moreover, the media coverage and attention paid to the issue of participation, especially the high visibility given to Japanese practices, also had an impact on the movement for more participation. In addition, the fact that Japanese models and practices have caught the attention of top executives has increased efforts among managerial circles to involve employees, in an effort to increase employee commitment and productivity (Kochan, 1985).

Although many of the experiments to humanize the workplace have taken place in nonunionized plants, quite a few unions have changed their position on worker participation. This has also had an impact on the growing movement toward participation and involvement. In the 1960s, for instance, most of the unions perceived programs for improving quality of worklife as undermining the role of the unions. In the 1970s and 1980s, as discussed above, large and powerful unions such as the United Auto Workers, the Communications Workers of America, and the United Steel Workers have introduced a variety of industrywide participation schemes (Kochan, 1985; Kochan et al., 1984; Parker, 1985). Collective bargaining agreements have also begun to contain clauses on labor-management cooperation. The 1973 GM and United Auto Workers was the first major one and helped launch a new era in labor-management relations (Cole, 1985; Kanter, 1983; Kochan et al., 1984; Parker, 1985). White-collar unions have generally been the leaders in bargaining over QWL issues, while the public sector unions, with their well-educated members, are the main supporters of joint labor-management committees (Kanter, 1983). Through participation, unions have increasingly been able to challenge one of the basic principles of the New Deal collective bargaining model, that ''management manages and workers and their unions grieve or negotiate the impact of management decisions through collective bargaining'' (Kochan, Katz, and McKersie, 1986: 179).

Labor and Management Interests and Orientation toward Participation

Participation does not take place without struggle, resistance, concessions, and compromises, since it affects interests and requires some power redistribution. It is a learning experience, as well as an adaptation to emerging socioeconomic needs, the outcome of which depends on how the parties involved react to the new situations, their power, as well as the strategies they develop to face the new challenges and reality. In the United States, the initiative to introduce and diffuse participation practices resides, for the most part, with management. Although some schemes and experiments might provide workers with a voice in the decision-making process or hold the potential for such a result, most of the participative reforms are merely mechanisms to increase managerial control and labor productivity through participative mechanisms rather than the ineffective traditional, adversarial labor-management bargaining approach.

The degree of worker influence and the scope of decisions which these participative schemes cover are limited, and their institutionalization has not been extensive or systematic in the United States, as in Japan or other European countries. Despite high turnover, absenteeism, or other related problems, until recently American management has not had to face any serious challenge that would require changes in traditional practices. A large pool of unemployed and casually employed labor exists in the United States to fill the less desirable jobs. This explains why American business did not feel the need to reform workplace practices to the same degree that Japanese management did during the 1960s.

Thus, unlike its Japanese counterpart, American management did not have any strong economic incentives to innovate (Cole, 1985; Fraser, 1983a). As a result, in the United States, upper level management did not provide the much needed leadership for a national organization, which could widely diffuse and implement participation schemes. Organizations such as the American Society of Quality Control, the American Productivity Center, or the International Association of Quality Circles, although they promote and advocate worker participation, still have not emerged as nationwide institutionalized organizations. There is no organization comparable to the Japanese JUSE in the United States (Cole, 1985).

The fact that labor unions have not been historically recognized as a legitimate force by big business has worked against building a national, coherent infrastructure to promote participation. Under these conditions, management and big business would exhaust any other possibilities (e.g., protective legislation, technology) before considering worker participation and QWL programs as possible solutions for economic losses and competitive disadvantage. In addition, a long-term antagonistic relationship between management and labor can explain why a national organization promoting participation has not emerged within the unionized sector in the United States. Some efforts to improve labor-management relations through participation schemes, such as those undertaken by the Work in America Institute, have not covered the 80 percent of the labor force that is not unionized.

In contrast, efforts within the nonunionized sector have made unions hesitant and suspicious about appeals for more labor-union cooperation. One of the main concerns is that management can use QWL strategy not to enhance workers' responsibility, autonomy, and power, but as a subtle way of manipulating and controlling workers and their work. The real motives behind appeals for worker participation are control, manipulation, and union busting (Cole, 1985: 570; Kochan, Katz, and McKersie, 1986).

Worker manipulation and control can be accomplished by giving management access to the specialized knowledge workers possess and by having workers assume the managerial role of monitoring worker performance and checking on each other, which can be detrimental to workers' solidarity (Parker, 1985; Wells,

1986). Under the pretense of worker participation, such practices further traditional Taylorist goals: That is, the appropriation of workers' knowledge in order to achieve greater managerial control (Thomas, 1985: 174). It is not surprising that even within unions, where top leaders have embraced worklife quality efforts (e.g., the Auto Workers or the Communications Workers), significant sections within them have nonetheless opposed such efforts (Parker, 1985: 1).

Critics of QWL and related participation schemes have raised the additional concern that such practices might undermine some of the prerogatives organized labor has gained over the years by espousing business unionism, without guaranteeing new ones. Those concerns and suspicions make sense, if we consider, first, the traditionally adversarial relations between management and labor and, second, the specifics of American industrialization, as well as labor's weak position as a political force (Cole, 1985). The struggle between management and powerful craft unions over control of the production process and the forms of remuneration that developed around the turn of the twentieth century had a strong impact on the forms of industrial unionism in the United States and on its basic orientation toward control of job opportunities, which participative reforms seem to threaten (Montgomery, 1979b).

Faced with increasingly strong international competition, management had serious incentives to cut down high labor costs, gain control over workers, and thus increase productivity and profits. This was accomplished through Taylorism by subdividing and reorganizing the labor process as a whole and by introducing new technology (Braverman, 1974; Montgomery, 1976). Consequently, unions faced a critical dilemma: either to continue their fight over control of the production process, or to fight to secure more material benefits and control of the distribution of job opportunities. Faced with strong management and government animosity, unions basically gave up the first radical option for the second, more limited one through which an extensive division of labor was legitimized. Unions in effect renounced any rights over the organizational aspects of production or over issues of investment, design, and marketing the so-called managerial prerogatives (Cole, 1985: 575).

The application of Taylorist techniques did not simply result in increased managerial control and increased productivity. In responding to those developments, unions stepped in and learned to develop strategies to protect workers' interests as well. As a result, precise job boundaries and pay rates for each job were established and negotiated through labor contracts (Cole, 1984: 47–49; Kochan, Katz, and McKersie, 1986: 28–29). Ultimately, unions protected workers' interests by taking wages out of competition and by preventing workers from competing against each other by establishing uniform standards within a single company or even within an industry. At the same time, workers' immediate interests were protected via grievance machinery. In effect, by establishing rights over wages, hours, and conditions of work, collective bargaining became the principal means whereby workers could influence the decision-making process in the American enterprise.

The U.S. collective bargaining system is characterized most by its detailed job control (Coleman, 1978: 181; Kochan, Katz, and McKersie, 1986: 22). In the name of QWL projects and flexibility, however, this traditional means of workers' participation could be seriously undermined, as the issues covered under collective bargaining threaten to become limited and as local contracts can be eliminated or abolished altogether (Parker, 1985: 47–50). Many QWL projects require flexibility, expansion of each worker's tasks, and the ability to assign workers interchangeably in order for business to succeed in the new competitive era. Frequently, this requirement means that workers have to give up their specialized knowledge and also that changes have to be made in traditional job classifications and lines of demarcation between skilled workers. Therefore, the concern exists that management will use workers' participation to eliminate the number of jobs, as has sometimes happened (Cole, 1985; Kochan et al., 1984).

Within participation schemes, workers are often moved to unfamiliar jobs, and their seniority cannot be used to protect them from the abuse of discretion exercised by management. In that respect, not only shopfloor power and job security could be at stake, but also safety and seniority rights (Parker, 1985). Although participation schemes help workers identify with managerial goals, such as increased productivity and better quality products, and therefore run the danger of being coopted (as some neo-Marxist critics have warned), they often do not share the immediate economic rewards of those efforts (Cole, 1984; Siegel and Weinberg, 1982). Increased productivity, and thus increased profits, do not always translate into securing existing jobs or creating new ones. Management might not invest at all, or it might invest in new technology. Such developments usually mean that more jobs are cut than created (Parker, 1985; Siegel and Weinberg, 1982; Wells, 1986). Therefore, the introduction of participation schemes could threaten important aspects of industrial unionism and basic prerogatives of labor.

Since unions have not been really supportive of the movement for more participation, and since management has not been faced with a strong incentive to innovate, we can understand the limited extent and scope of participation schemes in the United States. These schemes tend to be voluntary and cover mostly quality of worklife issues at the plant level. A critical question arises, however, as to whether unions today can afford a position of suspicion and defensiveness or indifference toward participative mechanisms. The number of unionized workers has been decreasing constantly since the middle of the 1960s (Dickens and Leonard, 1985). During the mid-1950s, approximately 35 percent of the nonagricultural labor force was organized. This figure declined to 19 percent by 1985. This decline would be even greater if just the private sector was considered (Kochan, Katz, and McKersie, 1986: 8).

As a result, the impact of unions' position on participation has been limited. We should not forget, of course, that gains in the unionized sector can also have a significant impact on the nonunionized sector by setting certain standards.

Beyond declining membership rates, another important factor seems to undermine the foundations on which traditional business unionism and union power are based. Market structures that created and sustained mass production processes have changed rapidly. Uncertainty, instability, and the competitive pressures of the 1970s, for instance, broke up mass production markets. More specialized markets emerged instead. As domestic and international markets for consumer durable goods became saturated, new, computer-based, flexible technologies developed to adjust to new and uncertain economic times. Given these conditions, job-control unionism could be proven inappropriate, rigid, costly, and inefficient, and therefore more vulnerable (Kochan, 1985; Piore, 1985; Piore and Sabel, 1984).

The question that arises, therefore, is whether the introduction of workers' participation in new, nonunionized plants with flexible work structures reflects the employers' position to avoid or even undermine unions, or whether it reflects deeper structural and organizational changes that require new strategies adapted not only by management but by unions as well. The history of antiunion corporatist practices, including the so-called right-to-work laws to outright union busting techniques, does not leave much space for doubting that capital will use any offensive mechanism to protect its interests.[7] Under the latter scenario, we could argue that unions need to make a choice, since markets, though powerful in their impact, do not totally determine structural conditions. As capital and management become defensive and use their resources and power to shape and affect market trends, unions might need to change their defensive posture. They may choose to utilize the potential which participative schemes might hold to redirect their focus and address long-term structural and technological changes in order to claim their viability as organizational means of supporting workers' interests. Within the context of plant closures, high unemployment rates, and labor concessions, it seems that labor unions will once more have to redefine their priorities and redirect their efforts in bringing changes that will best support workers' interests.

All these factors, especially the weak management incentive to innovate, explain the low degree of experimentation and diffusion of workers' participation schemes in the United States. It remains to be seen whether the continuing economic problems and the increasingly competitive disadvantage in which American business finds itself will push American management toward greater support for participative practices ideologically, financially, and organizationally. Because of socioeconomic pressures, the traditional American position of nongovernment intervention in business has occasionally changed to support labor-management cooperation activities. Of course, any sporadic changes introduced by American government cannot compare with the systematic support of Japanese government in its effort to diffuse small-group activities. Nevertheless, for the first time, in October 1978, Congress passed the Labor-Management Cooperation Act to provide a funding mechanism to "encourage and support the establishment and operation of joint labor management activities" (as quoted in U.S. Department of Labor, 1985a: VI). The money appropriated under that law was limited, however, and has reached only a small number of unions and businesses interested in participation activities (U.S. Department of Labor, 1985a: VI).

Concluding Remarks

Under current economic, technological, and international circumstances, efforts to promote participation fall within the category of isolated, piecemeal experimentation. Participation is not just another organizational formula or something that can be enforced to solve labor relations problems. Participation trends or movements are responses to socioeconomic and historic conditions. Their development and the forms they take depend on how participation affects the interests of the parties involved. Without a reevaluation of goals and interests pertaining to production, including labor interests and workers' growth and development, participative reforms will be limited and for the most part coaptive.

Responses to structural changes and developments often depend on the ideologies, organizational resources, and power to make the commitment needed to promote one's interests. It is often argued that the ingrained practices and habits of working life are difficult to change. Management and labor interests in the United States are frequently portrayed as being in opposition. It is simplistic, however, to argue that management seeks only greater productivity and thus greater profits, while labor wants only better working conditions.

Undoubtedly, profit is management's primary consideration. At the same time, management cannot ignore workers' power, as well as the value of workers' involvement in the production process and the potential effect of QWL processes in smoother labor-management relations, especially in times of increased international competition. For their part, labor unions at both the local and national level are increasingly faced with the dilemma of whether or not to endorse quality of worklife and similar practices. The pressure to support such developments usually has two origins. First, some pressure stems from the workers themselves, whose consciousness of quality of worklife issues is increasing, owing to higher levels of education and value shifts in the society (Kanter, 1978, 1983; Kochan et al., 1984; Tyler, 1986; Walton, 1979). Second, in light of worsening economic times, increased foreign competition, and internationalization of the economy, unions, like management, face pressures for better performance and higher quality products. These concerns and pressures explain, in part, the unions shift on participation. In previous years unions were openly suspicious and critical of worker participation schemes introduced by management, but their position changed somewhat in the late 1970s and 1980s. Although labor's overall position is still defensive, an increasing number of joint union-management QWL experiments and related processes indicate the need to adjust to changing economic circumstances (Graham, 1985; Kochan et al., 1984).

The unions' position on participation is very important in terms of the direction, scope, and outcome of such a movement. This is a critical turning point for the participation movement in American industry. Will the labor movement become part of the participation movement and thus exercise some kind of control over the whole process, as in Europe, or will the unions distance themselves from the movement and risk some of their most important prerogatives? In contrast to the Japanese case, American unions cannot afford to remain indifferent.

Equally important are the labor movement's power and its organizational ability to enforce any desirable position. The amount of resources unions can devote to participation is crucial in determining whether unions can develop their own strategies regarding participation programs or whether management can use participation schemes to coapt workers and undermine union survival. In that respect, unions in the United States face tremendous difficulties, because of bad economic times, declining membership rates, high unemployment, rapid industrial transition, a hostile national administration, and diminished public support (Dickens and Leonard, 1985; Kochan, Katz, and McKersie, 1986; Kuttner, 1986; Parker, 1985). Unions in the United States have only limited resources, and are weak in contrast to their counterparts in Europe and Scandinavia. Management has the decided advantage in resources (e.g., staff, time, information) and, therefore, the ability to influence participatory systems toward their goals (Martin, 1987; Parker, 1985; Sirianni, 1987b).

Because of these resource and power imbalances between management and labor, participative schemes introduced by management present a serious challenge for unions. If management were to win the loyalty of workers through participation schemes, there would be little need for unions. Furthermore, given the historically adversarial labor-management relations, we can better understand the unions' suspicions that participation schemes are part of management's strategy to further deter union recruitment, undermine union prerogatives, and even avoid unions altogether (Cole, 1984; Graham, 1985; Kochan, Katz, and McKersie, 1986; Parker, 1985).

When viewed from an optimistic side, participation schemes could allow unions to enhance their economic and organizational interests. Instead of adopting a defensive posture, unions could even try to gain control over participative processes, as some have already done (Kochan et al., 1984). Furthermore, unions could incorporate worker participation into the overall collective bargaining process in order to further their members' interests (Herrick, 1986; Kochan et al., 1984; Parker, 1985).

For this strategy to be effective, the following conditions have to be met: Unions must be accepted by employers; top management should be committed to the participation programs; and economic conditions must be favorable (Kochan et al., 1984: 187). If those conditions were met, unions could provide the leadership and direction needed to sustain chosen strategies. Existing participative arrangements would be legitimized, new participation schemes encouraged, and managements' initiatives to introduce such schemes challenged. In addition, the perceived need for strong unions would be recognized. As a result, the difficulties and problems associated with the passive and defensive union strategy could be transformed to potential advantages by a strategy of initiative, since participation schemes and what they stand for would be identified with unions. In the end, increased autonomy and responsibility, increased productivity and effectiveness, and better work life conditions could be associated in the public eye with unions (Herrick, 1986). It seems that in the 1980s this second position is gaining more support among unions (Kochan et al., 1984).

In Japan, participation in QCCs and small-group activities is widely diffused, whereas piecemeal experimentation is the case in the United States. This participation encompasses not only the production floor, but also offices, sales departments, warehouses, banks, insurance companies, as well as exchange of relevant experiences among business competitors (Cole and Tachiki, 1983; Ouchi, 1981). The statistical techniques and technical aspects underlying QCC practices were developed and have been used in the United States for more than a hundred years. The value and importance of human resources in a successful management process have been well known in the United States. After all, aspects of participative management originated in the United States long before they were transferred to Japan (Ouchi, 1981).

Differences between these nations are due mostly to the specific industrialization process, economic and labor market conditions, and different industrial relations traditions. Faced with tight labor market conditions in the 1960s, Japanese managers, with the help of the government, committed themselves to participative techniques. In Sweden and Norway, in the same period, a strong and united labor movement challenged the limited participation schemes. In Japan, since unions had secured basic rights for their members they never really challengeed managerial initiatives. In the United States, management has not been seriously challenged to consider participative solutions, and government has retained its generally noninterventionist position. Therefore, projects and experiments have been limited and have been initiated by management mostly to avoid unions or because of productivity problems. As a result of increased internationalization of the American economy and the challenges it faces both domestically and internationally, the need to search for new, more flexible participative systems of production has been felt in this country, as it was in Sweden, Norway, and Japan earlier. Most of these reforms have been introduced by management as strategies to increase production and as a way to coapt and control workers. But participation schemes in the United States as elsewhere have been caught in the middle of a power struggle and have not taken place without conflict. Although participation schemes have been used to coapt workers and undermine unions, unions have also initiated participation and they could shape it to their own interests. In contrast to Japan, Scandinavia, and Germany, where more collaborative labor-management relationships prevail, in the United

States the specific nature of the industrial relations system, with its antagonistic labor-management orientation, has helped deter the expansion of participation schemes.

NOTES

1. However, the cultural impact should not be ignored since it has bearings on the prevailing system of management. The Japanese cooperation within the company can be linked to the whole "shame culture" and the notion of indebtedness that is expressed in two types of repayment: *gimu* and *giri*. Each of these includes a number of obligations, including duty to one's work and superiors. For more details, see Briggs (1988: 62–63).

2. The strike that took place at the General Motors' Chevrolet Vega plant in Lordstown, Ohio, was one of the most publicized strikes in recent American labor history. Workers were not striking about wages, as was usually the case, but about quality of working life issues. Increased dissatisfaction and alienation among workers were the result of the monotony, frustration, and fast pace of work (e.g., workers had 36 seconds to complete their tasks), and workers demanded changes. See Simmons and Mares (1985: 44–45).

3. For a recent review of these and similar experiments, see Zager and Rosow (1982).

4. In 1969, only 3 percent of the labor force was unemployed; in 1982, the unemployment rate reached 11 percent. Productivity growth declined from an average yearly increase of 3.2 percent between 1948 and 1965 to an average of 2.4 percent between 1965 and 1978. In 1979, productivity fell even further. In addition, between 1968 and 1981 the average worker's real wages declined by one-fifth. For more details, see Reich (1983: 117–118).

5. Many Third World countries, for instance, are emerging as industrial forces. Much of the world's steel, textiles, rubber, petroleum, and other resources come from countries once considered backward. For more details, see Reich (1983).

6. Between 1950 and 1980, investment by U.S. companies increased sixteen times, from about $12 billion to $192 billion, while gross private domestic investment grew less than half as rapidly, from $54 billion to about $400 billion. Between 1957 and 1967, about one-third of all U.S. transportation equipment plants were located abroad. For chemicals, the ratio was 25 percent, and for machinery, it was 20 percent. By the end of the 1970s, overseas profits surpassed the profits made by the hundredth largest multinational corporations and banks inside the United States by more than a third. For some corporations the fraction was even higher. For instance, in 1979, 94 percent of Ford Motor Company's profits came from overseas investments while for Coca-Cola the percentage was 63. For more details, see Bluestone and Harrison (1982: 42–46).

7. By 1980, twenty states had passed those laws, which basically outlaw compulsory union membership whether or not a majority of workers in a firm voted for it. Over the years management has used more sophisticated techniques to keep unions out of their companies; for example, they use specialized firms that provide legal, psychological, and technical assistance. See Bluestone and Harrison (1982: 136, 179).

II

PARTICIPATIVE REFORMS IN PLAN-BASED SOCIETIES

5

The Ideology and Practice of Self-Management in Yugoslavia

The Yugoslav experience with self-management has captured worldwide attention because its experience is unique; it deviates considerably from workers' participation developments in both West and East. The federated and heterogeneous nature of the country has given analysts the opportunity to study and compare similar processes and phenomena elsewhere, especially in other Soviet-style societies, but under considerably different conditions. The Yugoslav experiment with self-management is unique in another sense: until very recently, it provided the critics of capitalism with a good example of an alternative vision to capitalism.

The development of self-management in Yugoslavia is also very peculiar in that it was not a response to demands from below, as in the case of Poland and Hungary. The party was the primary initiator of self-management, not in reaction to an internal crisis, as in other Eastern European countries, but mostly because of external threats. Self-management in Yugoslavia has become a permanent institution that permeates every sphere and aspect of society. It is not an isolated phenomenon affecting individual firms or industries, as is generally the case in the West, or a temporary solution to crisis as in Eastern Europe. In Yugoslavia, more than in any other country, workers organized on a self-management basis have extensive rights, at least on paper, in deciding about fundamental aspects of their working lives.

ORIGINS OF SELF-MANAGEMENT IN YUGOSLAVIA

Workers' participation in Yugoslavia was primarily a response to external pressures. Yugoslavia's expulsion from the Cominform in 1948 forced the country's elite to search for a new ideology and new organizational forms to support the departure from the overcentralized and bureaucratic Soviet model and thus legitimate its existence (Rusinow, 1977). As a result: "A doctrine of direct socialist democracy was developed calling for an immediate beginning of the state's withering away and the replacement of bureaucratic centralist decision making with direct participation of the population in the decision making based on a system of self-managing political and economic units" (Stephens, 1980: 66–67).

Political reasons notwithstanding, certain economic considerations prompted the introduction of self-management as well. Yugoslav leaders were hoping that workers' councils would stimulate economic development, productivity, and technological innovation (Comisso, 1979). Some cultural and historical aspects of Yugoslav society facilitated the reliance on self-management principles. Historically, the ethnically heterogeneous population of the country had always been distrustful of central administration and control. This attitude, together with the country's political instability and poor communications, had resulted in local, self-sufficient, and quasi-autonomous communities. In addition, during World War II, the notion of self-management had become an integral part of the Partisans' movement. After the break with the Soviet Union, this traditional form of decentralization facilitated a smoother transformation of the society toward democratic decentralization (Bean, 1985; Poole, 1982).

To justify and promote the new system of management, a whole body of theoretical formulations was utilized. Unlike other Marxist theorists, Yugoslav theoreticians argued that the private property relations of capitalism were not the reason for unproductive labor; rather, the reason was the bureaucratic structure under centralized planning with its unrealistic targets, administrative overhead, and subordination of the direct producers (Comisso, 1979). To avoid these and similar problems, Yugoslav communists made an important theoretical distinction between state and social ownership. Property was not to be controlled by self-elected privileged bureaucrats, but by the workers themselves.

This principle of social ownership was set forth in the first article of the Basic Law, the first law on self-management in Yugoslavia, enacted in 1950. With the introduction of this law, the state ceased to be the formal owner of the means of production. Instead, the law declared that the means of production would become "social property," owned collectively by the society (Poole, 1978: 153). Despite efforts to decentralize, the party's leading role in the society was never renounced. The introduction of self-management merely symbolized "the avowed intention of the Yugoslav Communists to disperse the power of the centralized state, and to create in its place a society of loosely connected, self-governing organizations" (Blumberg, 1971: 196). A new independent nation was developing that had left the Eastern bloc and was seeking new alliances in the West. The country needed domestic support and a united population, and it was hoped that the ideology of self-management and decentralization would help to accomplish those goals. In addition, "the Yugoslavs had to counter the destabilizing effect of market oriented production with some forms of solidarity, social equality and economic subsidy" (Zukin, 1981: 287). It was hoped that this goal would be accomplished by having people involved in the social and economic institutions of self-management. The power was eventually to be transferred from the party bureaucracies to the people, who would operate the socially owned means of production through workers' councils.

THE FIRST SELF-MANAGEMENT ORGANS AND THEIR FUNCTIONS

The workers' councils are elected on a one-person, one-vote basis and represent the entire working force of each enterprise. The workers' council meets approximately once a month and decides by a majority vote on the major policies of the enterprise. For instance, the workers' council manages the social property of the enterprise, plans the production process, fixes wage rates and prices, and determines investment policies. It elects a managing board annually to supervise daily operations. This board, whose membership should be three-quarters production workers, is directly responsible to the council. The director, who is responsible for day-to-day management and represents the enterprise before state agencies and in legal matters, has been increasingly subjected to the council's authority (Comisso, 1985; Lane, 1976; Rusinow, 1977; Stephens, 1980).

In 1952, for instance, enterprise directors ceased to be party appointees. Instead, the power to select enterprise directors passed to the local governments in an effort to decentralize decision making. A 1953 act determined that directors had to be chosen in open competition based on their education, experience, and competence. A few years later, in 1957, workers' councils were given more power: they became entitled to one-half membership of the selection committee instead of the existing one-third. Furthermore, in 1964, the director's unlimited term in office was restricted to four years. Finally, under the provisions of the 1965 reform, the workers' council not only had the right to determine the director's term in office, but could also remove him altogether (Blumberg, 1971; Comisso, 1987; Lane, 1976; Rusinow, 1977; Stephens, 1980).

In spite of efforts to decentralize and democratize the economy, and in spite of the formally given rights to the workers' councils, certain conditions limited workers' power in the first years of the reform. Enterprise autonomy was limited because of the central investment planning and certain price controls. Workers' councils were elected and were consulted, but they did not play any real managerial role. Resources were not available to utilize as councils wished, and at the end it was the enterprise directors who had the most power (Comisso, 1987; Rusinow, 1977; Stephens, 1980).

In contrast to other countries examined in this part of the book, the party leadership in Yugoslavia, for reasons explained above, were more committed to the goal of self-management. As a result, the leadership sought to decentralize both economic and political controls to the lowest level of the enterprise through a series of reforms. To that end, and through a series of measures, the direct, external influence of the state agencies gradually became reduced, and the directors' power, instead of being exclusively controlled by the state, became subject to greater workers' influence through their councils.

THE GOALS AND IMPACT OF THE 1965 REFORM

The 1965 reform initiated yet another phase of state decentralization by transferring control rights from the federations to the republics and local governments. Instead of centralized state control, republics and local governments were to supervise enterprises within their territory, at least in the initial stages. The 1965 reform also extended enterprise autonomy and initiated the period of market socialism in Yugoslavia (Comisso, 1979; Lane, 1976). Yugoslav firms did not have to fulfill goals set by the central political authorities; instead, their internal and external relations were to be governed by market conditions. In addition, the percentage of income retained by the enterprises was increased from 51 to 71 percent. This income could be used for consumption and investment purposes, and the workers' council could determine how to appropriate this income for these purposes (Stephens, 1980: 68). Finally, the 1965 reform made provisions for enterprises to receive flexible interest rates, allowing them to lend money directly to other enterprises as well as to participate in joint operations. The goal of all these measures was to promote capital mobility and to help enterprises become competitive in Western markets (Stephens, 1980).

Not surprisingly, the reforms did not take place without conflict and some negative consequences. Firms had an interest in seeking to diminish political control and administrative intervention. More autonomy meant greater incentives to become successful, greater control over profits, lower taxes, and more predictable sources of funding based on the firm's success. Workers also had an interest in gaining greater enterprise autonomy, since their incomes would increase as the politically determined high rate of enterprise savings would be eliminated. In turn, higher wages would stimulate higher productivity.

The enterprise elites, both managerial and self-managerial, were not united in their support for greater enterprise autonomy. They knew that, once their ties with the political elites that allocated resources were cut, they would have less control over resources and fewer resources to dispose. The political elites in the state administration and party apparatus were reluctant to support enterprise autonomy too. In fact, as Comisso (1987) argues, it was the split of national elites over the plan versus market option that promoted the 1965 reform. Higher wages could promote higher productivity, but they could also result in higher inflation rates. Cutbacks in the bureaucracy that the reformers envisioned could lower the social standard of living and thus further widen the existing regional inequalities. Most of all, increasing enterprise autonomy meant that the elites would lose their privileges and their political authority over enterprises (Comisso, 1987: 236–237). As Comisso has put it: "For national political elites, the loss of discretionary funds and regulatory authority meant losing a key set of rewards and penalties at their disposal for disciplining the political behavior of enterprise and political elites in the provinces'' (1987: 237).

The 1965 reform also had some negative economic results such as closing down inefficient enterprises, increasing unemployment rates, and promoting economic instability. The income gap among workers in the more and less profitable enterprises and in more and less developed regions became wider (Comisso, 1979; Lane, 1976; Stephens, 1980). The income differences were exacerbated by the division of the economy into high-, medium-, and low-wage industries. This meant that individuals with similar skills and in similar jobs received unequal pay and had unequal access to nonwage benefits. Workers became increasingly dissatisfied not only because of economic considerations, but also because the negative consequences of the reforms directly challenged the Yugoslav principle of distribution according to work.

Bitterness and resentment among workers grew even more as inequalities in the distribution of power within the self-managed enterprises became more obvious. According to the principles of the self-management model, every member was to have an equal voice in decision making. This proclaimed egalitarianism, however, did not materialize in practice. Numerous studies have shown, for instance, that managerial and skilled personnel had much greater influence than rank-and-file workers; that, although production workers comprised the majority of industrial employment, still they were not adequately represented in organs of self-management; that there was a decrease of power as one moved down the hierarchy of the enterprises; that the managerial staff dominated the majority of discussions; and that managers and experts not only did all the talking at the meetings, but also manipulated the decision making by carefully controlling the technical and economic information they presented to the workers (Blumberg, 1971; Burns, 1979; Comisso, 1979; Hunnius, 1973; Obradović, 1978; Stephens, 1980; Zwerdling, 1980).

Despite reform measures, the workers' decision-making power remained limited. Their lack of control has to be understood within the overall context of the generally low educational level of the Yugoslav working class (Obradović, 1978). It usually takes a few generations for a newly urbanized proletariat with low literacy and few skills to be in a position to exercise real control. In order to understand these results better, and in order to be able to understand similar experiences in other state socialist countries, some other aspects of the overall self-management system in Yugoslavia have to be considered.

First, self-managing firms in Yugoslavia operate within an environment wherein the ruling group, for the sake of political survival, chose early on to be supportive of self-management. Power and authority in economic and political life has shifted slowly from central control toward regional and local control, and the centralized economic management has been replaced by the growing autonomy of the enterprise and the growing role of the market, both internal and external. Second, in spite of the above-mentioned limitations and inefficiencies, the introduction of workers' councils meant that the direct, external influence of the state agencies began to be challenged, and the director's power, instead of being exclusively controlled by the state, became subject to the workers' influence through their councils (Comisso, 1987). Third, self-management through which people manage major aspects of their social existence has been ingrained within the overall fabric of the society. This does not necessarily mean that self-managing bodies always function according to the regulations provided by the law or that abuses and inconsistencies do not exist (Denitch, 1976; Popovic, 1984).

In all the countries described in this book, Yugoslavia included, there is usually a big gap between prescribed, intended changes and their actual translation in practice, between *de jure* and *de facto* participation, as the IDE group has called it. What distinguishes Yugoslavia from other cases is that its political elites were committed more than those in any other country to self-management. As a result, organizational resources and the means to support the idea of self-management exist (Tardos, 1984). This is reflected in the various stages of participatory reforms that took place in Yugoslavia as the country faced the problems presented by the changes.

This does not necessarily mean that the ruling class totally gave up its prerogatives in Yugoslavia. Having made the choice of self-management for ideological, political, and practical reasons, the leadership attempted various solutions to make the system work economically in order to preserve and legitimize its own existence as well. The increasing public discontent and opposition of the late 1960s, for instance, once more tested this basic premise of the elite's support for the self-managed economy.

During that period, unfulfilled aspirations for social equality and influence in the decision-making process resulted in increased discontent among disadvantaged groups, as manifested in strikes and work stoppages (Arzenšek, 1978; Comisso, 1979; Jovanov, 1978; Stephens, 1980). Between 1958 and 1969, two thousand strikes took place. By the mid-1960s, strikes occurred in all the major industrial sectors and in all the country's republics (Zukin, 1981: 298). A nationwide study between 1966 and 1969 revealed that, when considering external reasons, 90 percent of the strikes were due to the unfavorable position of the enterprise within the economic system. Where reasons inside the organization were considered, personal income was the primary reason (approximately 63 percent) and the underdeveloped stage of self-management (approximately 15 percent) was the secondary reason (Obradović, 1978). Most of the strikes did not last more than two days, they rarely spread through an entire enterprise, and the reasons for strikes were mostly monetary. Nonetheless, they represented a threat to the political leadership and to the self-management system it supported. The immediate response to the strikes was a quick acceptance of workers' demands and the replacement of directors, union representatives, and party officials of the enterprises (Zukin, 1981: 289). In the long run, all the pressures and the general economic crisis of the early 1970s (e.g., inflation, unemployment, increasing tensions among the nationalities, the indebtedness of enterprises to the banks, and persistent foreign trade deficits) pressed the political authorities to reevaluate the whole self-management program (Linden, 1986; Woodward, 1986). As a result, the 1974 Constitution and the 1976 Law on Associated Labor further decentralized governmental authority and economic management of the enterprise.

THE DEVELOPMENT OF THE SELF-MANAGEMENT SYSTEM IN THE 1970s

In order to raise the level of direct participation, enterprises were broken up into smaller independent units, the Basic Organizations of Associated Labor (BOAL). The enterprise, an integrated cluster of BOALs, would still operate on the market and it would be involved in other external relations, but only on the basis of power delegated to it by the otherwise independent BOALs. More importantly, all net income from economic activities was now a BOAL income, and it could be used and distributed under each BOAL's control. If the firm had more than one plant, the firm's workers' council was made up of representatives from each plant (Lane, 1979; Linden, 1986; Pejovich, 1990; Stephens, 1980). In addition, in order to raise the workers' effective influence in decision making, the 1974 Constitution forbade the election of managerial and technical staff to the councils. The intent of the proposed changes was to reduce the decision-making powers of the managerial class within the enterprise (Pejovich, 1990; Rusinow, 1977). Educational programs on self-management were also initiated to educate workers and to make them more assertive and thus eliminate the power advantage exercised by the managerial elites (Pastuović, 1978). Such provisions, however, tend to create contradictions that are not easy to resolve, since managerial dominance is deeply rooted in the structure of the economy (Tardos, 1984).

As Comisso (1979: 110) has pointed out, the reforms granted greater autonomy to enterprises with an "essentially oligarchic power structure at the onset. Thus, when the sphere of enterprise's discretion was enlarged, the already influential groups were in a better position to take advantage of it." Moreover, as the firms became more dependent on market forces for their efficiency and survival, financial and commercial operations started gaining greater importance over production, where the majority of the workers were concentrated. In addition, the need for rapid decisions in order to respond to market demands flexibly, and increased pressures for technological innovation, enhanced the influence of skilled workers, specialists, and executives over that of workers. Although the dependence on expertise and market forces resulted in the increase of influence among technical experts, as well as other pluralistic forces such as customers, suppliers, and banks, at least theoretically it also implied more freedom of the enterprise from political and bureaucratic manipulations.

CONCLUDING REMARKS

In Yugoslavia the technocratic and managerial elites have the incentive as well as the appropriate resources to press for more enterprise autonomy. Unions have also become more involved in self-management goals. Trade unions as well as party organizations within the firm, as in most East European countries, operate on the principle of following rather than challenging party policies. They are merely bureaucratic organizations in charge of supervising the implementation of party policies within the workplace. Their task is basically to monitor both the workers and management, so that their actions will not hurt the interests of the working people, as perceived by the party. They derive their power not from the working people, but from the support of officials within the party bureaucracy (Comisso, 1987). With the increasing autonomy of the enterprise and the introduction of self-managing bodies, the supervisory function of the trade unions gradually decreased. Although trade unions in Yugoslavia have not fully emerged as independent sociopolitical forces that defend the workers' interests, still their role is to strengthen the self-managing bodies and educate their members about self-management (Comisso and Marer, 1986; Singleton, 1970; Stephens, 1980; Zukin, 1981).

Yugoslavia's economic problems have worsened during the last few years, to the degree that many predict that the self-managed economy is not a viable economic system. Others blame the present crisis precisely on the system that was supposed to avoid such problems—self-management. For example, the national debt has assumed epidemic proportions. Inflation has made the dinar worthless. The rate of growth has been negative, and personal incomes are declining. In the late 1980s, the rate of unemployment reached double digits, increasing from 12 percent in 1980 to 14 percent in 1987. This, of course, does not represent the whole picture. As some correctly caution, there are more than 1 million Yugoslav workers working in the West, while many Yugoslavs return or stay in their villages, without full employment. For both reasons, it is difficult to estimate the real unemployment rates in Yugoslavia (Pejovich, 1990: 127, 130).

In light of this grave economic situation (Linden, 1986; Woodward, 1986), as well as the increased nationalistic, at times violent, sentiments among the six ethnic republics and the one province in the late 1980s and 1990s, it is very uncertain whether efforts to expand workers' power and increase enterprise autonomy will continue and whether the whole self-managed economy will survive the present crisis.

As many have demonstrated, the way the self-managed system has operated might in itself have contributed to the country's mounting problems. Thus, it might have invariably contributed to its own demise. As the economist Pejovich has shown, some specific elements of the self-managed system in Yugoslavia have negatively affected its performance and viability. First, the choice of organization is very important. A totally free-market society, for instance, features a number of organizational structures ranging from small business to multinational, to nonprofit-oriented businesses. In Yugoslavia such a choice does not exist; the firm has not emerged voluntarily, but is mandated by the law. Also, it has not proved its success by openly competing in the market. Instead, the ruling elite has mandated its existence and protects it from competition. In that respect, the costs of maintaining and enforcing the existing structure must be higher within the Yugoslav context than within the free-market economy.

Second, the increased bureaucracy that has grown over the years to supervise and monitor the self-managed firms adds to this cost. For example, the Agency for Social Book Keeping has to check every single receipt and approve every single payment of each firm.

Third, the location of decision making in the labor-managed firm creates a number of problems and contradictions, which might ultimately inhibit the effective and profitable running of the enterprise. The fact that all employees have to participate in the decision-making process rules out the right or the need of any individual with specialized expertise to make key decisions, and it can be a very time-consuming and counterproductive process.

Finally, the workers' council approves all the hiring and firing, including the director of the firm. The director is under pressure to conform with the council's preferences rather than follow policies that would maximize the value of the firm. Pejovich contends that two conditions have to be met in order for the labor-managed firm to be more efficient: first, to reward the manager with a broad range of property rights, including the right to hire and fire, and the right to be independent of the council's preferences; and second, to devise a new penalty-reward system that would allow the manager to pursue strategies that would maximize the firm's value. Of course, if all these changes were to take place labor's participation in management would cease to exist (Pejovich, 1990: 123–132).

This is not the place to evaluate such a position which represents growing concern over the direction the Yugoslav experiment will take. Suffice it to say that most criticisms of the self-management system are guided by monetary criteria. Then again the crisis and inadequacies of the system may well push the country to greater openness and serious consideration of capitalism. In view of the epochal events of 1989 in the Soviet Union and Eastern Europe and in view of the multiparty, free elections that are mandated for all federal units (free elections already took place in Slovenia and Croatia in the spring of 1990—see Denitch, 1990: 303), we can cautiously argue that those changes offer a possibility for increased public expression. The dynamic of power that resulted from the changes in Yugoslavia and elsewhere will determine the future of self-management in Yugoslavia.

6

Workers' Participation in Eastern Europe: The Cases of Poland, Hungary, and Czechoslovakia

THE CASE OF POLAND

With the exception of Yugoslavia, attempts to introduce workers' participation in Eastern Europe have been short-lived and associated with an outbreak of crisis, primarily in response to the inefficiencies of the Soviet system of management.[1] Take, for example, the widespread labor unrest in Poland in 1956, especially the Poznan uprising in June 1956 as well as the emergence of workers' councils during the Polish October.[2] All were outcomes of, first, the realization of the inefficiencies and excessive centralization of the economic system in general, and second, of the shortcomings of the industrial labor relations system in particular.[3] Trade unions, for instance, instead of defending workers' interests, were completely dominated by the government bureaucracy and were designed to maintain and increase labor productivity.[4] Although the managerial power of directors over workers was counterbalanced somewhat by the control and regulations of the administrative authorities, still it assumed almost dictatorial dimensions over the years. As a result, managerial misuse of power and abuse of workers were very common.

Managerial and trade union practices could not, however, totally stifle workers' resistance and the resistance of the lower personnel in the trade union hierarchy. In general, the people's courts that tried disciplinary cases took the worker's side. Moreover, during the 1955 trade union election campaign, the harshness of the regime, the trade union position, and the managerial abuses of power were thoroughly criticized. This in turn resulted in a period of relaxation of labor discipline, which gave workers the opportunity to formulate their demands. Consequently, the Poznan events followed and workers' councils emerged. These events should also be understood within the overall reformist political climate of the post-Stalinist period. Workers demanded to comanage industrial production to fight waste, mismanagement, rigid bureaucracy, and exploitation. Under those circumstances, "A major reform providing for an efficient machinery to deal with labor grievances and to establish tension-relieving mechanisms, to avoid regime shaking eruptions of the Poznan type, and to overcome the demoralizing effect of the unsatisfactory labor conditions became mandatory" (Grzybowski, 1957: 276–277).

It was not just the workers who became increasingly convinced that the reform was needed. The same sentiment was also slowly growing among officials within the party circles themselves.[5] Soon workers' councils were set up as spontaneously as in the 1944–1945 period, although conditions for their development were different in 1956. For instance, after the German forces withdrew from Poland, councils and committees began to spring up, which tried to conserve the plants by starting the operation themselves, arranging supplies and the like. However, the urgent need to industrialize during that time required centralization of economic decisions and strengthening of managerial authority.

In 1956, on the other hand, the negative consequences of overcentralization required that the economy shift to less centralist principles. Furthermore, the influx of poor and illiterate peasants into the factories required training and discipline. In fact, the filling of various management positions by the most able workers constituted the major form of participation in those years. In contrast, in 1956, such mobility and participation were no longer possible. Another form was needed to allow workers to participate to reduce corruption, inefficiency, and waste. As George Kolankiewicz argues: "The setting up of the workers' councils was a way of exposing the reality of the industrial situation, the bureaucracy of administration, the inexpert management and the subservient trade unions" (1973: 103).

Workers' Councils after the Poznan Uprising

The party's legitimacy had been seriously eroded, and the regime was compelled to face some pressing problems, including the misuse of power and worker dissent and alienation. Since the discredited trade unions could not renew confidence in the party and state institutions, the workers' councils could alleviate some problems (de Weydenthal, 1981: 188). As noted above, in order to strengthen its legitimacy, the party introduced the self-management system in Yugoslavia. In Poland, the party's legitimacy was also seriously eroded during the late 1960s and early 1970s. This was one of the factors that prompted the reevaluation and subsequently the change of the self-management system.

The situation in Poland in 1956 was not identical to Yugoslavia's during the above-mentioned periods. In Poland, the acceptance of the workers' councils and the whole propaganda of self-management were temporary solutions to the party's threatened legitimacy. As subsequent events proved, the party leadership was not ideologically committed to such goals. In Yugoslavia, on the other hand, self-management became an officially sanctioned means to legitimate the break with the Eastern bloc. The party leadership, therefore, had to commit itself to self-management on a more permanent basis, although conflict and resistance existed. Furthermore, the party leadership needed to make scientific management work as efficiently as possible, since Yugoslavia's separate and independent road away from the centralized Stalinist system was justified on the grounds that the self-management system was superior to the centralized Soviet-type system.

In Poland, the central elite tolerated the workers' councils as a temporary measure, until the party regained its strength. Nonetheless, the spontaneous emergence of workers' councils in Poland placed tremendous strain on the party leadership. As a result, in November 1956, the Sejm (parliament) formally sanctioned their existence. In that respect, the party leadership appeared to be responsive to popular demands, and thus its political domination was reaffirmed. Since workers, along with peasants, were the major elements on which the party based its legitimacy and support, the party had to accommodate their demands to some extent. On the other hand, the economic crisis could not possibly be ignored, and the political elite seriously considered that workers' participation could be one way to overcome the crisis, at least on a temporary basis.

The councils, which were subsequently established, represented at least two-thirds of the workforce in each factory and exercised considerable power in regard to major management and production aspects of factory life, such as expansion of the plant, evaluation of production plans, as well as work norms and wages. The councils were also granted the right to appoint and dismiss the company directors, an exclusive prerogative of the ministry and local party organization up to that point (Kolankiewicz, 1973). In effect, the power granted to the workers' councils was in exchange for their assuming responsibility for greater productivity and output as well as better quality products. This would subsequently lead to the improvement of standards of living, something that would help the party's legitimacy as well (Kolankiewicz, 1973; Stefanowski, 1977).

The 1956 Polish law regarding the rights and responsibilities of workers' councils resembles provisions of the 1950 law in Yugoslavia, according to which workers would actively participate in the management of their plants through their elected workers' councils. The Polish workers' councils, however, were the result of a spontaneous and unorganized movement that lacked the support of any major sociopolitical force in society. In contrast, councils in Yugoslavia were carefully planned from above, marking the beginning of a new political and economic era. This difference is of critical importance, since in Yugoslavia every attempt to give workers more power was based on the principle of de-centralization of the economy in general and of the enterprise in particular. In Poland, on the other hand, despite the official rhetoric of strengthening workers' councils, which were supposed to be the cornerstone of Poland's socialism, their power was merely limited by the plans and regulations of the centralized planning system. Some serious political and ideological considerations eventually determined the councils' fate. The spontaneous emergence of workers' councils and their subsequent ratification were in a way challenging the party's key place in the dictatorship of the proletariat, and the subsequent events proved that this could not be tolerated indefinitely. The councils' preoccupation with management and production issues took over basic functions of the party organizations and trade unions, but this could undermine the party's role. According to the principles of democratic centralism, the party plays the leading role in the society, and the workers' councils threatened this role.

The 1958 legislation on the Conference of Workers' Self Management (KSR), consisting of the workers' councils, trade unions, and party committees, eventually neutralized and undermined the workers' power (Kolankiewicz, 1973: 117). Through legalistic procedures and manipulations, workers' councils became part of the KSRs. Crucial decisions on social welfare, wages, and employment policies were beyond the councils' control, which in effect meant subordination of the workers' councils to the party and administrative authority (Woodall, 1982a). Managerial power was strengthened, and the conferences became a voting mechanism to approve plans submitted by management. Eventually, KSRs became production conferences, and after 1975 the workers' councils were excluded from the KSRs altogether (Norr, 1983).

By 1978, even the party's own research indicated that most workers believed that the KSRs were under total managerial influence (Kolankiewicz, 1982). If to all these are added the constraints of the micro-level of the enterprise, we can better understand the councils' limitations and their final demise. The establishment of workers' councils, for instance, was reluctantly accepted by directors and senior managerial personnel. The idea of having to fulfill orders coming from above, along with the fact that one's decisions had to be sent downward for discussion and criticism, was not a comforting one. Furthermore, party officials and union members were not interested in supporting workers' councils since the councils threatened their own roles and interests. Finally, the workers' movement itself posed some limitations. The movement was spontaneous and unorganized. Workers lacked the skills and art of the industrial management and organization. The working class had increased four times since the end of the Second World War, and most of the newcomers were from the countryside, with low educational levels, and were unadjusted to the factory work, let alone self-management (Blazejczyk et al., 1978: 19).

Worker Participation in the 1970s

Workers in Poland never stopped fighting for justice, freedom, and democracy and when appropriate, always made their intentions known. The people naturally always resented the imposition of a foreign system, and this resentment became more intense during the late 1970s as a result of adverse economic circumstances. Trust in the party's policies was fading, and its legitimacy was seriously questioned (Persky and Flam, 1982). As Norr has pointed out: "History and geography made it necessary, most of the workers recognized, to accept the existence of the system 'they' had imposed, but there was no use in waiting for them to start running it fairly, or in legitimizing it by 'pseudo-participation'; 1956 and its aftermath had exposed those illusions'' (1983: 7). Broadly speaking, events of the 1980–1981 period in Poland and the development of the self-management movement were the result of accumulated dissatisfaction among the working population owing to the widespread corruption, incompetence, and structural inability of the system to fulfill its promises to the supposedly ruling class of the society. Poland's history since the communist takeover has been marked by a series of violent upheavals. In 1956 and again in 1970, 1976, and 1980 specific economic grievances, usually over large increases in food prices, triggered the workers' agitation for participation in management and political influence over the established hierarchy of power (de Weydenthal, 1980; Pravda, 1979). The bloody 1970 repression of the workers' uprising along the cities of the Baltic coast further widened the gap between the people and the party. It also politicized the working class. Gomułka's dismissal and the subsequent reversal of economic policies owing to the workers' protest produced a direct effect on the hierarchy of power and justified workers' demands and criticisms of the established order.

With Gierek in power, workers' expectations increased, as promises were made for greater social welfare benefits, shorter working hours, more democratic trade unions, and the revival of the workers' councils (Norr, 1983). Despite the official rhetoric regarding socialist democracy, and as consequent developments proved, Gierek's goal was to modernize industry and increase the productive capacity of the economy by importing advanced technology from the West. It was a technocratic approach to solve the economic and social problems of the country based on managerialism rather than on workers' participation (Norr, 1983; Woodall, 1981).

Eventually, the functions of unions and the KSRs were restricted in preparing and implementing labor legislation according to the party's dictates, regardless of concerns voiced during the mid-1970s regarding the worsening economic situation and in spite of demands to expand workers' participation schemes. Considerable efforts were made to consolidate the party's hegemony in the decision-making process at the workplace, and demands for greater worker autonomy were opposed. By expanding opportunities of consumption and improving the standard of living, the party was hoping to restore political control over workers' activities, and thus validate its role as the main articulator of their interests. Political stability would be accomplished through economic advancement (de Weydenthal, 1981). Implicit to this strategy of stability was the reliance on political and institutional centralism and the reaffirmation of the one-man management principle (Woodall, 1981).

Such an instrumental and manipulative approach was ineffective in containing the workers' growing dissatisfaction, as proved by events in 1976 and especially 1980 (Norr, 1983; Woodall, 1982a). This approach could have been successful and won popular support if the government had been able to maintain high levels of economic performance. After the mid-1970s, however, it became apparent that such a condition was difficult to secure. As Nuti (1981a: 25) states, "Gierek's plan was adventurist and badly executed and came apart under the impact of extreme adverse international and natural conditions." The oil crisis, worldwide trade recession, and inflation resulted in industrial slowdowns, decline in exports, and shortages of food and consumer goods. These problems were intensified by widespread incompetence, negligence, and corruption (Nuti, 1981b).

As the government tried to cope with the growing inflation and the shortage of consumer goods by drastically increasing food prices, the working population responded with strikes in the factories and protests in the streets. The 1976 workers' outbreak and strikes posed serious challenges to the existing system. First, the party's credibility was as low as it had ever been since 1956; therefore, change in leadership and promises for reform would not be as easily believed as they had been in 1970. Second, the 1976 events had, as in 1970, successfully reversed the economic measures taken (e.g., the increase in prices) and once again exposed the system's vulnerability to collective working-class action. Third, the formation of the Committee for the Defense of Workers (KOR) in 1976 and the Social Self-Defense Committee (KSS-KOR) in 1977 united intellectuals and workers for the first time. It was from those groups and through debates and publications, especially the unofficial periodical *Robotnik* (Worker), that demands for free unions were shaped, and the idea of self-management was developed and eventually emerged as a movement in 1981 (de Weydenthal, 1981; Norr, 1983; Runciman, 1985; Woodall, 1981).

This accumulated experience and the lessons drawn from it led to another workers' revolt in 1980–1981. Although all the workers' protests seem to have been prompted by specific economic measures that were hurting them directly, we should not underestimate the political and ideological grounds of such revolts. It gradually became apparent to workers that economic reforms alone were not enough to meet their political needs. Of course, the Gierek regime attempted to negotiate and limit the confrontation on economic issues. It soon realized, however, especially with the establishment of the strike committees, that it was impossible to prevent workers from making political demands (Poznanski, 1986; Staniszkis, 1981). For instance, the twenty-one demands of the Inter-Factory Strike Committee (MKS), beyond the immediate monetary claims, had mostly to do with rights of expression and protection (e.g., right of expression, right of strike, right of forming unions, and the like) (Persky and Flam, 1982).

The strong emphasis on technocratic socialism during Gierek's regime, and the parallel expansion of the needed education, created some great contradictions pertaining to socioeconomic equality and working-class mobility. As a result, workers' attitudes were politicized. Over the years, the workers became increasingly more self-assured and more demanding (Kolankiewicz, 1982). In 1960–1961, for instance, there were approximately 78,000 graduates of elementary technical vocational schools. This was the major source of semiskilled workers in industry. In 1977, this number increased to approximately 366,000. Between

1970 and 1977, there was an approximately 63 percent increase in the number of elementary vocational school graduates (Kolankiewicz, 1981: 133). Although the educational qualifications of the manual workers had increased, opportunities for promotion were limited and entrance to senior industrial management positions was the prerogative of those from white-collar educational backgrounds. A 1974 Labor Code (article 52), passed by the Sejm, reinforced managers' position by giving them greater powers, especially in the area of layoffs. But a lot of the directors were not qualified for their jobs. Many of them, even those considered specialists, had not even finished elementary school. Directors also preferred to import foreign specialists rather than educating their own workers, in fear that these workers would form alliances with professional groups and challenge their power. Overall, then, the educated and qualified intelligentsia was denied opportunities (Kolankiewicz, 1981: 133). This kind of underqualification was brought about mostly through a *nomenklatura* policy, that is, a policy of promoting people who were not competent and knowledgeable so that the interests of insecure and less competent managers would not be hurt (Kolankiewicz, 1982). It was this group of managers, whose interests were threatened, that opposed self-management and economic decentralization in the 1980–1981 period.

The Emergence of Solidarity

The emergence of Solidarity and the subsequent demand for self-management and worker control in the 1980–1981 period have to be understood within the context of developments and changes that took place during the Gierek years. Higher educational levels soon produced many workers with qualifications that exceeded the level of jobs available. Therefore, instead of being a vehicle for upward mobility, education became a source of frustrated aspirations. Greater income and privilege differentiation between white-collar and manual workers also intensified the perception of social inequality and the notion of relative deprivation among workers. This, too, contributed to their frustration (Kolankiewicz, 1981; Woodall, 1981). In addition, management held wide powers, especially in the area of dismissals. Accordingly, we can easily see why workers perceived autocratic management as a major source of division within the workforce (Kolankiewicz, 1982). Under worsening economic conditions, the deteriorating industrial management system and the persistence of mismanagement and poor planning became politically very significant (Woodall, 1982a). It was mostly the working class that was negatively affected by such adverse conditions (Kolankiewicz, 1981).

The emergence of independent trade union Solidarity in August 1980 was both a response to prevailing disillusion and discontent, and an organizational means to defend workers' interests and to channel working-class aspirations into a new administrative order. However, since Solidarity did not want to be blamed for mismanagement, it did not wish to be drawn into joint responsibility for the management of production (Norr, 1987; Touraine, 1983). Nonetheless, in the famous Gdansk Agreement, the participation of workers' councils in management was recognized (Persky and Flam, 1982). Solidarity's major concern at the time was not so much to introduce workers' participation in management as to safeguard its existence as an independent trade union, free of party influences. Protecting workers' interests was its overriding concern, and there was fear that workers' participation in management could undermine such a defensive posture (Kolankiewicz, 1982). At first, then, Solidarity did not formulate any demands for self-management. That position was clearly reflected in its Draft Program of Current Action, in which it stated that "the independent union has no interest in interfering with affairs under the competence of management, nor to replace it, nor to be responsible for its activities" (as quoted in Norr, 1987: 268).

From the beginning of its existence, Solidarity exerted considerable self-restraint. On the one hand, it identified the centralized apparatus as the major cause of the country's problems, and it articulated a radical criticism of the regime. On the other hand, in view of the history of workers' movements in Eastern Europe, and taking into consideration the role of the Soviet Union in the region, Solidarity realized, and often had to remind its radical base, that communist rule could not be overthrown. Therefore, by accepting the party, Solidarity set up the boundaries of its limitations regarding the extent of socio-economic and political change (Staniszkis, 1981; Touraine, 1983).

New developments prompted Solidarity to change its position. What contributed to that shift of position? First, demands for workers' participation were raised within the grass-roots segment of the unions; second, party representatives and enterprise directors were replaced by union representatives; and third, spontaneous formation of workers' councils was taking place in various workplaces. Solidarity could not ignore such developments without losing its legitimacy. The new movement for self-management had the support of junior technocrats who had become impatient with existing waste and inefficiency. The movement was also supported by factory and regional-level activists who had become frustrated with the defensive position of trade unions that seemed to lead nowhere. Later, in 1981, it got the support of rank-and-file workers as well (Norr, 1987). In addition, the formation of the Network (Network of Solidarity Workplace Organizations), an association of seventeen key factories, became instrumental in promoting self-management as a dominant theme in political life and a vision for a new socioeconomic and political order. The first meeting of the Network in April 1981 was devoted entirely to the issue of self-management (Kolankiewicz, 1982). Throughout the summer of 1981 the movement grew stronger through the labor-management conflict at the national airlines, LOT. That conflict helped the leadership of the movement to realize that defensive trade unionism was not suitable for solving the problems labor was facing, especially because negotiations between the union and the party regarding reforms were not producing any results. Instead, self-management could become the basis of the badly needed strategy to overcome the crisis. Solidarity's National Congress in September, with an overwhelming majority, supported that position (Norr, 1987).

The Impact of Solidarity on Workers' Participation Schemes

Based on the Network's proposal, enterprises were to become independent, free of the party's control both organizationally and financially. In order to become more efficient and profitable, enterprises would have to follow the rules of the market instead of executing central plans. On the basis of the Network's plan, the democratically elected parliament would influence the economy and the enterprise functioning by introducing laws on taxes, tariffs, credits, and the like. In effect, enterprises would operate under three principles called the three Ss: *Samorzadnosč* (self-management), *Samodzielnosč* (independence), and *Samofinansowanie* (self-financing). Profit was to be one of the major goals of the independent enterprises (Norr, 1987).

In contrast to the West, appeals for participatory democracy in Poland did not seek to eliminate alienation and uplift the spirits of workers per se. Fears and suspicions raised in the West that workers' increased power in management affairs could jeopardize efficiency (due to their incompetency) were not considered to be valid in Poland either. Unlike the West, in Poland, the managerial hierarchy was subject to party control that brought about inefficiency and corruption. The crisis was very deep and the problems so severe that there were no grounds to claim that the proposed reforms could undermine efficiency. Therefore, the focus of the reform in Poland was on rationality and effectiveness. The goal was to overcome the economic crisis by offering a new alternative to the existing economic management and by making enterprises more responsive to market demands.

It was assumed that if the enterprises became independent, workers would be motivated to work hard and make responsible decisions. As a result, the inefficient, centralized, and corrupt management would cease to exist. Since the goal was economic efficiency, it was imperative that the most talented and competent directors be elected to oversee the overall running of the enterprises. The leadership of the movement was, of course, aware that the vast majority of workers did not possess the necessary expertise to do so. They were also well aware that workers "had the ability and the motivation to recognize those who did. Few believed that the primary object—economic rationality—could be attained by entangling the workers in technical and financial discussions for which they had little preparation" (Norr, 1987: 277).

As Nuti (1981a: 30) has pointed out, there was "an almost Friedmanite faith in the virtue of the markets and prices," and given the deep economic crisis Poland was facing at the time, it is doubtful whether a market economy could be effective. During crises, capitalist societies frequently centralize their authority, and as Nuti further argues, measures corresponding to war situations would have been more appropriate at that time than opening up the market. As the crisis became more profound and the movement proved unable to fulfill its claims, interest in self-management started to fade as well (Norr, 1985).

Undoubtedly, Solidarity had considerable powers to block decisions, but it did not participate in the economic decision-making process. This severely limited the impact and the future prospects of the movement (Staniszkis, 1984: 21). Judging from the debate on the social versus state enterprise between the Network and the party, we see that the party firmly resisted the idea of social ownership, although some of the authorities supported it. In its proposed draft law on self-management, for instance, the party used the notion of state enterprise to declare it as "the fundamental unit of national economy." In contrast, the Network's position was that the social enterprise was the basic unit of the economy "conducting independent activity on the principles of economic accounting, endowed with legal personality, owning part of the national assets and managed by organs of workers' self-management" (as quoted in Nuti, 1981a: 31).

On the basis of the Network's proposal, the enterprise was to be managed by its workers through their self-managed organs. The councils would decide about the strategic economic, organizational, and production aspects of the enterprise. The experience since 1956 has shown that whoever had the power to appoint the director would in reality be able to exercise considerable power in running the enterprise. The Network's position was that enterprise directors had to be accountable to the workers. In doing so, the directors would avoid the difficult position of always looking upward to please their party superiors (Kolankiewicz, 1982). To resolve that problem, and according to Solidarity's plan, the workers' councils were to be granted the right to appoint the director on the basis of open, public competition. (Nuti, 1981a). The workers' council or the entire workforce could also dismiss the director through a referendum (Norr, 1987). In fact, Solidarity and some party organizations acted on those proposals in 1981 and initiated public competition for management appointments. New directors were appointed with the support of rank-and-file and party members, who throughout the years had been intimidated by unacceptable appointments based on the *nomenklatura* system (Kolankiewicz, 1982; Staniszkis, 1984).

In contrast, the law proposed by the party clearly contradicted the above considerations and positions. It firmly reasserted the one-man management and central appointments. The founding organs (e.g., ministry or local government authorities) would have the right to appoint and dismiss the director, who was to manage the enterprise and represent it externally. The appointment and dismissal, however, were to be approved by the workers' councils. But this prerogative, along with the other, mostly consultative (e.g., approval of the annual plan, confirmation of the budget, approval of the direction of the enterprise), was undermined by certain loopholes in the party proposal. For instance, the director had the prerogative to veto workers' rights in case they "seriously undermine the social interest," something that was left undefined (as quoted in Kolankiewicz, 1982: 143).

Regardless of these limitations, demands for genuine worker control were increasing by the day. During the first round of Solidarity's Congress (September 5–10, 1981), demands for genuine self-management, abolition of the *nomen-klatura* system, and a national referendum on the issue of self-management dominated the meetings. The Solidarity congress made appeals to workers in Eastern Europe to follow the Polish example and to support the trade union movement. Unfortunately for Solidarity, such appeals were strongly criticized by the Soviet Union and by most party leaders in Eastern Europe as attacks on socialism. As a result, and despite the strong sentiments for self-management, the compromise reached between Solidarity's leaders and the government was quite different from Solidarity's position. The new law on self-management that was quickly passed by the Polish parliament stated that the government had the power to appoint the directors of enterprises in key sectors of the economy. The list of these enterprises, which comprised the nucleus of the self-management movement, was to be negotiated with Solidarity. As for the rest of the enterprises, the law stipulated that directors would be appointed by both the workers' council and the party together, while disputes would be settled in court (Norr, 1985; Nuti, 1981a). As subsequent events proved, such provisions never materialized, although workers in some plants elected their own councils to take over the management of the enterprise (Norr, 1987).

Poland after Solidarity and Concluding Remarks

This compromising position and the development of the movement as a whole have to be understood within the general context of competing interests and groups, of conflicts and tensions that operated in a desperate, paralyzed society. First, Solidarity's position on self-management directly challenged the power and threatened the prerogatives of the ruling elite and those in the administrative apparatus closely related to it. Although the need for reform was widely acknowledged, and most of the rank-and-file party members and some local party organizations had supported the notion of self-management, all the beneficiaries of the *nomenklatura* system strongly opposed it (Norr, 1987).

Second, the increasing politicization reinforced polarization among the opposing parties. Self-management was not perceived as simply another way of managing the enterprise, but as an indirect way to transform socialism. In turn, the politicization of the movement helped to consolidate the conservative forces of the party and to promote rumors about Soviet economic boycott and intervention. Neither side could ignore such realities. In reality, they were skillfully manipulated by both Solidarity and party leadership to serve their own respective interests and to keep people in line.

Third, all these fears were further reinforced by the broader demand for free elections and the polarization and fragmentation of political forces within the party. The party's legitimacy decreased considerably in the 1980–1981 period. Yet the party was unable to use any previous mechanism to absorb conflict and save face inside and outside the country. However, since Solidarity continued to negotiate with the party leadership, its authority was acknowledged, at least symbolically.

Fourth, the consequences and constraints of the socioeconomic and political crisis were felt not only by the party but by Solidarity itself. Signs of crisis and disorientation within Solidarity itself became apparent. As Staniszkis so convincingly has shown, the more politicized the movement became, the more it overstepped the boundaries of its self-limiting revolution set by Solidarity itself in August 1980. The movement was moving beyond trade unionism to become a social movement (Staniszkis, 1984). This generated tension and conflicts within Solidarity circles themselves, especially between pragmatists, who advocated negotiations with the party until common grounds were established, and fundamentalists, who advocated direct confrontation with the party (Norr, 1987).

It should again be stressed that Solidarity, by having acknowledged from the beginning the party's dominant role in the society, did not seek to take over the means of production. In effect, Solidarity was lacking substantial economic power that was very much needed. In turn, the deterioration of the economic situation (e.g., food shortages, huge foreign debt, lack of imported parts needed in manufacturing) and the prevailing inability to solve those real problems exhausted people's tolerance and made them less enthusiastic about self-management.

Self-management had been perceived and advocated as a kind of panacea for the country's socioeconomic and political problems; this perception, at least in the short run, did not correspond to reality. "It [self-management] had been packaged as the key that would open to resolution of the union's and the nation's dilemmas. When this promise began to lose its plausibility . . . enthusiasm for self-management waned" (Norr, 1987: 286). In December 1981, with the imposition of martial law, all the rights of the workers' councils granted by law in September 1981 were formally suspended. According to the official proclamations, this was a temporary measure because of the politically unstable situation. However, the need for reform was still acknowledged, since the leadership's legitimacy was in question. Therefore, in April 1983, workers' councils began to operate again.

A big discrepancy was obvious between the official rhetoric concerning the need for self-management and its manifestation in reality. Since the directors gained the right to overrule the decisions of the workers' council, their power was eventually strengthened. The right of the workers' councils to appoint and dismiss enterprise directors was not granted, even in those firms that were not the most crucial for the national economy. Moreover, if the government perceived councils as illegal (according to government criteria of course) or as a threat to the society's interests, the workers' councils could be suspended altogether (Holland, 1984; Norr, 1987). How can this discrepancy between rhetoric and practice, which is typical in all Soviet-type societies, be explained? On the one hand, the need for cooperation and for systematic reform to improve the economy is recognized. Such a position preserves the party's legitimacy, since the image presented is that the party is interested in improving economic and working conditions. On the other hand, the regime is well aware that a radical decentralized reform, such as the one promoted by Solidarity, entails serious challenges to the prerogatives of managers and administrative bureaucrats on whom the party's authority and power rests.

Political concerns, as in China, the Soviet Union, and the rest of Eastern Europe, posed some limitations for economic reform in Poland as well. The self-managed structures, which were retained during the time Solidarity was illegal, can thus be viewed as corresponding to the elites' need to widen their base for social support, and not as a genuine effort to decentralize the economy and give power to the workers. But the workers' councils had a symbolic value, and, although opposition was not coherent and organized, as in 1980–1981, it was still alive. The underground leadership, after initial hesitation, revised its position regarding participation in self-management organs and stressed the importance of legally exploiting every opportunity these participative structures offered, in order to fight oppression and defend workers' interests (Holland, 1984). Until the spring of 1989, when Solidarity was legalized again, Poland lacked any independent organizational basis to channel working-class demands and aspirations. Until that time, the existing councils could not freely articulate working-class needs and interests, although opposition and strikes in Poland never stopped.

Solidarity, which in 1980–1981 claimed about 10 million members, still enjoys tremendous popularity and has become a strong political force. Since Solidarity's relegalization, there has been hope that the workers' interests can be openly heard again. In June 1989, Solidarity won all the seats available to the opposition parties in the Polish parliament and all but one (260 out of 261) seat which it contested in the newly created Senate. These were the first free elections in Poland in more than four decades (Palmer, 1989: 22).

Poland's deepening political and economic instability and the popular support Solidarity enjoys resulted in the unprecedented formation in Eastern Europe of a noncommunist government. On August 16, 1989, a Solidarity-led coalition with two small parties—the United Peasants' party and the Democratic party which traditionally supported the communists—was formed and made such an extraordinary event take place. Although today the first noncommunist government might have some differences with Solidarity's leadership, these seem natural in a context of democratic pluralism, and undoubtedly Solidarity was the principal force behind the historic transformations that have taken place recently. Only time will show where these latest history-making developments will lead Poland. Interestingly, however, according to a statement of Poland's principal political forces on August 17, 1989, the need for political and economic reforms is widely recognized to resolve the political and economic crisis Poland faces (Tagliabue, 1989: A14). Solidarity's rise to power through democratic means, and the extraordinary political realignment, reflect the communist leaders' re-alization that political reforms are necessary if the economic crisis is to be resolved and political instability avoided.

In Poland, during times of economic crisis, there have been waves of interest in establishing workers' participation schemes. The 1956, 1970, and 1976 de-velopments worsened the authorities' ability to secure the workers' loyalty by appealing to official ideology. The existing shortages and tensions, and the overall inefficiency of the centralized system, combined with structural inequalities, generated tremendous pressures for economic reform in the 1980–1981 period as well. As a result, the independent trade union Solidarity emerged and chan-neled workers' frustration and demands for self-management. As in the case of other Eastern European countries, however, the structure of the economic system does not permit radical changes without challenging the political authority of the regime and its beneficiaries within the economic ministries and enterprises.

Solidarity's demands for self-management exceeded certain limits as deter-mined by party ideology and Soviet politics. Therefore, such demands could not possibly be materialized. More recent developments also indicate that ideological and political prerogatives cannot be sustained indefinitely when deep economic crisis threatens the society's very existence. The growing militancy and politi-cization of the population certainly has helped such a realization. The informal Brezhnev Doctrine, which limits the sovereignty of Moscow's allies, is no longer official policy, and the fact that the Soviet Union itself has undertaken political and economic reform under Gorbachev has also facilitated the recent develop-ments in Poland. These developments will definitely upset the balance of political power held in Poland for more than four decades. The Communist party's role is being seriously questioned, and any transition will not be easy or smooth, given that so many powerful interests are at stake.

THE CASE OF HUNGARY

In Hungary, the emergence of workers' councils in 1956 was short-lived, as in Poland in 1956 and 1980–1981. As in Poland, the workers' councils in Hungary were the result of profound dissatisfaction stemming from economic policies and the inefficiencies of the centralized system, as well as the party's policy of control. Khrushchev's de-Stalinization strategy helped, on the one hand, to bring to the surface antiparty and anti-Soviet sentiments, and on the other hand, it stimulated the emergence of nationalistic feelings. The spontaneous formation of mass organs in schools, communities, and factories reflected such sentiments and demonstrated the society's determination to change the relation-ship between the party and the people.

The 1956 Hungarian revolution, though short-lived, assumed more than re-formist dimensions. In that respect it was different from the Polish experience of the same year. In the Polish case, the workers' councils were mostly a way to improve economic management and a kind of safety valve to accommodate workers' dissatisfaction until the party regained control inside the factories. This was accomplished with the Conference of Workers' Self Management. In Hungary, the emerging workers' councils demanded the management of factories in an effort to smash the *nomenklatura* system and thereby free the factories from party domination, which was perceived as a source of inefficient performance. The workers' councils became the centers of political and national resistance as soon as the movement began to take radical, social, and nationalist dimensions supported by students and intellectuals as well as workers. Demands for self-management were voiced, along with demands for free elections, national independence, and even the withdrawal of Soviet troops (Kiraly, 1986). Under these circumstances, workers' demands for self-management ceased to remain purely economic and almost invariably carried political messages.

After the Soviet invasion, the workers' councils became the major centers of political and national resistance by establishing their own armed forces as well as an umbrella institution, the Center of Workers' Councils of Greater Budapest (CWCGBp) (Touraine, 1983). This institution coordinated the efforts of workers' councils of the major industrial complexes, articulated their demands, and later negotiated workers' demands for self-management with the Kádár regime. According to the Center's proposal on self-management, the factories belonged to the workers, who would only have to pay the state taxes, calculated on the basis of output and profits. The democratically elected workers' councils would elect the director and other management officials. The councils would also decide about all major financial, operational, and production aspects of the factories, including the social aspects of working life, financial matters, and foreign contacts (Kiraly, 1986).

It was soon realized that such demands would have been meaningless without accompanying political changes. Thus, self-management became not simply an economic demand; it was inherently associated with ideology and politics. In order for factories to be autonomous, and democratically governed by their councils, party interference and control had to cease. This is why workers included in their demands the radical reorganization of society (e.g., multiparty system, legislation to secure democratic institutions, civil liberties and rights, common ownership of the factories, and withdrawal of the Soviet troops) and a reexamination of the planned economy and its adjustment to Hungarian circumstances.

Inevitably, this politicization of the demands and the weak party leadership brought on the Soviet invasion, in sharp contrast to what happened in Poland the same year. The way the party leadership handles public dissent is crucial in determining the outcome of the conflict. Although anti-Soviet sentiments and strong nationalist feelings did not take the same dimensions in Poland as in Hungary, they were always present. In contrast to Hungary, however, events in Poland in 1956 were skillfully manipulated by the party leadership and, therefore, did not have the same results as in Hungary. Beyond the rhetoric of workers' management and economic reforms, Gomułka's position was firmly in support of the party's leadership and the Soviet-type socialism. The party never recognized the workers' councils' claim that they were the real alternatives in managing or even co-managing the means of production (Stefanowski, 1977: 13).

In that respect, Soviet interests in Poland were never seriously threatened. Nagy's leadership in Hungary, on the other hand, instead of leading popular feelings, followed them. Aiming at making his country politically neutral, and having announced his country's withdrawal from the Warsaw Pact, Nagy violated critical Soviet strategic interests in Hungary. At the same time, changes did not go far enough for the revolutionary elements within Hungarian society (Touraine, 1983: 25). As Triska and Johnson have pointed out: "The Hungarian revolution deteriorated into a nationalist, anti-Soviet, anti-coalition uprising. While Polish de-Stalinization was compatible with that of Khrushchev, the Hungarian was not. And while nationalism and anti-Sovietism were challenged through and transformed by the party in Poland, in Hungary they were not. Hence the strategy of Soviet-suppressed revolution in Hungary" (1975: 273).

The Soviet military intervention did not immediately destroy the workers' councils in Hungary because (1) the workers' councils had been established in the biggest industrial complexes; and (2) they had played an instrumental role in resisting efforts to restore the old system. Through their Central Workers' Council of Greater Budapest, the councils created a power center opposing the Kádár regime, which in turn was forced to legalize them. If the invasion was not able to destroy the councils in the short run, it contributed to their final decay in the long run. The invasion further radicalized the workers' demands and made clear the councils' limited role under party domination. The decree issued by the Kádár regime, for instance, confined the duties of workers' councils to economic management and denied them any political power. The invasion helped to crystallize the notion that, under state socialism, economic issues remain a mere extension of politics and ideology, and unless workers' councils had political power, any management rights granted to them would be meaningless.

Under those circumstances, the leadership of the Center pushed for the creation of the National Workers' Council. The Council would serve as a temporary parliament against Kádár's leadership and until free elections for a free national assembly took place. Because this move directly threatened the interests of the party and the Soviet Union, the councils were finally declared illegal. For a while workers resisted by striking and protesting. In the end, however, the councils were unable to carry out their plans, and they were finally dissolved owing to the terror and harsh penalties imposed on them (Kiraly, 1986).

Although workers' demands were suppressed, the need to reform never ceased to exist. In addition, the revolutionary experience of 1956, and similar experiences in other Eastern European countries, taught the party certain lessons: that the society should not be allowed to organize itself in similar ways; that systematic and careful steps had to be taken to avoid similar crises; that the party had to be in control of the change process, and at the same time it had to be flexible and paternalistic enough to know what was happening in the society and what needs were not being satisfied (Gorlice, 1986). Finally, the central authorities realized that it would be difficult for the society to tolerate strict central command once the state terror was lifted and that such a prospect wouldn't be economically efficient either.

Therefore, when the Kádár regime felt sufficiently secure politically, it began to make concessions. In 1962, for instance, amnesty was given to those who participated in the revolution, and the terrorist rule was relaxed. The political inactivity of the people was exchanged for some freedom to pursue more personal interests. Kádár's efforts to increase the standard of living and national production through agricultural reforms such as eliminating forced deliveries, and through participation in the second economy, helped the masses to pursue personal enrichment goals (Comisso and Marer, 1986; Gorlice, 1986). Finally, in 1968, a systematic effort was undertaken to increase the productive capacity of the economy as well as its efficiency by introducing comprehensive economic reform.

The New Economic Mechanism (NEM) Reforms

Before its introduction in 1968,[6] the reform was carefully prepared and evaluated by a number of well-known Hungarian economists. In contrast to Czechoslovakia, where, as we will see in the next section, reforms were under way during the same year, the party in Hungary was in full control, and it gave its decisive support to the economic reform, which was implemented according to its wishes. In that respect, the Hungarian reform resembles the Yugoslavian effort to decentralize, since the party in Yugoslavia initiated the reforms as well. The basic difference is the ideological basis on which the respective reforms rest. The Yugoslav emphasis on self-management, market socialism, and political decentralization is missing to a certain degree from the Hungarian reform of decentralization. The New Economic Mechanism (NEM) was to combine the central control of the socialist economy with the self-regulating market mechanism. But the concept of market socialism, which was associated with the Czechoslovakian heresy of Ota Šik and the Yugoslav model of self-management, was carefully avoided. There was no doubt that the party was in full control (Nove and Nuti, 1972: 352).

The Hungarian reformers not only escaped criticism from the Soviet Union, but they also got the approval of Brezhnev himself during his visit to the Tenth Party Conference in Budapest in November 1970. Basically, the New Economic Mechanism attempted to diminish the importance of the plan as the sole criterion in decision making. As in other Eastern European countries, the centralized plans did not adequately handle the complexity of the economy. Production was not adjusting flexibly enough to the rapidly changing demands of the economy. The results were mismanagement of resources, low growth rates, stagnating standards of living, scarcity of products and services, and balance payments difficulties (Comisso, 1985; Tardos, 1984).

On the basis of the principles of NEM, the enterprises were free to produce, market, and compete with other enterprises. The aim was to develop a link between production and demand, and with the notion of profit in mind to achieve a more efficient utilization of resources (Granick, 1974; Hohmann et al., 1975; Nove and Nuti, 1972; Révész, 1979; Tardos, 1984). The NEM also provided for a system of largely free prices, foreign trade, and the expansion of rights to workers in determining the operation of the enterprises they worked for.

Regardless of plans and promises, the implementation of reform, especially after 1972, became very limited. A new wave of economic reforms started in 1979, which included implementation of abandoned provisions under the initial 1968 plan. Despite the setback, the penetration of the market elements in Hungary is deeper than in any other Eastern European country except Yugoslavia. The Hungarian reform has also been praised for giving considerable freedom to enterprises and for taking steps to decentralize the economy, although certain administrative controls (e.g., central investment plans, price controls, taxes on profits) restrict the freedom granted to enterprises (Comisso, 1987; Granick, 1974).

In spite of Hungary's proclaimed adherence to expansion of the democratic rights of the workers, workers' self-management has still not been established in Hungary (Tardos, 1984). From the outset, the Hungarian elite ruled out the possibility of workers' self-management. Decision making would remain a managerial prerogative, although consultation committees would exist and unions would have more say within factories (Comisso, 1987; Volgyes, 1981). In fact, unions were given the right to veto management decisions (Schregle, 1976). This seems quite an impressive right, unless we consider that unions, as other state organizations, are not accountable to workers for their actions. Their function is more to supervise and control rather than carry out workers' wishes. They are fully backed by the party officials, and they have to implement their policies in order to safeguard their interests (Comisso, 1987).

Similarly, there are no mechanisms and provisions to make enterprise directors accountable to workers. Their relationship with the workers is not that of a leader to constituents, as in Yugoslavia, but rather of a superior to subordinates. Although their goals under NEM have changed (e.g., pursuit of profit instead of fulfillment of the plan), their authority nonetheless derives from the party, not from the workers. Furthermore, they have not given the incentives or the organizational means, as in Yugoslavia, to push for more enterprise autonomy. In Yugoslavia, management and the workforce have come to depend on each other to increase enterprise autonomy and efficiency. In order for the managerial elites to gain any economic or political benefits, they have had to push for enterprise autonomy. To that end they have had to gain the alliance of the labor force. In contrast, since the Hungarian directors represented the interests of the party, they did not have particular reasons to push for more efficiency and autonomy. As Ellen Comisso has put it: "With the adoption of NEM . . . Hungarian managers concentrated their efforts on creating the conditions in which their enterprises could now show an annual profit, just as they had previously concentrated their efforts on creating quantitative targets" (1987: 239–240). The more successful the enterprise became, the less discretion the directors had over enterprise resources, since this fell within the jurisdiction of the appropriate ministry and thus the party (Comisso, 1987; Comisso and Marer, 1986). The worldwide recession of the early 1970s, especially the world price explosion with its negative trade impact in both socialist and nonsocialist countries, forced the leadership to increase control and administrative intervention, although NEM principles were not fully abandoned (Comisso and Marer, 1986; Tardos, 1984).

Expansion of the Reforms Since the Late 1970s

It increasingly became apparent to the Hungarian regime, especially after 1973, that the economy could not be insulated from external market conditions and that the economic course followed since the retreat from the reforms was not working. Severe economic problems during the mid- to late 1970s (e.g., slow economic growth, increase in consumer prices, and increase in foreign debt) compelled the government to find ways to manage the crisis by reducing expenditures without restraining consumption. Since massive cuts in imports would promote social unrest, the government instead reactivated the reforms it had put aside. Starting in 1979, a new phase of economic reform began, which aimed to decentralize industry, make the economy more efficient, and change the industrial relations system within the enterprise. Measures were taken to expand operations in the second economy, to introduce new price and wage regulations, to break up large firms, and to make industrial ministries more efficient. The 1985 law on self-management, which would be gradually implemented over the years, as well as the establishment of Enterprise Contract Work Associations (ECWAs) since 1982, are also parts of the new reforms and have some potential to promote workers' welfare and increase their power within the firm. Based on the provisions of the self-management law, for instance, management of the firms will be transferred from the supervisory ministry to enterprise councils. Selection and evaluation of enterprise directors will be the responsibility of the councils. Among the councils' responsibilities are defining enterprise plans, approving financial statements, and allocating profits.

The significance of these provisions is limited since enterprise councils cannot operate in the largest corporations. The councils' seemingly extensive rights have been undermined by two important constraints. First, the councils can be elected by only part of the employees and, second, the selection of directors is subject to party influence, since the appropriate ministry can veto the councils' decisions in regard to the selection of directors (Comisso, 1987). Although the need to decentralize and to increase enterprise autonomy is widely acknowledged, the proposed changes do not reflect the intention to decrease control of the party and its administrative apparatus, and thereby introduce genuine self-managed structures.

Similarly, since 1982 small, semiautonomous subcontracting units within the firms, the ECWAs, have been introduced in an effort to reduce costs and eliminate bottlenecks. The goal is to overcome the inefficiency of the planning system by utilizing the most skilled and competent workers of the firm to ensure prompt and efficient outcomes, rather than increasing workers' power. Overall, ECWAs are designed to reduce day-to-day administrative interaction, allow firms to adapt more flexibly to domestic and international market conditions, become more competitive, and thus contribute to more efficient and profitable enterprises. In fact, ECWAs are characterized by higher productivity and improved quality control, as well as higher earnings among workers (usually 2 to 2.5 times more than working regular hours) (Stark, 1985: 26).

As noted in Part I of this book, the trend toward internationalization of the economy, new technologies and demands, as well as increased competition among economies and the saturation of mass-produced markets in industrial societies, has helped to develop more specialized products and has created the need for more flexible and participatory production systems. To a certain extent, the same logic underlies the establishment of ECWAs in Hungary. The more the economy opens up to international markets and worldwide competition, the greater the need to respond flexibly to the rapidly changing market demands and uncertainties. Those market demands and uncertainties are more accentuated in a country like Hungary than in the West, because of the uncertainties stemming from the planning system itself (e.g., shifts in planning targets and uncertainties of supplies) and the rigidities in the central regulations. By adopting ECWAs, the assumption is that firms would no longer have to depend on unreliable outside subcontractors. Furthermore, because of the mutual benefits for both workers and directors, through the ECWAs ties of dependency would eventually develop, which would allow firms to respond promptly to shifting market demands and to needs for new products.

ECWAs are small, self-managed units of up to thirty persons, characterized by a loose division of labor and equal pay among members. ECWAs are relatively autonomous, since their internal operation is the responsibility of their members, and not of the management of the enterprise. In sharp contrast to the Yugoslav case and the model of self-management envisioned in Hungary and Poland in 1956 and in Poland in 1980–1981, this type of self-management is contained within the ECWAs, and it does not extend beyond the ECWAs' boundaries. In addition, since workers do not have any voice in determining the rules regarding their formation, the workers' bargaining power within the ECWAs is limited. This resembles developments and experiments in the West, where management initiates participatory experiments without workers' influence in regard to their structure and functions. In the same way, experimentation in some countries in the West such as the United States and France is limited, and participation is not accepted as a prevalent organizing mode of the entire industry. Similarly, the establishment of ECWAs in Hungary constitutes small islands of workers' autonomy and power. The need to form an ECWA has to be determined and approved by the director of the enterprise, and ECWAs involve only a small part of the total workforce (Comisso, 1987; Stark, 1985).

These limitations, and the fact that work performed within ECWAs is better paid, can create conflicts, resentment, and antagonisms among workers. They therefore have the potential of breaking the unity of the workforce, as well as hurting the firm's overall performance (Comisso, 1987). On the other hand, the flexible and autonomous work experience within ECWAs, along with the opportunities for worker participation that the enterprise councils offer, has the potential of creating a value orientation among workers that would help to push for more control rights over their regular working lives.

This latter scenario has to overcome some serious constraints. Independent organizational means to push for such changes do not exist. On the contrary, the existing unions do not support the formation of ECWAs. This is understandable, given that the ECWAs' activities are regulated not by the Labor Code but by the Civil Code, and therefore fall beyond the jurisdiction of trade unions (Stark, 1985). Given the role of trade unions in Hungary, this opposition does not stem from the concern that the formation of ECWAs represents an effort to bust the unions, as might be the case in the West. Instead, as Stark correctly argues: "this opposition springs less from democratic impulses and the desire to offer protection to the 'non-unionized' than from the fact that trade union officialdom regards the partnerships as an invasion of what it has long guarded as its own institutional turf" (1985: 18).

Furthermore, we should keep in mind the political circumstances of the ECWAs' introduction. ECWAs were not introduced because the workers demanded them but because the party leadership perceived them as a good way to increase enterprise productivity and efficiency. As we would expect, there is significant opposition to the ECWAs among officials within the party leadership (Comisso, 1987). There are good reasons for such an opposition. ECWAs are not just forms of economic activity. First, they represent a challenge to the hierarchically organized enterprise structures under the administrative control of the party. Second, wage differentials between members and nonmembers of ECWAs, as well as increased competition, inevitably increase social inequalities and thus undermine the party's legitimacy. In fact, in order to avoid unfair competition, in 1985 the party imposed a 10 percent surtax on all firms with ECWAs (Comisso, 1987: 252).

Concluding Remarks

In Hungary, as in the other Soviet-type economies, economic reforms and efforts to decentralize the economy and to increase workers' power have to be seen within the limitations imposed by the political power structure. Economic and political structures are closely associated. Therefore, any comprehensive economic reforms and efforts to introduce genuine market mechanisms will inevitably lead to changes in the political apparatus, changes that overall are not very welcome. This does not mean that changes will not take place. Pressures for change, as was explained above, existed and will continue to exist. For legitimacy reasons alone, the political leadership will continue to take reformist steps, and the restructuring of the Soviet economy itself will reinforce and sanction such efforts. In addition, the more the economy opens up to international markets, the greater will be the pressures for reform.

As in the other Eastern European countries, however, the political system imposes certain limits with regard to how far these reforms might go. For instance, although the new NEM provisions legally enlarged the scope of the workers' councils' power, and the power of the ministries regarding the nomination of directors has been reduced to vetoing the choice of the councils, this does not necessarily mean that party control over the economy and the enterprise management has been reduced. In practice, the role of the ministries has been taken over by other government agencies, such as the Planning Office and the Material and Price Commission (Comisso, 1987). Therefore, unless the relationship between the party and society changes (the recent free parliamentary elections in Hungary are hopeful signs in that direction), reforms might take place and the industrial relations system might change somewhat. These changes will not necessarily translate into a considerable increase in workers' power, unless the political leadership is forced to do so under adverse economic conditions and increased politicization of the masses.

THE CASE OF CZECHOSLOVAKIA

Worker participation has a long history, and for many years it has been an integral part of the industrial relations system in Czechoslovakia. During the 1920s, for instance, works councils with advisory powers were introduced. Toward the end of the Second World War, works councils were spontaneously reestablished to facilitate production and smooth the transition to normalcy. As an important element of the organized working-class movement, which envisioned a special road to socialism, works councils strove for workers' control. In fact, the councils took over the management of the German-owned enterprises, and the decree issued in October 1945 gave them substantial control and economic rights (Kovanda, 1977; Svejnar, 1975). However, after the communist takeover in 1948, the works councils lost their extended powers. The fact that the once powerful and independent labor movement (ROH), which played a decisive role in the composition and functioning of the councils, lost its independence contributed a great deal to that outcome. Through various political manipulations, works councils were eventually transformed into transmission belts of ROH, which itself had become the transmission belt and victim of the centralization process of the Communist party (Kovanda, 1977: 269). The works councils were eventually liquidated, as ROH organizations became the official representatives of workers' interests. In practice, this meant boosting workers' morale and promoting competition in order to meet production goals dictated from above rather than promoting workers' interests through participation.

Khrushchev's denunciation of Stalin had much the same impact on Czechoslovakia as on the other Eastern European countries. The party became critical of its past Stalinist methods and thus more flexible in allowing public discussion and criticism. And, of course, workers' dissatisfaction with the existing centralized system gradually increased. The unreasonable production targets and the lack of workers' input soon resulted in low worker morale, lack of enthusiasm, and increasing levels of absenteeism. The relaxation period of 1956 allowed workers to translate feelings of discontent into demands regarding workers' participation in management through the establishment of workers' councils.

In August 1956, the party leadership, having perceived the introduction of workers' councils as threatening to its interests, as well as fearful that a Yugoslav-type self-management system might develop in Czechoslovakia, condemned the efforts of the reform as antisocialist and made clear that the unions were the only means to increase workers' participation in managing the economy (Svejnar, 1975). Still, the economic stagnation and recession of the early 1960s, owing to extensive rather than intensive industrial growth, and the rigid centralized system of planning and management, compelled the authorities to explore possible alternatives to overcome the crisis,[7] as Poland and Hungary had done a few years earlier (Fišera, 1978; Kovanda, 1976).[8] Economists were asked to work on proposals to improve the economy, and Professor Ota Šik became the most prominent spokesman of the reform.

The Economic Reform of the 1960s and the Changes That Led to the Prague Spring

The economic reform began to take shape when the idea of mass involvement in societal affairs and worker participation in management began to gain widespread public support, and references were made to the emulation of the 1945–1948 works councils experience. However, the eventual establishment of production committees and enterprise councils in the early and mid-1960s under the supervision of ROH, which meanwhile had been incorporated into the state power structure, did not intend to foster any kind of industrial democracy. Instead, the primary goal was to improve efficiency and increase productivity (Svejnar, 1975). A new socialist market system was adopted which was to combine market with state-guiding elements at the macroeconomic level. Decentralization was advocated to make the enterprises more autonomous in planning, production, and investment. Indeed, by the end of 1967 the central plan lost its exclusive power, prices had been decontrolled, foreign trade increased, and the government reduced or withdrew enterprise subsidies. This decentralization process seems similar to changes that took place in Yugoslavia in the 1950s. But the political situation in Yugoslavia was completely different from that in Czechoslovakia.

Regardless of delegation of responsibility to enterprises, the Novotný regime inclined toward a technocratic managerial model of management (Vitak, 1971). The internal management of enterprises remained the same, since it was the managers, not the workers, who had to make the decisions. The regime, unwilling to give up its prerogatives, was powerful enough to prevent any major reform toward industrial democracy. In 1966, for instance, the State Commission for Management and Organization (SKŘO) assigned a number of management experts the task of developing proposals regarding the management of the firms within the market economy. However, the party leadership did not endorse the suggested proposal that the firms should be able to make their own decisions. Such a change would have meant that the party would also have to give up its right to oversee the management of the firm, which in turn meant loss of substantial economic power for the bureaucratic administration (Kovanda, 1976).

Theoretically, the concept of self-management had not been fully developed during the first years of the reform to be presented as a serious alternative to the existing centralized system of planning and management (Svejnar, 1975). It is true that in some instances the workers forced the trade unions and party committees to intervene in management, change plans, and even set up their own self-managing type of bodies to cope with mismanagement. These were mostly isolated cases, however, and the idea of self-management did not gain momentum until late 1968 (Fišera, 1978; Pelikan, 1973; Vitak, 1971). At first at least, the working class was not the initiator or supporter of the plans for economic reform. Instead, progressive economists headed by Ota Šik, as well as intellectuals and students, were the major advocates of the reform (Kovanda, 1976; Pravda, 1973).[9]

At the time, Czechoslovakia was the most advanced industrial country in Eastern Europe. Its working class originated from craft and urban working-class backgrounds rather than pauperized peasantries, as in Hungary and especially Poland, and it comprised the most numerous section of the population. In the mid-1960s, 40 percent of this working population was engaged in "mechanized," "complex mechanized," and "automated work" (Kusin, 1972: 10). This is probably the major reason why workers in Czechoslovakia, in contrast to Hungary and especially Poland, have historically been characterized by sobriety and seriousness. Violent outbreaks and strikes are very rare events in Czechoslovakia's history (Pravda, 1979: 212).[10]

Since the 1948 takeover, this working class, with its long democratic tradition and its strong unions, had been gradually demoralized and depoliticized by the skillful tactics of the party. By official proclamations, workers had been the ruling class of the society, and the party was just ruling in its name. In reality, the working class was contributing to the decision-making process merely by executing centrally determined demands and by fulfilling party orders (Kusin, 1972; Pelikan, 1973; Skilling, 1976). The regime was careful with its policies, so that any measures affecting the working class, which comprised the majority of the population, would not be perceived as undemocratic. Therefore, "social security" rights were given to workers in order to compensate for possible frustrations arising from the inability to influence events in the economic and political sphere (Kusin, 1972: 11). In a way, therefore, the traditional dispositions of the Czechoslovak working class and the effects of the command economy and politics canceled each other out (Kusin, 1972: 12). As Valenta has pointed out: "The regime's policies are aimed at raising the social and economic status of the authentic workers—the embourgeoisement of the proletariat—and at exalting their social respectability. By assuring them of a continuously higher standard of living the regime strives to dull the workers' senses to the political conditions and any notions of class consciousness" (1981: 212).

In a period of low economic growth during which the need for economic reform was badly felt, as it was during the mid-1960s, workers found themselves courted by two main elements of the society. First, there were the proponents of the reform, mostly progressive economists and scholars, who were trying to convince the masses of the long-term benefits of the reform. Second, there were the antireformist elements within the socioeconomic and political apparatus, who were fearful of losing their jobs and taking the blame for mismanagement, and who denounced the reforms as threatening to destroy all the advantages of socialism. But workers were skeptical, and they did not join the reform efforts until much later.

Workers at first received the proclaimed benefits of the reform with considerable skepticism. This is understandable given that workers had for a long time been indoctrinated with the notion of being the ruling class of the society. Besides, the ruling party had skillfully managed to inflict intellectuals and workers with suspicion and antagonism toward each other (Skilling, 1976: 580). In addition, as in other Soviet-type economies, the introduction of market principles brought to light another serious contradiction of market reforms, namely, the prospect of unemployment, which became very painful for many workers. Moreover, the emphasis on productivity and qualification as criteria for remuneration threatened the egalitarian income structure that workers had come to expect (Pravda, 1973: 106). As the reform was progressing, unprofitable enterprises were closing down and product prices were steadily increasing. Meanwhile, since adequate information regarding the problems was missing and inappropriate measures were taken to alleviate the problems, the workers became increasingly anxious, bitter, and insecure. During the first stage of the reform, insecurities and dissatisfaction were skillfully manipulated by the adherents of the centralized system, whose interests were at stake with the introduction of the reform (Kovanda, 1976).

Any kind of sociopolitical organization that could present and articulate workers' needs and that workers could trust and identify with was lacking. Therefore, unless workers could see changes in the state apparatus and unless they had access to the means to exert power, and thereby influence policies that affected their lives, they were not inclined to accept the risks of the reform. Any kind of social change requires tremendous effort and time, so that the various social groups can articulate their demands and mobilize their constituencies. The situation in Czechoslovakia was not any different. In the serious and intense public debates during the first months of 1968, the extent and seriousness of mismanagement was made public and workers became aware of their real standard of living, which lagged far behind that of their counterparts in Western Europe. Only then did the workers begin to be more supportive of the reform.[11] For instance, they slowly became more assertive in demanding wage increases and better working conditions. They occasionally resorted to stoppages and strikes to secure the removal of incompetent managers and to ensure greater enterprise autonomy (Kusin, 1972; Pravda, 1973; Skilling, 1976). In some cases, they even set up their own self-managing bodies, but these ventures were isolated and they were officially opposed as efforts to undermine state socialism. As in the other Eastern European countries, the badly needed economic reforms were severely limited by the interests of the adherents of the centralized political and economic system.

The change of leadership in January 1968 provided a more supportive political environment for the reform, since reformers could form alliances at the top and thereby influence its scope and direction. Such developments helped to convince workers that the reform had firm political support and it could work to their advantage. The need for a new economic mode of management was widely accepted. The political changes merely helped to release frustrations and tensions, as well as to promote discussions and debates in searching for solutions and methods that could best combine efficiency goals with democratic ones in the enterprise. As Vitak has observed: "The people of Czechoslovakia were learning to their cost that the reforms for which the economy was crying out were cramped and confided by the political interests entrenched in the seats of power, while it was equally clear that the most perfect democratization system would be doomed if it failed to cure the economic ills" (Vitak, 1971: 254).

In the first months of 1968, three alternative solutions regarding the compatibility of efficiency and democracy were articulated, each reflecting the differing views of economists, politicians, and trade union officials. The first one, supported mostly by the conservative economic planners, favored the so-called managerial method of management. It sought to combine the latest forms of enterprise management used at the time in the West, with some kind of democratic enterprise administration. Second, many union officials within the trade union movement were against the formation of new bodies such as workers' councils, since such bodies threatened to undermine trade union rights and privileges. Instead, they were supporting the position that trade unions should be entrusted with the control of enterprise management. Finally, the third model that was eventually adopted advanced the notion that workers' councils represented the most suitable way to manage democratically and efficiently the Czechoslovak enterprises (Svejnar, 1975: 16–17).

The political changes of that year also helped to bring to surface issues that the SKŘO's proposal had raised before but that were never publicly discussed. The most important issue was management of the autonomous enterprise and the accountability of the managerial personnel. Several positions were articulated during 1968, but the one that clearly gained widespread approval was workers' participation in management through workers' councils (Kovanda, 1976; Kusin,

1972; Pelikan, 1973; Pravda, 1973; Skilling, 1976). The SKŘO proposal contained three alternatives regarding the power and the composition of workers' councils, and as a result a lot of discussion and debate took place. According to the first position, the councils would have token powers, which basically meant that management would have unlimited powers, and its close ties with party officials would be kept. The second option, the so-called weak model, provided for limited workers' power. The workers' councils could appoint and dismiss the director and possibly other top management executives, but this could happen only once every four years. Furthermore, the workers' councils could decide once per year about the distribution of profits. But the councils would not have any power with regard to other, strategic aspects of company affairs. Most likely, then, the councils would eventually follow management's recommendations. Finally, according to the third, strong model, the councils, in addition to the above powers, would have substantial rights regarding strategic aspects of enterprise management. These would include deciding on matters such as finance, technology investment, major changes in the firm, and personnel and production aspects.

As far as the composition of the councils was concerned, the SKŘO team favored the concept of the *thirds*. Specifically, only one-third of the councils' members would be elected by workers. Another third would be represented by outside experts from research institutions and universities, while the last third would be represented by the government (Kovanda, 1976: 40–41). This concept of thirds was rejected by members of the intelligentsia and workers. Discussions regarding the experience of self-management in Yugoslavia and the Czechoslovak experience of 1945 abounded, and the issue of workers' self-management began to gain the support of social scientists, the press, and gradually the emerging labor movement, especially during the Prague Spring. The economist Ota Šik, being a member of the new administration, was charged with applying the reform. Having to overcome the resistance of the central bureaucracy to self-management, Šik appealed to workers' initiative. By the spring of 1968 the workers had become a strong political force, mobilizing support for the national leadership and intelligentsia through strikes, mass meetings, and demands for worker control over enterprise management (Kovanda, 1976).

Despite its initial passivity, reservation, and even fear and hostility toward self-management and the formation of workers' councils, the Trade Union Movement (ROH) played a very decisive role in those developments (Kusin, 1972; Pravda, 1973; Skilling, 1976). Trade unions with their established network of organization were also seen by the reformers as the most appropriate channel to articulate working-class demands (Kusin, 1972). In Czechoslovakia, as in the other Eastern European countries, however, trade unions were centrally organized, and their primary goal was not to defend workers' rights but to mobilize workers' initiative for more productivity. The central trade union apparatus only slowly became involved in the democratization process (Fišera, 1978: 10). At the early stage of the Prague Spring, the workers strongly criticized the hierarchical structure of the unions. Workers sought to democratize the labor movement, whose top organ, the Central Labor Council (URO), was very conservative and not supportive of the Dubček leadership (Fišera, 1978). Widespread elections within the labor movement resulted in the replacement of union officials and of the leadership of ROH itself (Kusin, 1972; Skilling, 1976).

In addition, the Action Programme issued by the Communist party of Czechoslovakia in April 1968 gave much needed official party support to the notion of workers' participation as well as an ideological basis for its further development (Fišera, 1978). During the subsequent months, and as more detailed plans were elaborated and forces capable of implementing them became crystallized, the reform program took a more definite shape. The democratization of the labor movement and its new leadership, as well as the widespread support workers' self-management was gaining, resulted in a change in ROH's initial position on workers' participation in management. It became apparent that trade unions could not afford to take the blame for blocking progress by supporting old, inefficient, undemocratic practices. Thus, the labor movement progressively began to support the self-management movement, and its already well-established network of organization proved crucial to diffusing workers' councils.

As discussed before, in Western Europe similar concerns prompted unions to consider and support workers' participation. In Sweden during the 1960s, for instance, unions could not ignore the employers' initiation of changes that could undermine their role within the enterprise. As a result, unions collaborated with management to design the changes together. In this case, unions were strong and in a position to impose their demands and even help to escalate them. Unions in the United States, on the other hand, although they face similar problems of legitimacy, do not support participation goals for ideological reasons. Their weak position does not allow them to shape and channel existing demands and needs for participatory democracy either. Not until very recently did some unions, for reasons of survival, begin to support participation goals. In Czechoslovakia, concerns about the unions' legitimacy were reinforced by the revolutionary circumstances of the period and strengthened its supportive position for participative goals.

Subsequently, during the Prague Spring a new compromising position within the ROH leadership emerged in respect to the role of the trade unions within the enterprises. Unions and workers' councils would be independent but collaborate with each other (Svejnar, 1975). People working in the new socialist enterprises (instead of state enterprises) would have a dual status. On the one hand, employees would be represented by the unions, and thus the defensive role of the unions would be preserved; on the other hand, employees would share the social ownership and management of the enterprise through their elected councils (Kovanda, 1976; Vitak, 1971). The Action Programme had stated that the councils' main responsibility was the economic management and the long-term direction of the enterprise. The unions' responsibility, on the other hand, was to defend human, social, and other interests of the workers in an organized way (Fišera, 1978:30).

Unions were indeed instrumental in setting up workers' councils. Two-thirds of all the preparatory committees to set up councils were formed on union initiative (Vitak, 1971: 256–257). ROH became the primary force in getting councils started, especially after the invasion (Kovanda, 1976: 49–50). It is important to note these efforts since any institutional, organized leadership to implement the party's proclamations was missing, despite the party's endorsement of the workers' councils in its Action Programme. Whether this was an indication of the party's new policy that it no longer held the monopoly of power, it is difficult to determine, given the existing opposition to workers' councils among some party officials (Pelikan, 1973).

In June of the same year, the government, pressed by radical economists and confronted with the establishment of workers' councils in various workplaces, issued guidelines regarding the formation of workers' councils and warned against any excessive spontaneity (Svejnar, 1975: 17). Šik, having been personally involved with the implementation of the reform, realized the serious constraints the movement for self-management was facing and changed his initial position. Instead of supporting the idea of the thirds, he called for councils, whose decisive majority would be elected by the whole workforce, having weak but nonetheless real powers (Kovanda, 1976: 46). Šik came to realize that certain people, such as incompetent managers and ministry officials, were not going to leave voluntarily. They were the biggest obstacle to reform, and a mechanism had to be found to strip them of their power. Workers' councils had an interest in getting rid of incompetent managers. Since the model of one-third worker representation did not give workers decisive powers, it had to be abandoned.

Czechoslovakia after the Invasion

Inevitably, the August invasion had a very powerful impact on the society: The invasion not only made clear the limitations of the reform, due to the external interference; it also crystallized the positions of the radical and bureaucratic forces inside Czechoslovakia. The workers' councils movement was expanded and deepened organizationally and ideologically after the invasion. The fact that the number of councils increased after the invasion demonstrated their importance as safeguards of democracy. It was the best defense of the population against the neo-Stalinist and bureaucratic forces that they were regaining strength after the invasion (Pelikan, 1973: 15). The invasion strengthened the old bureaucratic forces as well. These conservative forces and the Soviet leadership, both threatened by the existence of the workers' councils, forced the government to restrain their activity and declare them illegal. Eventually, the government was pressed to reverse its position and expressed its support for the ongoing process, because of the strong organized reaction of the working class against the initial undemocratic decision (Kovanda, 1976; Pelikan, 1973; Svejnar, 1975).

In April 1969 Dubček was replaced by Husák, which ended the government's indecision and the instability of the period. The latest struggles and gains of the unions over the composition and jurisdiction of the workers' councils (e.g., the Bill on the Socialist Enterprise) became irrelevant, when in March 1969, while the issue of socialist management was still debated, President Svoboda blatantly declared that "associations of the workers' councils will not be allowed, since they would constitute a new political power" (as quoted in Pelikan, 1973: 16). In May of the same year the liquidation of the workers' councils was announced. According to the official position, they had become anti-socialist pressure groups (Pelikan, 1973: 16). Although the workers' councils were not the primary reason for the Soviet invasion, their emergence on a broad scale and their gradually politicized nature after the invasion became a threat to the planned restoration of the Soviet model of socialism. As Kovanda has put it: "No longer was the struggle between 'conservatives' and various 'progressives': now it was a more clear cut struggle between revolution and counterrevolution. The space for some 'middle' way, for some reforms . . . was rapidly diminishing" (1976: 47).[12]

The censorship was restored, and communication became problematic. The councils lacked any formal and legal support, since trade unionists, intellectuals, and supporters of the reform were dismissed and often prosecuted. The councils eventually died out, and the short-lived experimentation with democracy ended. The councils operated in the biggest and most prestigious firms. In terms of their composition, employees were getting two-thirds to four-fifths of all seats, the rest being representations of outside interests and people nominated by the directors or sometimes by government departments (Kovanda, 1976: 50; Vitak, 1971: 258). With regard to their powers and functioning, their short life and the lack of thorough studies on the issue makes it difficult to draw firm conclusions. By reviewing some evidence, however, some general comments can be made. The daily management of the enterprise was the responsibility of the director and his managerial staff. This structure resembles the executive council of the Yugoslav model. This management body was appointed, and its power considerably restricted by the council. Issues of top management personnel and remuneration as well as long-term matters of policy such as investment, distribution of revenues, and mergers fell within the responsibility of the council (Kovanda, 1976; Pelikan, 1973; Vitak, 1971).

The structure of the elected councils reveals that employees in the councils, of whom at least two-thirds were manual workers, were concerned with issues of responsibility, competence, and experience (Vitak, 1971: 260). The early years of socialism, when less educated workers were promoted to managerial posts, were long gone. Increasing levels of education combined with blocked mobility have brought frustration and dissatisfaction among workers. This frustration and alienation is also present in the West where the increased levels of education and workers' aspirations clash with the boring and fragmented tasks they have to perform. However, unlike the West, management in Eastern Europe often displays visible lack of knowledge and competence, which heightens workers' frustrations. In the Czechoslovakian case, approximately 70 percent of the delegates were thirty-five to forty-nine years old, and engineers and technicians constituted more than 60 percent of the council members. Twenty-nine percent of all council members had college education, while in 1966 only 20 percent of the enterprise directors had similar education (Fišera, 1978: 15; Kovanda, 1976: 51; Pelikan, 1973: 15; Svenjar, 1975: 20). As discussed above, the issue of competence and responsibility was raised in Poland as well; incompetent directors were ousted and new ones elected during the 1980–1981 period.

In a society with an economy planned from above, where there was little individual or mass responsibility, and where the antagonism between manual and intellectual worker had been skillfully fostered by the Novotný regime for such a long time, these voting patterns are very interesting. They clearly reflect the workers' dissatisfaction with the mismanagement and incompetence of the previous directors. They also demonstrate the workers' maturity and determination to pursue the long-term goals of the enterprises (Fišera, 1978; Kovanda, 1976; Svejnar, 1975; Vitak, 1971). Thus, concerns and fears that critics often raise in both the West and East—for instance, that workers would pursue only short-term wage interests—were not substantiated. This is most probably due to the nature of the working class as discussed above. The Czechoslovak working class is characterized by long industrial traditions and higher educational and cultural standards than those in other countries that have introduced workers' councils, especially Yugoslavia. These differences, including the high value placed on education and skills, were reflected in the voting patterns and preferences (Kovanda, 1976: 51). There is no doubt that the presence of highly trained and experienced councils during that initial stage of autonomous enterprise operation under market conditions would have benefited the enterprise. Some observers, however, were skeptical about future problems, owing to the overrepresentation of technical intelligentsia and/or skilled workers, as in the case of Yugoslavia. Others supported the view that the councils' composition would shift, once the quality of the management improved (Kovanda, 1976: 52).

Concluding Remarks

What might have happened is pure speculation, since the whole process was abruptly interrupted. But the popular support the councils enjoyed, the democratic climate of the elections, the fact that labor unions, despite their initial reservations and doubts, strongly identified with the council movement, and the fact that councils had some political support from the party leadership, were all positive aspects of the overall reform that pointed in the direction of the further democratization of Czechoslovakian society. The councils' attempts to coordinate their activities on the national level, just before their abolition, suggests their emergent character as a serious socioeconomic and political force (Svejnar, 1975: 27–28).

There were limitations to the process of democratic reform determined by the relationship with the Soviet Union. Whether that experiment could have survived, the intervention aside, is difficult to say, since strong conservative, antireform forces were present within the country itself. On the other hand, we must remember that the party enjoyed a great increase in popularity during the Prague Spring, and Dubček, forced by public and progressive party opinion, would have probably proceeded with more drastic reforms (Skilling, 1976: 842). Legalization of the councils' powers, popular support, state and trade union support, along with enterprise autonomy, would have been some of the requirements toward industrial democracy. But the economic reform had already spilled over into other spheres of society and thereby created a polarization between progressive and conservative forces. It subsequently placed the basic aspects of the communist power system in question. Soviet intervention was thus inevitable.

NOTES

1. For more details and discussion of the economic inefficiency of the socialist economies and how it manifested itself, see Burks (1973); Flakierski (1985–1986, vol. 24: Chapter 1); Zielinski (1973: Chapter 1).

2. In June 1956, because of the authorities' prolonged failure to deal with wage grievances, workers in Poznan, the largest Polish railway engine and carriage factory, struck. A peaceful protest march which was joined by workers from other Poznan factories was eventually suppressed by the army amidst much bloodshed and massive arrests.

3. Alex Pravda (1979) discusses how the same factors determine the incidence and shape the nature of workers' dissatisfaction and opposition in Poland, Hungary, and Czechoslovakia. Since participatory schemes are often just one manifestation of worker dissent and opposition, Pravda's analysis helps us better understand workers' options and the way they manifest themselves based on historical, socioeconomic, and political circumstances.

4. According to the principles of democratic centralism, the labor-capital conflict cannot exist, since the party manages the national economy in the name of the working class, which actually rules. Therefore, theoretically at least, the defensive role of the unions cannot exist.

5. Gomułka himself, in his speech to the Eighth Plenary session of the party (October 1956), admitted that "It is necessary to change a great deal in our system of People's Government, in the system of the organization of our industry, and in the methods of the State and Party Apparatus" (as quoted in Grzybowski, 1957: 272).

6. Careful preparatory work preceded the reform, so that there would not be a major reorganization of enterprises or an increase in the unemployment rates. Furthermore, the reform was somewhat easier to implement, since enterprise autonomy had been increased between 1957 and 1967 and the number of obligatory plans had already been reduced.

7. According to Kusin (1972: 2), this crisis must be understood by noting that in 1968 Czechoslovakia, despite serious deficiencies in certain areas, was not at the verge of social or economic collapse. He points out that "reform themes . . . were formulated as an alternative national aim of a long-term nature, rather than as a plan for an immediate rescue operation."

8. Given the long democratic traditions of Czechoslovakian society and the maturity of its working class, during the 1950s Stalinism took extremely repressive forms. Thus, the official reaction to the Soviet signals for de-Stalinization in Czechoslovakia was very slow in comparison with Poland and Hungary, most probably because of the fear that oppositional forces would emerge. For more details on the issue, see Skilling (1976).

9. This can most probably be explained by the enforced inaction of the previous twenty years. Furthermore, enterprises had not changed very much organizationally, and new leaders at the factory level had not emerged in adequate numbers. See Kusin (1972: Chapter 1).

10. The famous 1953 Pielsen revolt was among the few violent outbreaks in Czechoslovakian history. As in most outbreaks in Eastern Europe, it resulted from monetary measures that as a consequence had wiped out much of the workers' savings and lowered their standard of living.

11. Still the support given depended on the socioeconomic position and thus the interests of different sectors of the working class. The working class, as other groups (intelligentsia, farmers, nationalities) that supported the reform, was not united by the same interests. Unskilled workers, for instance, given the prospects of unemployment and instability that the reform raised, could have perceived the reform as threatening. Secure, high-level managers, on the other hand, saw the reform as an opportunity to conduct business more efficiently and profitably. For more details on this issue, see Skilling (1976).

12. According to Skilling (1976), the central theme of Soviet propaganda and the main justification for the intervention were not the reforms as such, but the risks they entailed in creating a counterrevolution that could have resulted in a possible return to capitalism and bourgeois democracy.

7

Workers' Participation and the Politics of Economic and Industrial Reforms in China

Since late 1978, when Deng Xiaoping consolidated his political power, China has undergone a number of sweeping economic reforms that have had serious consequences for the country's political, economic, and social structure.[1] The reforms have attempted to reverse past practices of party domination over every single aspect of life ranging from control over economic resources and organization to ideology, bureaucracy, law, and foreign policy. The dismantling of collectivization in agriculture and the introduction of the family contract have been quite successful in raising agricultural productivity and the farmer's standard of living.

China's experimentation with industrial reforms, particularly with worker participative structures, has also figured prominently in its attempt to transform the command economy through decentralization and democratization practices as well as increased enterprise and individual responsibility. However, in spite of the official rhetoric industrial reforms in China have not been successful in breaking away from the Soviet central-planning model and the problems associated with it. Industrial reforms in China have been fragmented, at times reversed, and not as widespread or successful in achieving their aim as hoped.

This chapter presents a brief background of the industrial reforms; explores the ideological and practical reasons behind the introduction of post-1978 worker participation schemes; describes the structure and functions of the existing workers' participation schemes; and discusses the challenges and efforts to democratize management within the enterprise.

FIRST STEPS TOWARD INCREASED AUTONOMY OF THE ENTERPRISE

At its Third Plenary Session on October 20, 1984, the Central Committee of the Communist party of China, with its Decision on Reform of the Economic Structure, approved a nationwide experimentation with industrial reforms. The main objectives of the reform—openness of the economy, reliance on market forces, and decentralization of decision making—were touted as a pressing necessity, required to accelerate the restructuring and modernization of China's overall economy (*Beijing Review*, October 29, 1984: I–XVI). The Decision demonstrates the leadership's commitment to apply on a national scale what had already been launched on a trial basis in 1979. The Chinese leadership had introduced the reforms in ten pilot factories in Sichuan and later in other parts of the country (Goldman, 1987: 204–205). One of the major goals of the reform was to increase the autonomy of the enterprise, and this was manifested in the introduced experiments. Taking steps similar to those in East European countries, China, too, attempted to reduce the administrative and financial dependency of the enterprise on the central authorities. Earlier, for example, enterprises were operating on rationed supplies, and their operations were financed at no cost. Their goal, as determined centrally, was to produce specified quantities of products. Increasingly, after the introduction of the reforms, enterprises have not had access to free investment and working capital in the form of grants. The banks, instead of the central authorities, have lent capital to enterprises by incorporating interest charges in their transactions and carefully scrutinizing their clients.

Under the old system, the production process was cut from the demand and supply forces of the market, and the state, through its plan, determined production and fixed prices. Under the new system of decentralization, the mandatory old plan has been loosened, price controls have been relaxed, and market demands now substitute to a certain degree for the central planning and the industrial ministries. The number of targets given to enterprises has been decreased, and enterprises can keep a portion of their profits above specified amounts for plant renovation, minor expansion, housing, and bonuses allocated to employees (Goldman, 1987: 205; Solinger, 1986: 106–107; Walder, 1984: 64). As discussed in more detail below, the workers' decision-making power was to be expanded through participative democracy organs and by bringing into play the initiative, knowledge, and responsibility of the workers within the enterprise. In that respect, Chinese reformers not only supported the financial independence of the enterprise, but also sought to extend its organizational autonomy and increase its decision-making power.

Such reform efforts were in direct opposition to Mao's preoccupation with the class struggle, and his policies to dismantle individual material incentives and instead cultivate the collective interest for the society's well-being. The proponents of the reform heavily criticized the concentration of power in a vertically structured, administratively directed command economy. In general,

Mao's policies were blamed for increased bureaucratization, evasion of responsibility, gross inefficiencies, increasing financial losses, and threats to the vitality of the national economy (Solinger, 1986: 106–108; Walder, 1982: 227–232).

Although China had enjoyed 10 percent average annual industrial growth throughout its history as the People's Republic, in 1977 almost all financial measures of productivity showed important declines. In an effort to revitalize the degenerated normative system which was claimed to be responsible for the society's social problems, the Maoist regime pursued strict austerity measures, including abolition of bonuses and a freeze in wage increases. By adopting such a policy, Mao's leadership eventually stripped away any kind of incentive for workers and managers alike. This in turn demoralized workers and increased their dissatisfaction, which was manifested in every aspect of work performance ranging from attendance, tardiness, work intensity, attention to quality, and machinery (Walder, 1986: 213). Mao's aim was to decrease inequality, but as Walder (1986: 205) correctly points out, by freezing wages in order to accomplish equality, the opposite happened: new inequality was created, as people grew older and got stuck in frozen wage structures. The abolition of group bonuses also had detrimental effects since it

took away the incentives for a thorough assessment of co-worker performance and undermined the link between individual performance and collective income . . . there were few incentives for managers to enforce rules and keep up labor discipline. There were no bonuses for managers; financial criteria used to judge enterprise performance were loose and themselves rarely enforced; and labor productivity was not a major constraint on the fulfillment of plans, especially when compared with the more pressing problems of ensuring supplies of materials and parts and their prompt delivery. (Walder, 1986: 193, 205)

Consequently, labor productivity, although it had more than doubled in the first fifteen years of the People's Republic, declined by 5 percent in the decade after 1965. Total factor productivity, although it had increased by 43 percent between 1952 and 1965, fell by 11 percent in the following decade (Walder, 1984: 67). The reform in China was not necessitated by the slow decline in growth, as for instance, in the Soviet Union. To be sure, China was and still is one of the poorest countries in the world in terms of per capita gross national product. More than 800 million people live in the countryside, using primarily hand tools to make a living. Approximately one-fourth of the population is illiterate or semiliterate (Chu-Yuan Cheng, 1988: 253). The problem basically has been that the system is inefficient and very wasteful.

As Andrew Walder (1984: 67) explains, in a poor country like China, industrial reform was urgently needed. First, more investment was needed in the transportation sector and energy production to prevent the further decline of economic growth. Second, in contrast to some Western and Eastern European countries, as well as the Soviet Union, China has had labor surplus rather than shortage.

As a result, unemployment became problematic, especially in the urban cities, as increasingly more people were joining the labor force. To eradicate the problem of unemployment, new jobs had to be created, especially in light industry, where there was demand for consumer goods. Third, to validate the leadership's commitment to the improvement of impoverished living standards, there was a need to increase wages and housing space, both of which had declined by 20 percent since the mid-1950s. To be sure that people would be able to spend their increased income, there was a need to invest in consumer goods production. Indeed, light industry grew 50 percent, and the purchase of consumer goods in urban areas between 1978 and 1981 increased 26 percent per capita (Walder, 1986: 225). The need for reform was urgent, and China, as Eastern European countries had done much earlier, undertook the task of modernization and reform at a very fast pace.

MEASURES TO DEMOCRATIZE THE ENTERPRISE THROUGH WORKER PARTICIPATION

As other Eastern European countries and the Soviet Union earlier, China attempted to make enterprises and workers more independent and responsible for their own success or failure. It also aimed to democratize the authority structure of the enterprise by incorporating workers' initiative and creativity into the decision-making process. The primary reasons behind the regime's desire to democratize the enterprise were economic, political, and ideological. First, by incorporating workers into the decision-making process, it was hoped that productivity would be increased and the quality of products or services improved. In that respect, as in the West and other centrally organized countries, the leadership perceived worker participative structures as very instrumental in its effort to increase productivity and modernize the economy (Cole and Walder, 1984).

Second, some serious political considerations prompted the regime to consider participative reforms seriously. The strategy of promoting participation by mobilizing the human resources and initiative of the managers and workers was seen as a way not only to accomplish productive efficiency, but also to stabilize the country politically. Deng Xiaoping and his supporters had been politically persecuted during the Cultural Revolution and were fully aware of the political chaos, gross inefficiencies, and corruption of that period. The plan was to democratize the management structures and in that way to be able to dismantle the overconcentration of power, to eliminate the subculture of cult personality management, nepotism, and the arbitrary decision-making process and corruption that had prevailed during the Cultural Revolution and had paralyzed the country (Walder, 1982).

Third, as a result of the Cultural Revolution, the party legitimacy had eroded and the regime had a difficult time attracting young people into the party ranks within the workplace. The party was in need of articulating a new ideology that would justify worker participative forms and attract workers' support for the party and party policies. We should remember that, because of the peasant origins of Chinese society, the party had always been at odds with the Marxist notion that the proletariat is the leader of the society. Mao Zedong had glorified the peasants, although he had tried not to cut totally the party's ties with the working class. However, the 1982 Constitution explicitly states that "The People's Republic of China is a socialist state under the people's democratic dictatorship led by the working class and based on the alliance of workers and peasants" (Constitution of the People's Republic of China, 1982, Article 1). According to the official rhetoric then, by participating in the democratic management of the enterprise, the working class assumes its leading role in the workplace, in the party, and in society in general. The reformers knew very well that if their goal to reform and modernize was to succeed, they had to gain workers' support and loyalty. Such political support of the workers, especially the young ones, whose ties with the party were loosening, was essential, especially because young workers under thirty-five make up approximately 60 percent of the Chinese workforce (Wilson, 1987: 301).

Fourth, the East European experience with reform undoubtedly had an impact on China's attempt to reform its own economy and power relations within the enterprise. Reforms in Yugoslavia, Hungary, and Poland attracted special attention in China, although the Soviet Union's de-Stalinization process and Liberman's notion of decentralization and market reform also had an impact on Chinese reformers. For instance, major East European writings were translated into Chinese and studied by Chinese reformers. Chinese specialists were sent to Eastern Europe to familiarize themselves with the reforms. In addition, prominent East European economists, such as Ota Šik and Wlodzimierz Brus, who were instrumental in shaping democratic reforms in their own countries, also consulted the Chinese reformers as they began to institute the reform in China (Goldman, 1987: 203–205; Wilson, 1987: 303).

As Jeanne Wilson correctly points out (1987: 303–304), discussions in China pertaining to reform issues lack the theoretical Marxist analysis that characterizes the public debates of democratic reform in some East European countries. For example, although signs of alienation might to a certain extent have justified Deng Xiaoping's reforms, in the debates for reform the link of alienation to relations of production within the workplace—a major element of the Marxist analysis—was missing. Instead, emphasis was placed on pragmatic considerations. As Wilson further points out, the Chinese interpretation of democratic reform differs from the East European formulation on another point. In contrast to East European approach, where democratization is promoted in order to cope with the emerging complexities of industrialized society, the Chinese reformers view democratization as a means of socialist construction. In that vision, the role of the party is crucial, and despite depoliticization aims, political controls still penetrate the structure of workers' participation schemes. Thus, it is not surprising that Chinese reformers would hold up contemporary Hungarian reform efforts as a successful example of workplace democracy, while the workers' councils of 1956 wouldn't be a point of interest to them (Wilson, 1987: 303–304, 312).

Since 1978, the Chinese leadership has attempted to restructure authority relations within the enterprise by distinguishing between administrative and political power, and by instituting mechanisms to allow workers to exercise their power within the enterprise. In one of his speeches on economic reform, the then First Secretary of the Communist party, Hua Guofeng, summarized that goal as follows: "The general orientation of the reform is to transform the overcentralized management by the state (central and local authorities included), extend the decision-making power of the enterprises and the power of their workers and staff to participate in management, transform regulation through planning alone into regulation by the market, and transform management relying mainly on administrative organs and methods into management relying mainly on economic organs as well as on economic and legal methods" (*Beijing Review*, 1980, vol. 38: 14–15). There are three sources of authority within the enterprise, as envisioned by the reformers: the workers' congress, the managerial personnel, and the party. The party's monopoly of power within the enterprise would be diminished by reinstituting the system of managerial responsibility (which was abolished during the Cultural Revolution) and by allowing for mechanisms of worker participation in management. As a result of the reforms, the workers' congress has the authority to make some policy decisions. Management is responsible for the daily administration of the enterprise's operation, whereas the party is entrusted with a secondary supervisory role and with the ideological work within the enterprise. This restructuring of authority relations, which resembles the Yugoslav model of self-management, was first tried out in a number of selected enterprises during 1980. During the same period, reformers in China were stressing the importance of increasing the power of workers' councils as a way of shifting the power dynamic within the enterprise and advancing the workers' interests (Hong, 1984: 56–57; Laaksonen, 1984: 305; Wilson, 1987: 305).

Antireform forces, feeling threatened by the direction the reform was taking, in 1981 succeeded in halting its progress.[2] In June 1981, the Central Committee of the Chinese Communist party issued the Provisional Regulations Concerning Congresses of Workers and Staff Members in State-Owned Industrial Enterprises, where the role of the party within the enterprise was declared to be quite strengthened. According to those regulations, enterprises were to "set up and perfect the system of congresses of workers and staff members under the leadership of the party committees so as to give full scope to the workers' and staff members' sense of responsibility as their own masters and ensure their democratic right to manage their enterprises" (Provisional Regulations, 1981: 16). The congresses of workers were to cooperate with the directors of the enterprises who were to assume "responsibilities for production and administration under the leadership of the Party committees" as well (Provisional Regulations, 1981: 16). Such stipulations show that the party was becoming more conservative regarding the scope of the reform. The leadership was essentially adhering to the fundamental principles of democratic centralism rather than responding to the demands of market socialism. However, despite changes and occasional setbacks, the leadership has tried to detach itself from the operative enterprise management and over the years (at least until 1989) has continued its commitment to enterprise democratization (Hong, 1984: 60; Wilson, 1987: 307).

To accomplish that goal, first, elections were advocated for the selection of directors and deputy directors, who are responsible not only to the party but also to the entire workforce represented by the workers' congress. Based on a *Beijing Review* report (25, no. 26, 1982: 5), as of June 1982, 95 percent of large and medium-size Chinese enterprises had established workers' congresses. The same report reveals that a substantial number of enterprises, grass-roots units, and government organizations democratically elected their directors and other administrative personnel. Second, according to a decision of the Central Committee of the Party on Reform, "the factory manager responsibility system under the leadership of Party committee" is now replaced by the "factory manager responsibility system." The official position was that the present conditions in the modern enterprise, such as detailed division of labor, technological complexities, and the need for cooperation, necessitate a system whereby the director or manager assumes full responsibility under the direct support of the party organizations within the enterprise (Wilson, 1987: 307). In effect, then, the management system that was developed bears a close resemblance to the Soviet one-man management that had been adopted to a certain degree in China in the pre-1956 period (Laaksonen, 1984: 305; Wilson, 1987: 307).

During the same period, measures were taken to incorporate workers into the decision-making process and thus fulfill the overall Chinese vision of democratization as a process of reducing the party's monopoly of power and expanding the power of other groups within the enterprise. Workers could participate and have an impact on the decision-making process of the enterprise they worked for through two institutions of democratic management: their congresses and unions. Based on Article 2 of the 1981 Provisional Regulations, the workers' congress is the "organ of power by which the workers and staff members take part in decision making and management and the supervision of cadres" (Provisional Regulations, 1981: 16). Congresses are established in both state and collectively owned enterprises and convene twice a year on a two-year term, which is renewable. Representatives to workers' congresses are elected by employees, both workers and staff members. To guarantee workers' incorporation into the decision-making process, workers should comprise at least 60 percent of the total number of representatives, and the congress should be representative of the various groups within the enterprise across sex, age, occupational, technical, administrative, and party lines. The congress's responsibility is to elect its presidium, which also consists of "workers, and technical personnel, administrative personnel, and leading cadres of the enterprise's party, administrative, trade union and Youth League organizations'' (Provisional Regulations, 1981: Chapter III, Articles 8 and 11).

The congress is entrusted with the following rights and responsibilities. First, the congress formulates the yearly production plans and targets of the enterprise which are submitted to the relevant higher industrial authorities in their districts for coordination. As noted above, the director is responsible for making the daily administrative decisions, but he must consult the congress before the end of each year about his plans. The congress, for instance, has the right to discuss and examine the director's work reports, his plans for production and construction, issues of technical innovation and transformation, and overall major issues in management for which it can adopt appropriate resolutions (Provisional Regulations, 1981: Articles 5 and 6).

Second, the workers' congress is responsible for formulating and administering policies on welfare and the reward and punishment system of the enterprise. For instance, the congress deals with questions such as housing allocation, medical benefits, retirement pensions, wages, bonuses, and the criteria of their distribution. It also examines and approves collective agreements signed between management and the trade unions and is responsible for devising and enforcing the rules pertaining to rewards and penalties (Provisional Regulations, 1981: Article 10).

Third, the workers' congress enjoys the power of removing from office incompetent directors (Solinger, 1986: 109). Most importantly, the congress has the power to elect the factory management (Hong, 1984: 62). This holds true for the collectively owned enterprises, while the state-owned ones have the option of either electing or appointing their managers. Even in those cases, however, some provisions exist to take into consideration the workers' input. In addition, directors' choices of deputy directors have to be approved by the workers' congress.

As of 1987, the system had not been implemented nationwide, and only some test-point enterprises were selected to introduce the new participative system (Wilson, 1987: 309). Regardless of all these changes, it should be remembered that the party's role within the enterprise remains essential. Efforts to institutionalize workers' congresses and managerial elections as formal mechanisms of workers' participation in management should therefore be viewed as a reflection of the Chinese model of attempting to integrate centralized leadership with democratic management.

THE ROLE OF THE UNIONS IN THE
WORKPLACE DEMOCRACY

During the 1980s, trade unions became more visible in the workplace. They seem to have assumed a new, revitalized role as mass organizations representing workers' interests, at least according to the official rhetoric. This is quite a shift from the role traditionally assumed by the unions in China. The All-China

Federation of Trade Unions (ACFTU) has been supportive of the party's policy, often siding with management against striking workers or approving cuts in their wages. Indeed, this was the case during the period after the 1949 Liberation (Hearn, 1977: 161–162). In essence, Chinese trade unions, as the trade unions in most Soviet-type societies and in accordance with the Leninist principle, have been functioning as transmission belts between the party and the masses, as organizations representing the interests of workers led by the party. Unions, for instance, would ideally promote increased production among workers. This was the case during Mao's period, when production was the main focus of trade union activity (Wilson, 1987: 310).

Unions in China have occasionally performed a more (Western) traditional union-oriented function: that is, to defend workers' interests, especially against excessive bureaucratic demands. For a while during the 1950s, for instance, and until they were suspended in 1967–1968, unions were instrumental in exposing exploitative conditions resulting from the drive for increased productivity (Hearn, 1977: 163). During the last decade, the leadership seems to have emphasized as the unions' primary role that of defending working-class interests. The unions have become more visible in the workplace, and they are closely related to the workers' congress. Unions, for example, are entrusted with educating their members about economic reforms, mobilizing and organizing the workers' congresses, as well as handling their daily tasks when the congresses are in recess.

This twin mechanism of workers' participative democracy raises some serious questions as to the efficacy of the unions' aim to truly represent workers' interests at the workplace level. Although unions in China are viewed mostly as representative bodies rather than as direct channels through which workers can participate in the management of their enterprises, still the integration of unions and workers' congresses raises some serious concerns. Unless there is a complete overlap in their functions, there is always a strong possibility, as Hong (1984: 66–68) correctly points out, that conflict will arise from this twin scheme of worker representation. For instance, the unions' presence at the production level implies that union officials have to fulfill the classical shop steward task of resolving shopfloor grievances. Unions could easily avoid this role in the past simply by choosing to act as "transmission belts" for enterprise management. Besides, it is doubtful whether these union representatives have the negotiation skills to assume that role successfully. Moreover, as Hong further argues, "challenges to managerial decisions, if inspired by members' job interests and demands, are liable to throw the union into embarrassing confrontation with the enterprise's democratic authority—the workers' congress, for which ironically, the unions deputizes" (1984: 68).

These contradictory demands can have dangerous repercussions for the future of the unions and workplace democracy in general in case of strikes. The official position is that, under ordinary conditions, strikes should not take place in a socialist state like China, where workers are the masters of their enterprises and have many means of channeling their demands and resolving their grievances.

Reflecting that logic is the elimination of the right to strike from the 1982 Constitution which was first approved by the 1975 Constitution. Under extraordinary circumstances, such as bureaucratic abuse and manipulation, workers can strike. The interpretation of *extraordinary circumstances* aside, this implies that, theoretically at least, the leadership recognizes the potential for conflict between worker and the party interests. If the unions determine that workers' demands are reasonable and strike is decided as a last resort to conflict resolution, the responsibility to organize it lies within the unions (Wilson, 1987: 317). This implies "the undesirable or even dangerous propensity for unions to drift to syndicalist opposition against authority" (Hong, 1984: 68).

The emergence of a labor movement in China resembling labor movements in the West could provoke further demands for independent labor unions. This has been attempted in China, although efforts to establish Solidarity-style trade unions have not been successful (Hammond, 1982: 24). The potential for labor unrest and nationwide mobilization Solidarity-style is recognized, feared, and has actually informed the leadership's position to enlarge the scope of the unions' authority within the enterprise. Such a position has not been solid, and contradictions always emerge since, despite experimentation with worker participative structures, overall the principles of political centralism remain intact in China. Independent unionism would threaten the current power relationship between the party and the ACFTU. The ACFTU in China is highly centralized, and its regional offices are accountable both to the party authorities of their district and to the superior levels of authority within the ACFTU's bureaucratic structure (Hong, 1984: 68–69).

It is not surprising, then, that regardless of the expanded role envisioned for the trade unions and the recent emphasis placed on the unions' primary role as defenders of workers' interests, the guidelines issued by the Second Session of the Tenth Congress of the ACFTU contradict such intentions. According to those guidelines, "national, transregional, and transindustrial mass activities should by all means be discouraged" (as quoted in Wilson, 1987: 316). Such positions contradict intentions for increased democratization. They also validate fears that the prospects of workplace democracy are limited in China as long as the leadership is not addressing the contradiction that is inherently built in its effort both to modernize and yet maintain its political control over economic and management activity.

HOW WORKERS' PARTICIPATION WORKS IN PRACTICE

Undoubtedly, the shift from the strict command economy to the mixed plan-and-market economy of the 1980s and the efforts to democratize the workplace have raised the living standards of many Chinese, especially in the countryside. They have also increased people's appetite for more economic and political changes. The democracy movement of 1989 with hundreds of thousands of people demonstrating at Tiananmen Square dramatically demonstrated those aspirations, as well as the people's desire for the party to live up to its own promises for accomplishing such goals (Pomeranz, 1990: 243). The bloody crackdown on the students' and workers' movement raises serious questions as to whether the present leadership is willing or able to accommodate pluralistic interests and respond to escalating demands for democracy and decentralization of the economy that go beyond the boundaries of acceptable discourse as defined by the party. The same concerns can be raised in regard to the prospects of the workers' congress and unions as viable channels of workplace democracy.

To continue its economic growth and its drive for modernization and increased productivity, China under Deng Xiaoping has come to realize the importance of economic decentralization. However, economic decentralization cannot by itself guarantee the successful implementation of workplace democracy, if the party continues its tradition, albeit reduced in the last years, of interfering with economic decisions and if it continues to dominate the structures of workers' congresses and unions. There is no doubt that the leadership under Deng Xiaoping was able to relax some central controls over the economy. As of 1985, for instance, the number of manufactured products under mandatory planning had been reduced from 123 to 60, and the materials allocated through the State Planning Commission and the Central Bureau of Material Supply were also reduced from 256 to 65 (Solinger, 1986: 108). In addition, the regime introduced some market mechanisms into the economy, following closely the example of the Hungarian reform. These have not necessarily worked in practice as envisioned, and excessive bureaucratization and political controls are still pervasive.[3] An attempt has also been made to reduce the pervasive political controls over the enterprise management and to institute a process of depoliticization within the enterprise (Wilson, 1987). As elsewhere in the Soviet-type economies, however, important decisions that affect the enterprise's success are taken above the enterprise level and not through worker participative structures (Goldman, 1987: 209–210).

Regardless of formal proclamations and publicized intentions, no clear indication has yet emerged that the leadership is ready to give up one of the basic tenets of democratic centralism, that is, the party's leadership over the society. Although political control over the population has been diminished over the years and popular concerns can be raised through official channels (at least until the recent crackdown of the students' movement), still the regime firmly supports the socialist character of the country. According to the Chinese model, this means collective ownership of the means of production and adherence to the four principles of Marxism-Leninism-Maoism, the leadership of the party, the socialist road, and the people's proletarian dictatorship (Lee, 1986: 79).

A more critical glance at the way participation structures operate reveals this leading role of the party within those structures as well. For instance, as noted above, the party's dominant role in the workers' participative structures is assured by placing leading cadres of the various party organizations to preside over the workers' congress. Within trade unions the same pattern can be noticed. Unions are obliged to respect the party line and support its policy. As with the workers' congress, party members hold the highest positions in the union hierarchy, and the leaders of the unions are usually members of the enterprise party committee. Further political controls are ensured by the party's prerogative to approve personnel choices. Moreover, although workers have the right to vote for their delegates, workers' congresses have had the chance to select their directors in only selected enterprises. In both instances, however, evidence points to the party's control and manipulation of candidacy choices for leadership posts, raising concerns and criticisms among workers that their congresses have become a mere formalism (Wilson, 1987: 312–313).

Finally, how the issue of the director's accountability within the enterprise will be handled is of great significance, since the given solution will affect the scope of powers entrusted to workers' participative structures. Will the director be accountable to the party or to the workers' congress? The powers of workers' congresses might seem extensive, but in reality they are only consultative, or at best supervisory (Hong, 1984: 73). Their effectiveness in managing the enterprise is limited by the fact that all their decisions are dependent on the director for implementation. The current system of director accountability under the implicit leadership of the party seems to contradict the professed goal of increasing workers' power under the system of market socialism. The biggest obstacle to accomplishing that goal is the party's intervention in the enterprise's affairs. Theoretically, over the last few years the party's role within the enterprise has increasingly been a backstage one, in an attempt to unite all the groups within the enterprise in the drive for efficient production and modernization. Mass mobilization and the party's preoccupation with ideological tenets seem to have decreased; instead of focusing on the class struggle, the party now emphasizes economic development and modernization. The reality, however, differs from the official intentions. Beyond the formal channels described above that reinforce the party's powerful position within the enterprise, informal ties and relations between plant directors and the party representatives, as well as workers and their superiors, produce a unique system of pervasive political controls.

CONCLUDING REMARKS

Based on the official party rhetoric, political standards should not play a role in evaluating one's performance, but political controls over workers are still alive. Although the political standards seem to have been dropped, the party still defines what is acceptable behavior. The party still "spells out an elaborate framework of general beliefs from which citizens cannot dissent in public discourse" (Walder, 1986: 231). For instance, ideally, ideological positions should not be a criterion for wage raises and bonuses. Yet "those who are singled out for violating political standards are regularly deprived of bonuses and raises" (Walder, 1986: 232). In addition, the party monitors workers' behavior through dossiers, by keeping files, and by imposing and monitoring self-criticism sessions

(Walder, 1986: 231–232; Wilson, 1987: 312). Because workers have limited opportunities to fulfill their needs through institutionalized means, informal channels throughout the spectrum of enterprise authority have been developed over the years, and there is no sign that their influence has been diminished due to the recent economic and political reforms. The party secretary within the enterprise in accordance with formal policies should serve the factory director, support his decisions, and help create conditions that promote productivity. In reality, however, as Walder (1986: 236) points out: "much depends on the informal balance of power of different leadership cliques and the relationship between the plant director and the party secretary: e.g., how long each held the post and their respective backing from above."

At another level, workers themselves need to utilize similar informal channels to pursue their own personal interests, given their substantial economic dependence on the enterprise for their livelihood (Walder, 1986: 56–74). Although the workers' economic dependence on the enterprise has decreased substantially, owing to the increased supply of food and goods and the easing of rationing, still Chinese workers more than workers in the Soviet Union and other East European countries rely on their enterprises to obtain access to scarce resources such as jobs, welfare provisions, and housing (Walder, 1986: 237–238). Such pervasive economic dependency promotes the cultivation of close, highly personalized, cordial relationships between workers and higher party and managerial authorities. Such a solution seems to be the only effective way to pursue one's interests in light of the recent reestablishment of the one-man style of management. Granted, the director's decisions are to be guided by certain standards of skill and performance measured with certain statistical techniques and examinations, but as Walder (1986: 237) pointedly observes, "they (shop managers) still retain as much personal discretion as before, especially in promotions, distributions, and sociopolitical services, where the relevance of production statistics and examinations is limited."

Because the formal structures of workers' participation are not equipped with discretionary powers to counterbalance the arbitrariness that the informal system breeds, the overall pattern of political manipulation continues to exist. In addition, this informal system of filling workers' needs individually "serves as a powerful deterrent to the unsanctioned collective expression of worker interests (Wilson, 1987: 315). There are some warning signs that the reforms have in many ways increased corruption. Because the economy runs partly by plan and partly by market guidelines, individuals always have opportunities to move goods from the planned sector, where prices are low, to the private sector where they can gain more profits. Also within the nonstate sector there are a number of people who use their connections to get coveted licenses, preferential access to materials, and the like (Pomeranz, 1990: 243–246).

The peculiar nature of the Chinese labor market has also reinforced the leadership's ability to prevent organized group activity, which is a necessary condition for promoting and helping to accomplish workers' interests. To a certain degree, all Soviet-type societies have managed by placing overlapping political organizations within the enterprise, to prevent organized opposition. In contrast to the Soviet Union and most Eastern European countries, however, China has a vast labor surplus. This factor, together with the absence of a mature working class with democratic traditions, makes it extremely doubtful that workers would be able to collectively mobilize for genuine economic and political reforms in China (Wilson, 1987: 318). This does not necessarily mean that dissatisfaction, opposition, and even resistance do not exist within Chinese society. The 1989 democracy movement would challenge such an argument. Although last year's events in 1989 seem to prove that an effective organized resistance is lacking in China, at the same time they demonstrate that in the long run the government cannot politically or economically afford to have people's morale, especially the workers', get worse. In the short run, the Tiananmen Square events and the political repression that followed them[4] cast some serious doubts on whether the government was willing to address the pressing economic and political problems through democratic decentralization.

The leadership has also tried systematically over the years to gain workers' compliance through some other economic measures, such as increases in wages, bonuses, and generally upgrading the overall standard of living. From 1977 to 1983, for instance, wages increased by 18 percent and bonuses were restored and expanded, while the number of service establishments tripled from 1978 to 1982 (Walder, 1986: 225). The implementation of economic and political reforms as propagated by the leadership demands certain sacrifices and risks. Certain institutional guarantees and rights such as job security, small wage differentials, and worker benefits that workers grew up to expect are now being threatened by the reforms and the introduction of market forces. Unequal income distribution, class privileges and differences, bankruptcies, increased inflation, corruption and unemployment are only some of the adverse consequences of the reforms undertaken (Goldman, 1987: 219). Some people have also managed to get more out of the reforms, which resulted in increased resentment among various groups from teachers to soldiers, whose income remained stagnant. Moreover, by the spring of 1989, inflation was up to 35 percent in many cities, hurting mostly salaried employees who did not have access to second incomes. In addition, because of the country's indebtedness, the government initiated some austerity measures. Peasants and workers, for example, were asked to take payments and yearly bonuses not in cash but in other forms such as long-term government bonds. These measures have increased conflict and resentment among the overall population (Pomeranz, 1990: 243, 245).

In a socialist country like China, such negative outcomes of the reforms will be extremely difficult to justify. This without doubt will have a strong impact on the workers' overall support for reform. Other countries, such as Hungary earlier and the Soviet Union currently, have undertaken similar reforms and have faced similar dilemmas as the Chinese have been facing for the last few years. The need to modernize is compelling, but it would also be extremely difficult to justify an enterprise's bankruptcy in China given that the enterprise, as pointed out earlier, is not merely a source of income, but a major determinant of housing, medical care, pension, and overall well-being. The party has to convince workers that all these changes that seem to threaten their stability now will be beneficial to them and to the society as a whole in the long run.

A final point should be made: As expected, people in the factories, party, and military bureaucracies, whose positions and privileges are threatened by the decentralization process and the diminishing role of the party, also oppose the reforms. Despite Deng Xiaoping's systematic effort to rejuvenate the political, military, and economic bureaucracies with people who support his policies, the question still remains whether his successors will be willing and committed enough to the reforms he started. Without question, the fate of economic reforms will eventually determine the prospects of the movement for more autonomy and democracy within the enterprise. As has been argued, economic reforms are bound to escalate demands for more democratic freedoms in the society and thus in the economic enterprises. The question is whether popular demands and pressing economic and social problems will force the party to compromise some of its prerogatives and to give up some of its discretionary power that permeates the economic structures of the country. Eventually, the degree of such compromise will determine the future of the existing worker participative structures as a means of channeling the workers' interests.

NOTES

1. For more information on Deng Xiaoping's efforts to consolidate his political power, to restructure the state bureaucracies that had been decimated during Mao's regime, and to rejuvenate the society's leadership core with candidates who had the appropriate educational, technical, age, and political qualifications, see Clarke (1986: 119–132).

2. Wilson (1987: 306) suggests that the emergence of Solidarity in Poland might have had an impact on the setback of the reform. Solidarity's emergence contradicted the Marxist-Leninist position that the party was to assume the vanguard role in the society. Presumably what was happening in Poland alarmed and strengthened the antireformist movement in opposing the expansion of workers' powers through their congress.

3. Beyond the political repression, there are also very serious shortages of goods which are caused by bureaucratic accumulation and supply bottlenecks. There are, for instance, serious coal shortages across China, yet, for bureaucratic reasons, coal sits on the ground in Shaanxi Province. For this and other economic problems that plague China, see Ken Pomeranz (1990: 243–246).

4. The political repression followed the June 1989 crackdown on workers and hit unemployed youth the most. Measures have also been taken to avoid the coordinated opposition by intellectuals and students. High-ranking officials who were sympathetic to the causes of the democracy movement have been purged. The entering class at Beijing University has been cut by 60 percent, and all incoming freshmen have to take a year of military training before they proceed with their studies. On the basis of some media

reports, the signs of indoctrination are very obvious. Finally, open opposition, within the country at least, has been weakened by the fact that many people committed to democratic causes, as well as prominent influential people, have been arrested or forced to leave the country. See Pomeranz (1990: 243–246).

8

Participatory Reforms in the Soviet Union

Yugoslavia, Eastern Europe, and China have taken measures to deviate from the Soviet model of management through economic reforms and some schemes of worker participation in management. Although serious deficiencies and limitations have been pervasive in the Soviet system, the kind of crisis and public outbreak that developed in some East European countries and necessitated economic reforms has not taken place in the Soviet Union, at least until the last few years (Nove, 1980a). Under Gorbachev, the Soviet Union has been challenged not only by nationalist riots and demands for greater political and economic autonomy from the non-Russian republics, but also by an alarming increase in rates of dissent and opposition of various other social groups.

Only a few years ago, the history-making events of the Polish worker unrest (of 1980–1981) evoked little sympathy from the Soviet public, with the exception of some isolated strikes and protest actions confirming the Soviet people's reputation as being passive, cynical, and conservative. Since the early 1980s, some reform-minded intellectuals, academicians, and scientists within the Soviet Union have used the Polish example to press for reforms inside the Soviet Union, arguing that the Polish crisis was not just an isolated event caused by the peculiarties of the Polish socialism, but rather the result of endemic overall deficiencies that characterize all Soviet-type societies. Some even argue that the 1980–1981 events in Poland motivated the initiation of reforms in the Soviet Union under Gorbachev by demonstrating the "economic, political, and social bankruptcy" of the Soviet system (Teague, 1988: 40–43). Still, the Soviet people have not been organized to systematically demand reforms.

If the Soviet public seemed immune to any democratic influences from the neighboring countries in the past, since the early 1980s it has grown very aware of the serious problems that plague the nation, and it has increasingly demanded strategies for their solution. Elections, public protests, strikes, and simple encounters with politicians and the press, all demonstrate that the Soviet people recognize and are able to express the need for the country's political and economic democratization. Perhaps the most notable example of this trend—the independence movements in Lithuania and other republics aside—is the critical stance and opposition of the Soviet coal miners in 1989 and again in the summer of 1990. Their strike and opposition are very significant because they underscore the importance of political reform as a prerequisite of any meaningful economic and social reform as understood by possibly the most organized and powerful segment of the Soviet working class. For instance, in 1989 the coal miners in Ukraine went on strike about traditional grievances such as low pay and unsafe working conditions. In 1990, their demands had become more politicized: First, they requested the resignation of Prime Minister Ryzhkov, and then they made clear that the government does not have their trust. The miners ignored Gorbachev's personal plea to refrain from industrial action, walked out of their jobs, and strongly demanded the dismantling of the party, a sentiment that, according to some estimates, is being shared by millions of other workers in the Soviet Union (Karabel, 1990).

The need to restructure the economic and political basis of the society has been increasingly felt not only by the Soviet people, but also by politicians, intellectuals, scientists, academicians, and the Soviet leadership itself, starting in the most recent years with Andropov and culminating under Gorbachev. Two fundamental reasons made the reformers appreciate the necessity of changing the overcentralized and insufficient planned economy: (1) economic efficiency, and (2) the need to preserve the party's legitimacy. The elite came to realize that, in comparison with the West, Japan, and even some newly industrializing countries in East Asia, the Soviet Union did not fare well in the international competition owing to the immense inadequacies of the centralized system. The regime was also pressed to save its legitimacy in the eyes of the population by raising the population's standard of living by introducting *perestroika*, that is, restructuring the economy (Wu, 1990: 95).

THE NEW ECONOMIC POLICY REFORMS (NEP) UNDER LENIN

The Soviet Union reached a relatively high level of material production in a relatively short period of time after the revolution, and up to the 1950s at least the economy was growing very rapidly.[1] Compared with its prerevolutionary, backward, agrarian economy, within seventy years of Soviet rule the Soviet Union has become one of the most powerful industrial countries in the world. Nonetheless, the Soviet economy has been criticized in the West as wasteful and inefficient, and its growth rate has declined since the 1950s (Goldman, 1990a, 1987; Lane, 1985; Yanowitch, 1985). Moreover, the centralized Stalinist system with its emphasis on heavy industry, wasteful use of resources, and the inefficiencies of its oversized bureaucracy has come under attack in the Soviet Union as well, especially under Gorbachev (Goldman, 1990).

This is not the first time that the Soviet system has been under scrutiny and criticism. Since the 1917 revolution a number of attempts have been made to reform the economy. Elements of worker participation have also appeared in the reform process. In discussing some of these efforts, it will be possible to identify the reasons behind efforts to reform, and the similarities and differences with similar efforts in Eastern Europe, as well as assess the prospects for democratic worker participation under the challenges Gorbachev's reform is facing.

Lenin himself introduced the New Economic Policy (NEP) in 1921, and it lasted until 1928. Serious socioeconomic and political problems prompted its introduction. Foreign intervention and the civil war had devastated the economy. Compared with the pre-1913 period, for instance, production had declined five times (Aganbegyan, 1988: 46). NEP was introduced to replace the wartime economy which was totally centralized and to help effect the transition from the old agrarian economy to a command economy, a transition that had created serious adjustment problems. The workers' abandonment of factories, for instance, and the peasants' revolt against grain requisitions by the state, as well as natural disasters such as droughts, resulted in the breakdown of both small- and large-scale production. NEP was designed to address some of these problems.

Some state controls were relaxed, and freedoms and private initiatives in agriculture, small-scale industrial production, and retailing were encouraged. For instance, farmers, after paying small taxes in kind, were allowed to sell their products for profit; freedom to trade was allowed for small-scale production and services; party and trade union intervention within the enterprise was relaxed; administrative commands in state enterprises were replaced by self-finance and cost accounting principles; and, finally, competition in the open market between state enterprises and private entrepreneurs as well as cooperation between foreign capitalists and the Soviet industry was encouraged. The goal was to help the economy grow and sufficiently meet the needs of the population (Aganbegyan, 1988: 46; Draper, 1987: 287–289).

When Stalin came to power in 1928, NEP was interrupted. Competition, free enterprise, and market forces were totally discarded. The emphasis shifted to collectivation in agriculture, rapid and extensive industrialization, and increased centralization. The central plan replaced the market. Through the Gosplan, the central planning organization, the planners made five-year plans, determining who would produce what by using specific materials and who would receive the goods produced. Finally, quantity of production, not profit, was the criterion to judge a factory's success. As Goldman (1987) points out, although such a quantitative approach contributed to significant increases in industrial production in the last few decades, it also produced some negative results that became increasingly difficult for the Soviet leaders to ignore. For instance, the Stalinist model seemed suitable for building a heavy industry; it also seemed to function well in the early period when any production seemed better than nothing. Later, the need for stylish and better quality products became apparent. In addition, the system encourages the wasteful use of raw materials. Increased production is rewarded by superiors in both material and nonmaterial ways. Therefore, since production is determined by the gross value output measured in rubles, the Soviet managers have an incentive to use the most expensive raw materials and components. All these elements of the economic system have served as a continuous pressure for change in the Soviet Union.

THE *SOVNARKHOZ* REFORMS UNDER KHRUSHCHEV

The period 1955–1956 to 1964 marked yet another cycle of reforms under the leadership of Nikita Khrushchev, the so-called *Sovnarkhoz* reforms. Unquestionably, political considerations were behind Khrushchev's efforts to reform. In the name of the reform, for instance, a large number of his political opponents were displaced from the central apparatus. Economic considerations also played a key role. As the system became increasingly centralized, local authorities had lost control over the operation of their enterprises and thus waste and inefficiency became abundant. In an effort to rationalize a division of labor within and between regions, Khrushchev abolished the major industrial ministries; ministries were replaced by regional economic councils, called *sovnarkhozy*, where many of his political opponents were displaced.

The councils undertook to evaluate the economy of their region and then determine how the economy could become more efficient. Such a goal would be accomplished either by shifting production among the region's enterprises or by discontinuing production and importing the necessary products from other areas, if it was more efficient to do so. The increased local control and the ability to coordinate economic matters in the different regions were expected to reduce the burden on the transportation system as well as to cut down on the waste and inefficiency of having to coordinate every activity through Moscow.

Eventually, the reforms failed for political and economic reasons. *Sovnarkhozy*, as one would expect, came to favor their own enterprises over others, and thus local interests, rather than efficiency considerations prevailed. The fact that, during the period of the *sovnarkhoz* reform, the growth rates for national income and labor productivity declined, and those declines were linked to the *sovnarkhozy* regardless of their cause, did not help the reform efforts either. Dissatisfaction with the *sovnarkhozy* grew, and by early 1963 their number declined from 100 to 47. Another reason why the reforms failed was that bureaucrats in the ministries resented the fact they had lost their power. Besides, the *sovnarkhozy* were considered inefficient since they were unable to make some decisions on their own and certain functions were still performed centrally. Eventually, the number of state committees, which were established to replace the ministries, grew and in a way substituted for the old ministries, until Kosygin reestablished the old ministerial system in 1965 (Goldman, 1987: 49; Hewett, 1988: 223–227).

THE KOSYGIN REFORMS

The relaxation in censorship during the period of Khrushchev's rule, regardless of the failure of his reforms, permitted concerns to be raised and debates to take place as to the overcentralized and inefficient Stalinist system. They also set the stage for yet another cycle of reforms, the so-called 1965 reforms undertaken by Alexei Kosygin. Throughout the 1960s, the need for decentralizing the economy grew. Awareness of the waste and irrationality of the system at the micro-level also increased, and the need for greater enterprise autonomy became apparent. Economists were debating their theories, and they were drafting proposals describing how to implement them. Among them was Professor Evsei Grigorievich Liberman, who together with his colleagues attracted a great deal of attention in the West by suggesting decentralization of party controls over the economy. Liberman advocated the replacement of quantitative production quotas with management's own plans based on orders negotiated with customers.[2] Limitations would still exist as obligatory plan indicators would be sent to enterprises, albeit fewer in number, and the plans were to be approved by the central authorities. Once approved, however, it was up to management to devise the wage fund, profit plan, productivity targets, and the like (Draper, 1987; Nove, 1980b).

In an effort to eliminate waste and encourage more efficient use of resources, the 1965 economic reform strove to increase enterprise autonomy. The centrally fixed plan assignments were to be reduced, and the shares of profits that could be retained and allocated within the enterprises were to be increased. Both measures were expected to function as incentives for more efficient production within enterprises. The use of economic levers such as profits, prices, and bonuses would be increased, and managers could decide on issues of technology, the number of workers to be hired, and the like. Although the autonomy of the enterprises increased, the ministries still had considerable power over them, and ultimately, this contributed to the reversal of the whole reform process. For instance, all important capital investments, as well as the allocation of the most important material supplies, remained under ministerial control. Furthermore, any tasks that were related to the introduction of new technology, and thus any effort of innovation and expansion, were centrally determined. The extensive power which ministries and central authorities had over enterprises and their directors can best be understood if we add that the central authorities also had control over the careers and bonuses of upper management (Draper, 1987; Hewett, 1988; Lane, 1985; Yanowitch, 1977).

The debate over the new enterprise incentive system prompted the authorities to experiment with some of those ideas. At the Bolshevichka, a factory for men's clothing and at the Mayak, a factory for women's dresses, some of those ideas were put into practice. For instance, profitability, and not quantity, became the basis for evaluation. Sales were openly negotiated in the market, without central interference. In 1965, the experiment was expanded in 400 consumer goods enterprises, and by January 1967, 2,500 more firms had adopted the new incentive scheme.

As the number of enterprises experimenting with the new incentive scheme grew, so did the opposition of the ministers and middle-level officials. They were placed in the middle of a cross fire: their power was eroding, yet their responsibilities remained fairly intact. Ministries, for instance, were still accountable for underfulfilled production plans, while managers had more authority for daily operations and were encouraged to seek profits rather than plan fulfillment. Since real market forces were lacking, it was inevitable that ministerial officials would interfere with the firm's day-to-day operations and the reforms would fail (Goldman, 1987: 53; Hewett, 1988: 229–230). Consequently, the 1965 Law on Socialist Enterprises, which provided for enterprise wide-ranging rights, became a dead letter, since the central authorities never took any serious measures to defend and advance the rights of the enterprises (Aganbegyan, 1988: 61).

The autonomy and freedom of an individual enterprise remained limited because of extensive organizational and political controls, as was the case with similar piecemeal reform efforts in Eastern Europe. The reform was very limited in scope and not all-society embracing. Whereas changes were to take place in the main state and collective farms, they were not accompanied by similar changes in ministries and in other state and party organizations. Instead, the state apparatus grew, new departments developed, and the central economic institutions expanded (Aganbegyan, 1988: 62). The market mechanism of the Yugoslav type was never intended to be a factor in the Soviet economy. Consumer demand, a factor that could determine production, was absent, and directors were still under orders as to what and how much was to be produced. Furthermore, wages were still centrally determined and were not based on output. Even the use of profits was subject to indirect party and union controls. Although the manager had control over the details of the daily operation of production, the planning process per se remained within the jurisdiction of the appropriate ministry. Having a new ruling group emerging within the enterprise could not be easily tolerated, since such a prospect could pose a serious threat to the interests of the ruling elite and its administrative apparatus.

Therefore, in spite of the official rhetoric about the democratization of management, the reforms were never directly aimed at changing the structure of authority within the firm. Whatever the limitations of managerial power might have been, the one-man management principle within the enterprise and the overall power distribution remained intact. Hierarchical social relations that imply subordination, dependence, and inequality persisted. The workers' position in the power structure did not change either, Managerial positions, for instance, were not rejuvenated by new recruits from the overall working population. More importantly, workers did not participate in working out the plans of their enterprises, nor did they have any say in deciding how the funds for incentives were to be used. Under those conditions, their interest in the reform faded away, and the reform itself failed to materialize its promises (Aganbegyan, 1988: 62; Yanowitch, 1977).

ECONOMIC PROBLEMS OF THE 1970s AND INCREASED INTEREST IN WORKER PARTICIPATION

If the reforms failed regarding the issues discussed above, they proved successful in other respects; they prepared the groundwork for the subsequent public discourse as it pertained to the democratization of management. They also facilitated the extensive coverage of participatory issues in the Soviet sociological and economic literature. It gradually became apparent that serious problems, such as low worker morale, worker discontent, alienation, and inefficient work performance, could be solved by reorganizing the management process to become more participatory in its structure. This did not result, however, in increased workers' control or self-management of the Yugoslavian type (Yanowitch, 1978, 1985). To understand this difference, we have to know how the Soviet society operates as a whole. According to the official rhetoric, the society is highly participatory. Workers are the ruling class of the society and participate in it merely by belonging to the various production conferences and by being members of the various social organizations, such as party and trade union committees. The fact that they are not able to formulate any policies, voice their demands, or genuinely participate in decision-making processes is conveniently overlooked. Therefore, any proposals for changing the distribution of power are presented as improvements of a system that is already participatory. Obviously, such assumptions would from the start limit any attempts to genuinely change the distribution of power within the firm. Therefore, efforts to humanize work, to improve working conditions, to systematically structure job promotion procedures and rules that deal with vacancies, and finally to expand and institutionalize the brigade or team system have to be understood within this context (Yanowitch, 1985).

All these attempts are responses to similar problems faced in the West, although their causes, degree, and intensity might be different. In the West, for instance, autonomous work teams and similar participatory schemes are responses to the growing discontent, low morale, and indifference among the workers. The problem is more acute among the young workers and those who are well educated, whom managers have a difficult time motivating and retaining in low-skilled, boring jobs. Similar schemes have also been introduced in the Soviet Union in a search for more appropriate management methods that would better accommodate the changing workforce and its expectations. They are manifestations of the need for a more humane, less rigid, and, therefore, more efficient style of supervision that can improve working conditions and thus work attitudes (Aganbegyan, 1988; Goldman, 1987; Hewett, 1988; Kingston-Mann, 1988; Yano-witch, 1977).

In the late 1960s, following the raised expectations created by the 1965 economic reforms, some Soviet researchers proposed elections within the workplace to reduce managerial authority and counterbalance it by increasing opportunities for workers' involvement within the enterprise. The proposals reflected the need to respond to the country's mounting economic problems. The most influential proposal was authored by Ia. S. Kapeliush in 1969 under the Institute of Concrete Social Research and the Institute of Public Opinion of the newspaper *Komsomolskaia Pravda*. Based on the results of a public opinion survey, the recommendation was to introduce elections for certain managerial positions. By participating in the elections, and through their elected representatives, workers would be able to influence the way the enterprise was operating.

Despite the apparently overwhelming support of the workers, engineers, and technicians (90 percent of those questioned supported the proposal), elections were introduced on only a limited experimental basis because of strong opposition from various other groups. Opposition to the idea of elections was particularly strong among upper-level management, with one-half of plant directors and more than one-third of shop chiefs voting "no" on the issue. Party and trade union officials were not particularly supportive either, with one-quarter to one-third opposing the elections (Yanowitch, 1985: 120–121). These results are not surprising given the way the Soviet economy is organized. A number of managerial personnel did not welcome the prospect of being monitored by subordinates while being accountable to the higher authorities for their decisions (Yanowitch, 1977: 413). In addition, there were no institutional mechanisms to insure the implementation of an election process. Although workers supported the idea of elections, they lacked independent organizational resources or mechanisms to implement such proposals. Moreover, given the role of party and union organizations within the workplace, it would be difficult to imagine that elections would not be manipulated by party and union members. When we take these conditions into account, we can readily understand why the idea of elections has not been implemented in any comprehensive way, although proposals about elections have surfaced and elections in brigades have taken place again under Gorbachev (Aganbegyan, 1988: 168; Hewett, 1988: 327, Yanowitch, 1985).

Since the late 1970s, there has been yet another wave of renewed interest in worker participation issues. Attempts have been undertaken to redesign and restructure work and pay arrangements through the extension of the brigade system, which was first introduced in the building trades in the middle 1960s and then was extended to other trades (Aganbegyan, 1988: 169; Kingston-Mann, 1988: 12–13). The brigade form of management was adopted to alleviate problems associated with extreme division of labor, fragmentation, and routinization of tasks. It offered opportunities for job enrichment, enlargement, and rotation and thus allowed more flexibility and worker involvement in the shopfloor decision-making process. The brigade system of management aimed to motivate workers by providing incentives for work and thus boost attitudes toward work and work performance.

As the comparable autonomous work groups in the West, the members of the brigades work jointly on a set of interrelated tasks and share control of the production process and the rules that guide it. The aspect of cooperation in relation to the brigade way of management is very important since, until the late 1970s, the brigade system was largely confined to such industries and production processes where the employed technology requires collaboration of efforts (e.g., steel production). Focusing on the system's social advantages, a new ideology similar to the West's sociotechnical perspective subsequently developed. That is, a specific technology can be compatible with diverse ways to organize work.

A 1979 decree of the party and Council of Ministers expanded the brigade system to include other industries, including the chemical and machine-building industries, and to provide incentives for the workers involved. With the rapid advancement of technology, a need arose for more coordinated collective efforts to organize complex technical systems and to further accelerate technological progress. In a sense the institution of brigades was a response to that need. Similar kinds of developments had already taken place in the West, where the nature of technological development required a more cooperative type of work and coordination (Aganbegyan, 1988: 168; Kingston-Mann, 1988: 13; Yanowitch, 1985: 135).

It was expected that cooperation would be reinforced and higher and better productivity goals would materialize, providing output norms and wage payments were based on group rather than individual output, and providing overall production depended on group rather than individual uncoordinated efforts. In addition, the brigade system was promoted on the basis that the most efficient system of management is the one "in which decision making is entrusted to the maximum number of individuals at the lower range of the management hierarchy" (as quoted in Yanowitch, 1985: 137). In that respect, the brigade system sought to improve the social relations between managers and the managed through worker involvement in shopfloor decisions.

Regardless of the official rhetoric and the promising results of the first brigades as in the areas of cost effectiveness and labor productivity, the implementation of the brigade form of participation was blocked by serious constraints. It is not surprising, for instance, that any attempt to introduce workers' participation would undoubtedly meet the resistance of groups whose material and power interests were threatened by such development. Surveys have shown that managerial personnel considered the brigade an inappropriate source of managerial authority and that lower level supervisors, whose authority was threatened, were not enthusiastic about enhancing the decision-making powers of the work teams (Yanowitch, 1985: 149–153).

Plant managers, facing the loss of their power while pressed from their ministerial authorities to show that the transition to the brigade way of management was progressing, often did not comply with the official principles of the brigade operation. In effect, brigades existed in name only, and many workers continued to work and get paid on an individual basis. Brigades were supposed to be autonomous and free of administrative controls and interferences, work on a contract with a state enterprise, and organize work based on democratic principles decided among the brigade members. Ministries, however, soon began to interfere with the operation of the brigades and set plans for them. Since the power distribution within them remained the same, as in traditional enterprises, workers reportedly became dissatisfied with the way the brigades operated. Because the appropriate conditions were not present for the effective functioning of brigades, their promising start as self-managing work organizations failed to materialize. Apparently, however, all this accumulated experience and experimentation with participative forms of management have informed Gorbachev's efforts to restructure the economy, since some forms of management discussed here have been revived under Gorbachev (Aganbegyan, 1988: 169; Yanowitch, 1985).

SOVIET REFORMS IN A COMPARATIVE CONTEXT

Efforts to create genuine participatory forms, where workers can influence decisions, have not been successful or widespread in the Soviet Union, despite the increasingly strong appeals for democratization of management and worker participation. To become meaningful, any workers' participation scheme requires that decentralization of decision making at the plant level be accompanied by overall relaxation of central controls at the societal level. Decentralization is one of the basic requirements of democratization. In the Soviet Union, however, market mechanisms as they operate in the West do not exist, except on a very limited basis, and therefore, the incentives to respond to market demands are lacking. The reforms require changes in economic and authority relations, changes that would threaten the vested interests of the existing economic and political elites. Understandably, groups ranging from the central system down to the managerial personnel, whose privileges rest on the authoritarian system of management, would resist efforts of change.

Managerial personnel, for instance, do not have any strong reason to support participative schemes. During all cycles of reform in the Soviet Union, middle management has been especially against power redistribution efforts. This has also become problematic under Gorbachev, and apart from other political opposition, this is one of the difficulties he is facing in restructuring the economy and society. Unless fundamental economic reforms take place, the prospects of a genuine workers' participation seem remote, since it would be difficult for managerial personnel to accept a system that makes them responsible for fulfilling orders from above and at the same time holds them accountable to their subordinates. Not surprisingly, then, any serious effort to redistribute managerial authority and to reduce the barriers between the managers and the managed has not taken place.

The Yugoslav self-management approach in its societywide scope is rejected on economic, political, and ideological grounds, and there are no indications that the party is willing to give up its monopolistic role in the society (Lane, 1985; Nove, 1983). Although Gorbachev is talking about restructuring the economy, and the idea of self-management is increasingly gaining momentum, the role of the party within the new envisioned system remains central (at least until very recently, since the operation of other parties is now allowed). The Chinese model with its relaxed central controls, expansion of foreign trade, foreign investments, and joint ventures with foreigners, has not been viewed favorably in the Soviet Union either, although recently there has been more discussion about all these issues and some steps have been taken in similar directions. Inflationary trends, increased income, and regional inequalities, as well as increased bottlenecks and duplications, are considered negative consequences of the introduced reforms in China. Critics in the Soviet Union, for both ideological and economic reasons, do not welcome such results.

The East European experience of economic and work reforms is well known and is followed very closely in the Soviet Union. No systematic effort has been made, however, to integrate the lessons of that experience in their own attempts for reform, although the Eastern European experience, especially that of East Germany, has in the past informed the positions of reformers in the Soviet Union (Goldman, 1987; Hewett, 1988). Hungarian reforms, for instance, do not seem to provide the Soviets with an appropriate model suitable to their own historical experience and needs. In contrast to Hungary, the Soviet Union is a big, heterogeneous country, where it would be difficult to separate the demand for decentralized economic control from the demand for political independence and self-determination within the dissenting ethnic republics. Critics also point to the adverse effects of market forces on the Hungarian economy, such as balance of trade problems, zero economic growth and high inflation rates (Goldman, 1987: 165). The events of 1980–1981 in Poland were also received with mistrust and skepticism in the Soviet Union. However, the fascinating developments in Eastern Europe in 1989, especially the apparent defeat of the Communist party, have prompted a renewed interest and seem to have had a strong impact in the Soviet Union. As recent reports and media accounts indicate, there have been debates on whether and to what extent the changes that have taken place in those countries should be adopted in the Soviet Union.

Until the very recent past, the Soviet reformers were apparently more inclined to the East German model than to the Hungarian or Polish. Indeed, the German Kombinat system, which became dominant in 1979–1980, has attracted much favorable attention in the Soviet Union. Under this system, factories with similar product lines are organized into large Kombinate whose goal is to stimulate innovative production, increase foreign trade, and reduce as much as possible the obstacles posed by the centralized and bureaucratic system. The Kombinat system seemed more appealing to the Soviet Union for both ideological and economic reasons. Through the Kombinat system, East Germany sought to strengthen the effectiveness of the centralized system rather than decentralize it as Hungary has done.[3] The fact that the East German economy, regardless of its growing economic problems, seemed to fare much better than the other Eastern European economies, contributed to the Soviet Union's favorable disposition toward that system. Such a system might require some ministry consolidation or reassigning of middle-level managers. Changes like that, however, would not be difficult to introduce since they have already taken place to some degree in the Soviet Union (Goldman, 1987: 167–173; Hewett, 1988: 300–301). The recent dramatic changes that have taken place in East Germany itself, its economic unification with West Germany, its denial of socialism, and its adoption of capitalism not only will change the way the East German system will operate, including the Kombinat system, but will also force the Soviet Union to reconsider its position in view of changes in the Soviet Union itself.

Until very recently, the Eastern European experience with reform has been viewed cautiously in the Soviet Union because of its political consequences. The fear that economic reforms and workplace democratization will feed social and political demands and the danger of such spillover effects cannot be ignored in a society where political control and social stability are the keys to existing power relations. Nevertheless, reforms in Eastern Europe have been monitored carefully, to determine whether they can be applied in the Soviet Union. Gorbachev himself in his speech at the Twenty-Seventh Party Congress in February 1986 emphasized the need to take into consideration any positive lessons from the Eastern European experience with reform. He pointed out that "a considerate and respectful attitude to each other's experience and the employment of this experience in practice are a huge potential of the socialist world" (as quoted in Karen Dawisha, 1988: 21). More recently, despite opposition, Gorbachev and other reform-minded economists and politicians have admitted that the only way to save the economy, which is at the verge of breakdown, is to expand market reforms. Undoubtedly, the reforms and changes in Eastern Europe will be closely watched.

Another important point is that in contrast to Poland or Czechoslovakia, workers in the Soviet Union have not initiated or supported reform efforts. Although some isolated cases of organized protest have taken place and although indirect pressures for reform increase by the day, workers have generally reacted to reforms with indifference, skepticism, and even resistance. Such an attitude is not unexpected in a country where workers have been deprived of meaningful participation in the political, social, and economic life for several generations. The system does not prepare citizens for responsibility, and often represses initiatives for independence. Therefore, as the Soviet people have grown increasingly urbanized and educated, their exclusion from political power has bred apathy and cynicism. The results of this alienation are indeed horrifying: falling standards of labor discipline, widespread corruption, rising alcoholism, overall moral decline, and, most alarming of all, steady decline of economic growth (Teague, 1988: 40; Yanowitch, 1985: 162).

Under these conditions, efforts to increase workers' initiative and responsibility by incorporating them into the decision-making process have met with workers' skepticism and suspicion. They are perceived as yet another mechanism to increase their productivity. Workers lack any independent institutional mechanisms to channel their frustrations and demands. Trade unions, to which workers and managers belong by law, operate primarily as production organizations identified with the party authorities rather than with the workers. Furthermore, until very recently, the legitimacy of the party and party organizations did not seem to face serious challenges as has happened in Poland, for example. As a result, workers in the Soviet Union have not sought alternative channels to represent themselves, such as independent unions, which could promote their interests and unite them to push for workplace participation.

As in Eastern European countries, workers in the Soviet Union, at least in the short run, are threatened by reforms as well. Some of their basic rights, such as employment security and wage benefits, are at risk during this early period of reform. Relocations, mergers, and the closings of unproductive plants are unavoidable consequences of the transition stage of any reform. No doubt, economic transformation and market reforms will be very painful and will badly hurt the working class. The impact of increasing unemployment rates, higher prices, and plant closings has already been felt dramatically in Eastern Europe and to some extent in the Soviet Union itself. It is also becoming increasingly clear that the Soviet people don't trust the official rhetoric and are reluctant to accept the rise in prices, the increasing unemployment and social inequality, and the overall falling standards of living (Karabel, 1990: 88).

THE PROMISE AND CHALLENGE OF REFORMS UNDER GORBACHEV

For the last six years Gorbachev has made a serious and long overdue effort to modernize the Soviet economy, regardless of all the above challenges and difficulties and occasional setbacks in his attempts. The need to reform the economic system and change authority relations within the workplace has been recognized by economic and political authorities as well as academicians, scholars, and increasingly by workers and the general public. Headed by Gorbachev himself, proponents of the reform point to the inefficiencies, limitations, and abuses of the overcentralized system. The central planning system has outlived its usefulness, and it now hinders rather than promotes economic growth (Aganbegyan, 1988). Central planning has become problematic, and the Soviet Union needs desperately to find ways to stimulate individual initiative (Goldman, 1990).

The system fails to involve its citizens in participating and responding creatively to existing economic problems. This not only inhibits economic growth, but also generates cynicism and alienation, resulting in a number of social problems from drunkenness to drug addiction to apathy and bureaucratic abuse (Kingston-Mann, 1988: 13–14). In his book entitled *Perestroika*, Gorbachev talks about these problems and openly criticizes the sluggish and arbitrary state system. According to Gorbachev, exaggerated centralism, red tape, and the public inertia they breed, must be overcome if the Soviet Union is to move into the modern world. He has repeatedly emphasized the pressing need to "activate the human factor," to find ways to encourage creativity and reward initiative (Gorbachev, 1987; Teague, 1988). Tatiana Zaslavskaya, an economic sociologist, has also extensively discussed the problems of the overcentralized system, the need for reform, the challenges it would face, and the requirements for its successful implementation. According to Zaslavskaya, the old centralized system has become anachronistic. In her writings she talks about the need to create a situation whereby tapping people's creative potential will create better results.

Not only is the system unable to cope with the demands of a complex and modern industrialized economy, but also the socioeconomic composition of the population has changed, and the system cannot cope with the peoples' new expectations and demands. In contrast to the poor and uneducated peasants of the 1930s who were probably grateful for a job in a factory, the workers and managers of the 1980s are better off, better educated, and a lot more sophisticated. They are becoming impatient with low-quality, outmoded products and are unwilling to be treated as small cogs in a centralized and bureaucratic system. More importantly, after many years of sacrifice, and with the openeness of the society, the working class has become increasingly more demanding. They resent and more openly protest the low standard of living and the inflexible nature of the planning system (Goldman, 1987: 71, 1990: 29; Hewett, 1988: 277).

The Third Industrial Revolution generated by high technology and computers requires new changes in the economic and production process. For instance, in an era of rapid technological change and economic interdependence, as well as new societal needs, the self-contained and centralized Stalinist model cannot successfully fulfill societal needs and international trade demands. New technologies have substantially shortened the life cycle of a product, not only in high technology but in basic industries as well. If a product becomes obsolete within one to three years instead of ten years as was true in previous decades, then Soviet planners and manufacturers cannot possibly compete successfully in the international market. The new technology requires innovation, flexibility, and increased responsibility; the emphasis of the Stalinist system on discipline and conformity is ill suited to responding to these requirements. Emphasis on quantity rather than quality has been built into the system for so long that it would be extremely difficult for it to master new and rapidly changing technologies without some fundamental structural changes (Goldman, 1987).

More than any other reformers in the past, Gorbachev has had to confront these new challenges and has come to the bitter realization that economically and technologically the Soviet Union lags behind the United States and some of the most advanced industrialized European countries. The USSR cannot successfully compete with Japan or even with countries such as Korea and Taiwan. The growth in GNP fell from 3.7 percent in 1971–1975 to 2.7 percent in the five-year period between 1976 and 1980, and between 1981 and 1985, Soviet growth fell a full percentage behind the average of sixteen other industrial countries. In February 1986, Gorbachev himself revealed that during the last fifteen years the growth rates of the national income fell by more than 50 percent. Despite some reform measures, the real standard of living in the Soviet Union has declined considerably in the last few years, and some blame Gorbachev's reform for that (Draper, 1987: 293–294; Goldman, 1987: 15, 1990: 26; Hoagland, 1987: A20).

As is increasingly recognized, it is no longer possible to handle all economic questions and problems from Moscow. In order for the Soviet Union to be able to advance to higher economic and technological levels, the centralized system must be restructured. In June 1987, the Central Committee Plenum approved the *Osnovnye Polozheniia*, a set of principles that were the basis on which the Gorbachev reforms were to be implemented. Four basic assumptions underlie the reforms. First, the Soviet economy would remain a centrally planned economy, but planning would be limited to the most nationally important variables, while economic activity at the micro-level would be the responsibility of the enterprise. Second, the success and failure of individuals and enterprises would be determined on publicly specified rules on the basis of economic and not political criteria. The obvious consequences of that principle is that economic inequality would be inevitable as companies would go bankrupt and people would lose their jobs. The economist Vladimir Kostakov, for instance, predicted that, by the end of the century, between 13 and 19 million jobs would be eliminated. Such grim predictions undermine the whole philosophy of the "social contract" in Soviet-type economies as it specifically relates to full employment and job security, and it is only natural that it would meet popular opposition (Teague, 1988: 53). Of course the assumption is that the state would not allow extensive unemployment, as in the West, and measures would be undertaken to find jobs for people who need them. Third, since enterprises would be responsible for their own success and failure, it would make sense for enterprises to make their own decisions, free of party or government interference. Finally, the fourth principle assumes that people would participate in the management of the enterprise. Without this right, any failure of the enterprise would be blamed on the state-appointed management and allow workers to be absolved of any responsibility (Hewett, 1988: 349–350).

On the basis of these four principles and as a result of the recognized need for reform to meet the new demands, a number of steps have been taken to implement the reform. As of May 1, 1987, for instance, private and cooperative businesses could be legally opened. Individuals and families were allowed to start their own private business. The law permits twenty-nine kinds of business, mostly service-oriented activities like repair shops and hairdressing but also handicraft and clothing and shoe manufacturing. In reality, the law has legalized the private and illegal informal activities that were taking place in the secondary or black market economy. Cooperative businesses, such as restaurants, have opened up in most Soviet cities, something that would be difficult to do in the past when there was only the black market. The law also promotes competition for adequate and better quality products and services.

These provisions resemble Lenin's NEP program of the 1920s, although they are not as far reaching. For instance, the production of certain products such as medicine, weapons, and copying machines for social and political reasons are not allowed. In addition, as with cooperatives, private businesses are not permitted to hire other people, and only those who don't work for the state sector (e.g., students and pensioners) can work full time. Regular workers can work privately when they have free time or when they retire. Private businessmen should register their business in order to pay taxes on their profits and should get their supplies not in the market but from the state. Local soviets are legally obliged to help them in that process. Under the provisions of the Law of the State Enterprise, since 1989 all state enterprises are free to sell 30 percent of their products outside of the state sector. Under the provisions of the same law and in the spirit of decentralization, as of April 1989, enterprises were authorized to do their own exporting and importing without the interference of the Ministry of Foreign Trade (Goldman, 1987: 80–85, 1990: 31–33; Hewett, 1988: 325; Kingston-Mann, 1988: 18–19).

One of Gorbachev's goals is to decentralize the economy and to allow more autonomy at the enterprise level, in an effort to unleash the productive and innovative capabilities of the working population. Soviet economist Aganbegyan, who has been Gorbachev's adviser on *perestroika* policies, argues that one of the negative consequences of public ownership under socialism could very well be the lack of any feeling of individual or group ownership. The results of such an attitude could be devastating: "workers may use public resources uneconomically . . . The attitude to machinery in state factories is quite different from that, say, to personally owned cars" (Aganbegyan, 1988: 196). In order for economic management under socialism to be effective, the feeling of co-ownership should be cultivated in every single worker. He also argues that self-management is the most important means to strengthen that feeling (Aganbegyan, 1988). The Law on Socialist Enterprises, passed in June 1987, took into consideration some of these issues and expanded the rights of the enterprises and the autonomy of management within them. Provisions have been taken to decrease the direct and detailed management stemming from the central authorities.

In the summer of 1986 Gorbachev called for the introduction of "self-management" in the workplace. As he had emphasized many times, the goal was "to activate the human factor by going over to new ways of managing the economy" (as quoted in Teague, 1988: 55). The workers were to be given more incentives in order to become more responsible for their economic performance. One such incentive is the right of workers to effect changes by using their abilities and will through self-management. Based on the 1987 law, top enterprise management is to be elected by a workers' conference for a five-year term. The posts for managerial positions have to be openly advertised, and people interested in the jobs have to submit their preference to be decided in free elections. However, the elected managers still have to be approved by a "superior organ," such as a branch ministry or a state committee.

Workers have also been given the power to recommend the dismissal of a manager whose performance is perceived to be unsatisfactory. Enterprise directors in cooperation with the workers' council, which is chosen by the workers' conference, are responsible for the enterprise's performance. The directors, for instance, have powers over hiring, firing, use of assets, supplies, and capital investment. This does not mean that central planning has been abolished altogether. Ministries can still be in operation, but there are fewer than before. Ministries are responsible for the overall performance of their sector, but they use economic measures such as prices and taxes to influence their enterprises. The important issue here is that enterprises have an incentive to become efficient and profitable, because only a fixed amount of the profits is subject to taxation; the rest goes to wages, bonuses, research, and development as well as investment. The success or failure of the enterprises ultimately depends on their productivity levels (Aganbegyan, 1988, 1990; Goldman, 1987; Hewett, 1988; Linz, 1988; Roucek, 1988; Teague, 1988).

It is too early to assess the effectiveness of those changes, and only speculations are possible at this point in time. A very serious consequence of the overall approach is that, on the one hand, central authorities can extract only limited amounts of money from profitable firms. This provides an incentive for enterprises to become as profitable as they can; it also increases the interest of workers in participating in the management of their enterprise. The fact that a group of workers can form a brigade and sign a contract with the enterprise for a given job also increases workers' interest in giving their best performance and in gaining autonomy. As a result of all these changes, Gorbachev's strategy to link private and social benefits with one's work could materialize. On the other hand, the same measures imply that income inequality, even for people who hold the same jobs, is inevitable. Job security cannot be guaranteed, as many companies cannot rely on the state to bail them out and unprofitable enterprises would inevitably go bankrupt.

By giving workers incentives for more control over their working and economic lives, Gorbachev might eradicate some of the negative effects of leveling which have stifled economic growth. The threat of unemployment, for instance, could work in positive ways to bring people out of inertia and make them produce to the best of their abilities. On the other hand, the prospect of inequality and unemployment, which was officially abolished in 1930, could generate frustration and opposition within certain segments of the population. The younger generation, which is better educated, less traumatized, and frustrated by years of stagnation, might be more willing to take advantage of the opportunities provided by *perestroika*. The less qualified workers who have been accustomed to the security the system offers them are fearful of the reforms and will oppose them.

The older generation who went through wars, purges, and revolutionary sacrifices would be less willing to come to terms with the prospect of increasing inequality and adapt to the proposed changes.

Gorbachev has proposed to cut surplus workers in the factories they supervise and in the various ministries. For those people, as well as the middle and upper level of party bureaucrats and conservatives, the proposed reforms threaten the basic principles of socialism and their own interests and cannot be easily tolerated (Draper, 1987; Goldman, 1987; Hewett, 1988; Hoagland, 1987; Kingston-Mann, 1988; Lee, 1987).

CONCLUDING REMARKS

The need to restructure the inefficient centralized Soviet system has been recognized, which is a very important first step for any meaningful change. In times of crisis, the Soviet Union has made reform efforts in order to respond to the growing discontent of its increasingly educated population as well as to the need to advance economically and technologically within the world economy, and thereby maintain its position as a superpower. The party has until recently, been in control, and the society has managed to avoid the crisis of the Polish experience. As a result, the main initiator and manipulator of any reforms has been the party itself. Because of the structural constraints of the system, the Soviet population has, until very recently, been unable to generate any serious pressure to increase its power.

Reforms in the Soviet Union have not been able to produce extensive changes and introduce democratic rights within the workplace. This can be explained on the basis of the linkage between political and economic structures. Thus, any kind of economic reform is bound to generate opposition in a Soviet-type system. Moreover, independent organizational means for the working class to advance its interests have not been available until recently. Without question, some positive changes have taken place, and the new cultural openness, or *glasnost*, will promote further changes since freedom of expression and greater communication are prerequisites for scientific inventiveness, creativity, and experimentation to accomplish the badly needed economic and technological progress.

Ironically, however, the same openness has caused some formidable results and presents some serious challenges to Gorbachev's efforts for further reform, and indeed for his political survival. Although Gorbachev was recently reelected party general secretary at the Twenty-eighth Communist Party Congress, the party as a powerful political force is undermined by internal conflicts and schisms as well as by increasing public mistrust. Boris Yeltsin, the president of the Russian federation and Gorbachev's most vigorous critic and strongest opponent, resigned from the party in the summer of 1990, followed by a number of other influential political leaders, some of whom have already announced the formation of their own parties (Quinn-Judge, 1990b).[4] Although the results of the composition of the new politburo have proven his success in influencing the Communist party, Gorbachev still has to convince his political opponents as well as the Soviet people, who have grown to distrust the present leadership, that his proposed reforms will succeed (Quinn-Judge, 1990a).

The reforms face enormous difficulties, which is only natural inasmuch as groups whose interests are at stake will fight for their rights and those who have the resources and the power will try to exploit the fears and anxieties that the proposed changes will generate. The communist hard-liners, fearful of losing their power, and the state bureaucrats, whose entrenched interests are challenged by the weakening of party control and by Gorbachev's transfer of power to lower levels, such as soviets or councils, will fight, and have fought, the reforms as well. At the same time, Gorbachev and his allies have to face the so-called liberals or radicals. Headed by the powerful Yeltsin, they are critical of Gorbachev's progress in the reform process, blaming the present leadership for the lack of comprehensiveness in reforms and the half measures the leadership has taken so far.

This is not the first time in the history of the Soviet Union that reforms have faced enormous difficulties and bureaucratic opposition. Previous reforms have failed because of similar resistance; Khrushchev, for one, was deposed in his efforts to shake up his party bureaucracy. The difference at the present time is that because of the increased openness and political pluralism, public discourse, as well as the new opportunities that have opened up to the working class, changes might increasingly be forced from below, as in Poland, instead of from above. In the long run this may prove to be a major positive development toward the democratic transformation of the country and the workplace. In the short run, unless Gorbachev can block the resistance of groups that oppose his reforms, without undermining the legitimacy of his leadership, and unless he is able to consolidate the support of the groups that genuinely believe in his reforms, the impact of those reforms will indeed be limited.

NOTES

1. Economist Aganbegyan indicates that, compared with the prerevolutionary period, by 1941 the Soviet Union had made quite good progress. The social product had increased five times; illiteracy had been overcome; and unemployment had ended. For more details, see Aganbegyan (1988: 47).

2. To pique managers' interest in the pursuit of profits, Liberman suggested that the profits be placed in three funds: the incentive fund, to supplement the wages of workers; the cultural and housing fund, to improve the workers' living conditions; and the development fund for new machinery. See Goldman (1987: 52).

3. For more information on the Kombinat system and its relevance to the Soviet experience, see Goldman (1987: 167–173).

4. Article 6 of the Soviet Constitution guaranteed the party's "legal" monopoly of power. A recent decision of the party's Central Committee to remove that article signifies that political pluralism is possible in the Soviet Union. See Howe (1990: 133).

9

Conclusion: Cross-National and Cross-System Comparisons

In the preceding chapters, the numerous national participation schemes have been described and analyzed in an effort to understand the factors that determined their origins and conditioned their development. In this chapter we undertake cross-national as well as cross-regional/system comparisons. The goal is not to compare national experiences with worker participation schemes on a one-to-one basis. Instead, we discuss a set of broad dimensions and theoretical propositions, which hopefully will increase our theoretical understanding and help us better explain the divergent nature of worker participation schemes.

WORKER PARTICIPATION SCHEMES AND LABOR MARKET CONDITIONS

Participatory forms of management require that the traditional industrial relations system based on conflict be modified to allow for cooperation and the incorporation of workers into the decision-making process. Such cooperation, which both labor and capital do not always welcome, entails labor participation in decisions that go beyond labor's traditional concerns of employment, wages, fringe benefits, and conditions of work. Historical evidence indicates that this will more likely happen when specific labor market conditions threaten established industrial relations as well as economic and industrial interests (e.g., growth, productivity, and efficiency). Such challenges require integration of workers into the organizational process of the enterprise and more collaboration of labor and management in order to face the industrial problems at hand.

During periods of economic growth and reconstruction, for instance, labor's power increases, and its bargaining power is strengthened. During those times, management and/or government are under more pressure to incorporate workers into the decision-making process. The same is true during periods of war, when labor power increases owing to the overall shortage of labor. In other words, when labor market conditions in a given country are tight, the possibility is greater that workers will be incorporated into the decision-making process through various participation schemes.

Although labor market conditions differ from one country to another, the link between tight labor markets and the development of workers' participation is present, regardless of the country's socioeconomic and political system. For example, faced with labor and energy shortages, and in an attempt to secure and increase war production, both England and the United States during the Second World War encouraged labor-management cooperation by establishing joint labor-management committees. During the postwar reconstruction period, productivity committees were established in Norway in order to increase productivity, while in Czechoslovakia during the same period the strong labor movement supported the emergence of labor councils as part of its strategy to accomplish socialism. Similarly, in France and Germany, the immediate postwar reconstruction period, which was also marked by shortage of labor, increased labor's bargaining power. Since capital and big business had been discredited, unions and leftist parties were in a strong position both ideologically and politically. Those circumstances fostered the development of codetermination and enterprise committees in the two countries, respectively. Furthermore, during the 1960s both Sweden and Japan, faced with severe labor shortages, introduced and strongly supported the diffusion of new participatory work structures. In the United States on the other hand, the abundance of cheap labor during the same period was one of the major deterrents to the introduction and expansion of participatory schemes.

The two wartime and postwar periods generated labor shortages and the need for labor-management collaboration for national reconstruction. Similarly, tight labor market conditions increased workers' bargaining power and therefore generated the pressure for workers' participation schemes to emerge. In cases where industrialists had collaborated with the occupying forces or had helped in war production, a political climate developed, which was favorable to workers' demands for more control. Finally, the losses of the war, and the overall deprivation of standards of living compared with the prewar conditions, radicalized attitudes and accelerated demands for more worker power. As indicated in the foregoing chapters, the forms participation schemes took and their overall development depend on the organizational and political capacity of the trade unions, the specific mode of industrial relations, and the general political and international challenges these countries faced.

PARTICIPATION SCHEMES AND THE SOCIOECONOMIC AND POLITICAL CONTEXT

Pressing economic problems, coupled with increasing international competition and worker alienation problems, can function as powerful forces to make managerial elites and the government consider participative solutions. Similarly, political crises can generate the need for worker participation schemes. In both capitalist and socialist economies, political or economic inadequacies, coupled with workers' radical demands for more power, have generated pressures for workplace reforms, including worker participation. Usually, the rhetoric of workers' control is used, and the emerging participatory schemes might be tolerated in an effort to legitimate the existing political order, to accommodate workers' dissatisfaction, and, at least temporarily, to avoid the crisis at hand. The Polish experiences of 1956 and 1980–1981, the Hungarian revolution of 1956, and the French crisis of 1968 are all cases in point.

During the late 1960s and early 1970s, pressures to accommodate the social needs of the workers grew stronger. Those pressures, together with the needs generated by the new, accelerating technological demands, were accommodated by introducing participatory schemes such as problem-solving groups, semiautonomous work teams, quality of worklife projects, quality control circles, and the like. It was assumed that workers' involvement and participation in those schemes would increase their autonomy, responsibility, and competence. This in turn would enhance their quality of worklife and would help alleviate problems of high absenteeism, high turnover, strikes, poor quality, and, in general, alienation-generated problems.

New technological developments, the saturation of the markets with mass-produced goods, rapidly shifting market demands, and the need to respond flexibly to such demands in order to compete within the international market have also accelerated the spread of participation schemes, at least in the industries affected by such changes (Piore and Sabel, 1984). The new technologies have increasingly become more flexible and require a better educated and skillful workforce. As these developments take shape, issues of delegation of authority, workers' autonomy, and participation become an essential part of increasing numbers of enterprises. In previous periods, the need to respond to basic consumer demands was satisfied by utilizing the mass production model to carry out economic activity. At first, the emergence of workers' participation schemes was due mostly to political, ideological, and labor market conditions, as well as to the alienation problems caused by the extreme division of labor. The new cycle of participation that started in the 1960s and accelerated in the 1970s and 1980s seems to suggest that the need for more participative and flexible production systems stems from demands inherent to industrial structures and the changing nature of technologies and market demands.

Corporations in the United States during the 1970s and 1980s, for example, began to introduce labor-management cooperation committees, flexible styles of management, job enrichment, and job enlargement projects. Because of worsening economic conditions and the increased international competition, especially from the Japanese, it was hoped that these schemes would help reform industrial structures that were characterized by narrow job classifications, detailed rules and regulations, as well as routine and intensified pace of work. In Norway too, rationalization of production, applied during the expansion period of the 1950s, resulted in plant closures, dissatisfaction, and alienation. Since productivity was declining, alternative solutions had to be found. As a consequence, during the 1960s debates over the notion of industrial democracy emerged, and experiments and alternative forms of work applying the sociotechnical perspective were introduced. Enhancing the quality of worklife by restructuring work and rigid organizational structures in order to reduce strikes, turnover, and absenteeism was also sought in Sweden during the 1960s. Similarly, in Japan during the same period labor unrest and turnover associated with routinized jobs, as well as labor shortages, severely undermined modernization, economic growth, productivity, and the product quality goals of the nation. Faced with the rising costs of borrowing technology and increasing international competition, Japanese industry began to make better use of its human capital by introducing flexible, autonomous, small-group activities. Centralized, bureaucratic, and rigid structures of authority at the workplace adopted during the expansion period of the 1950s were also causing alienation problems among workers in France during the 1960s. Job enrichment schemes and semiautonomous work teams were supported by the government and some innovative managerial circles in order to facilitate labor-management cooperation, and thus meet overall economic expansion goals.

Although some firms regard participation as a means to become more responsive and face the demands of the new competitive markets, this does not necessarily apply to all countries, firms, industries, and sectors. Many of the new jobs that have been created in this era of rapid technological development, in the West at least, are routinized, low-paying, and boring (Bluestone and Harrison, 1982). Some management leaders and labor unions, faced with the prospects of shifting production operations, closing-down business, and so on, owing to the increased international competition, make surviving the challenge and saving jobs their priority rather than pursuing participative goals (Howard and Schneider, 1987). The specific conditions confronting each industry and nation, as well as the dynamic of power within the industrial relations system and the country itself, determine what approach is followed.

Worker alienation and job dissatisfaction are characteristic of state socialist as well as capitalist countries. In the socialist countries, these problems are compounded by the excessive centralization of the economic and political system and the ineffectiveness they breed. Thus, in the Soviet Union and Eastern Europe they have reinforced the need to improve economic performance by restructuring work.

Since the 1950s, the Soviet Union has taken some measures at both the macro- and micro-level by increasing enterprise autonomy to remedy its pressing economic problems, especially declining economic growth. For example, in the late 1960s and 1970s, humanizing the workplace was considered a remedy to the problems of absenteeism, low worker morale, and inefficient work performance. As in the West, semiautonomous teams, job enrichment, and job enlargement schemes were introduced along with the brigade system as a strategy to motivate workers and increase productivity. More recently, under Gorbachev's leadership, new efforts to restructure the economy and reform the workplace have been undertaken in response to the need to improve the country's economic and technological situation.

Similarly, in Yugoslavia during the 1970s economic problems such as inflation, unemployment, strikes, and worker discontent forced the elites to reevaluate the whole self-management program, to increase enterprise autonomy, and to take measures to ensure actual workers' control. Decreasing levels of productivity, poor quality production, and workers' alienation and dissent, resulting from the inefficiencies of the centralized economic system and rigid and authoritarian work structures, were among the serious problems Poland faced in 1956 too. By ratifying the workers' councils that had emerged during the crisis, the party hoped to relieve not only the tension of the period, but also the economic problems, since workers would share responsibility for industrial production.

The economic stagnation of the 1960s in Czechoslovakia motivated the authorities there to explore alternative solutions to the rigid, centralized planning system and organization of management. But as in Poland in 1956 and 1980–1981 and in Hungary in 1956, demands for workers' participation extended beyond the goal of improving productivity by eliminating worker alienation. They included co-management or self-management of industrial production in order to avoid rigidity, inefficiency, and waste. This development and the fact that economic demands took on political dimensions differentiate the workers' councils of Eastern Europe from quality of worklife experiments, job enrichment, and autonomous teams of the West and the Soviet Union. It helps us understand the challenges and limitations such schemes face.

Economic crises might generate the need for economic reform in both market and nonmarket economies, given that political and economic costs involved in such a process do not outweigh the losses. There is a great difference, however, as to how participation schemes might further develop in the two systems. The power dynamic of independent forces competing for their interests within the context of open market conditions and the opportunities and constraints they pose determine more or less the outcome of such schemes in the West. In the socialist countries, the centralized system and the lack of market forces have prevented independent forces from developing in the same manner as in the West, and incentives to innovate are blocked by political and bureaucratic constraints built into the system. As these countries attempt to introduce market reforms, they find themselves confronting another formidable challenge: the need to ignore the "social contract" as it pertains to the issue of employment security. Increasing public discontent and protest will be unavoidable in these countries, which will experience unaccustomed high unemployment rates. This situation is potentially very dangerous, not only for the success of those reforms, including participative reforms, but also for the political stability of these countries.

These countries may respond differently to crisis situations, owing to leadership style, as well as to economic development and the background of the working class before the communist takeover. The overall structural and political constraints remain the same. However, the historical evidence presented in this book indicates, for instance, that, as a response to its threatened legitimacy, the party leadership might be forced to reform and introduce participatory schemes. In every single crisis in Eastern Europe, demands for worker control were suppressed after the initial stage of compromise because of the challenge they presented to the interests of the beneficiaries of the system. Hungary could be considered an exception to this rule. Reforms there were carefully planned and designed by the party, and their development was gradual. Therefore, over the years a slow but steady progress took place toward decentralization.

In Yugoslavia, too, some measures and reforms introduced in the last four years and again in late 1989 have produced some promising results, reducing the federal deficit considerably and bringing down inflation. Yugoslavia is evolving toward a democratic parliamentary society, and reforms there seem more promising. The Yugoslav communists have not had to deal with a strong opposition in enacting their reforms, and historically they were not perceived as an instrument of foreign domination, as communists and other Soviet-type economies were. Moreover, the reforms in Yugoslavia were introduced slowly over a long period of time, and most of the people seem to support reforms that will improve the self-managing economy, but without the domination of the Communist party (Denitch, 1990c).

EDUCATION AND VALUE ORIENTATIONS

It has been argued throughout this book that low worker morale, dissatisfaction, low motivation, and the like must be understood in conjunction with the rising standard of living, value shifts, and rising levels of education. This argument draws on Maslow's (1954) theory of hierarchical needs; that is, as people's basic needs are satisfied, as their education and their standards of living rise, their values and aspirations change too. Therefore, people are less prone to be satisfied with rigid, hierarchical, monotonous work tasks. Instead, they pursue self-fulfillment and self-realization goals. To a certain extent, demands for increased responsibility and involvement at work through various participative schemes satisfy such objectives. Standards of living, educational levels, and value priorities may differ from country to country because of the specific socioeconomic and political circumstances of a given country. Nevertheless, especially since the 1960s, intergenerational differences within each country and the transformation of value priorities have taken place as a result of the rising standards of living and higher educational attainment.

The demands for workers' participation that emerged in Western Europe and the United States during the mid-1960s are one manifestation of these changes. New Left ideas, including the basic notion of opposition to the established order and support for direct participation, spilled over to the workplace. Traditional authority structures were contested everywhere, including the workplace. Dissatisfaction and overall alienation problems with monotonous work structures reflected the increased expectations regarding one's right for self-fulfilling, satisfying work, as well as the right for more control over decisions affecting one's worklife.

It is argued, therefore, that when value shifts and priorities cannot be accommodated within the established industrial order, and when increasing educational attainment fails to become a means to fulfill expectations regarding working life, then the need for more participatory work structures increases. The case of Japan during the 1960s is indeed reflective of such changes. Immediately after the war, Japanese workers were striving for employment security. By the mid-1960s, higher educational accomplishments had raised the expectations of young high school graduates. Those young workers were not willing to accept or stay in boring blue-collar jobs. During the same period, increasing levels of education and rising expectations helped to escalate demands for more control over worklife in Sweden and Norway, as well as in the rest of Europe.

Similar patterns can be observed in the state socialist countries. There alienation is compounded by the increasing levels of education. In contrast to the Western industrialized countries and Japan, however, the educational levels of the bureaucrats and managers are often very low. In effect, workers' alienation problems are compounded even further. For example, efforts in the Soviet Union in the mid-1960s and 1970s to expand the brigade system and to improve quality of working life similar to the West should also be understood within the context of rising educational levels. Aspirations for satisfying, creative, self-fulfilling jobs, fostered by extended schooling, could not be realized, not only because of the monotonous, rigid jobs, but also because of the unattractive, manual, and heavy jobs which were the concomitant of the Soviet Union's backward technology.

In Poland as well, expansion of education to meet the needs of technocratic socialism during the Gierek regime soon had negative consequences. Economic development lagged behind the rate of growth in educational attainment. Education, instead of helping to fulfill expectations regarding upward mobility, eventually became a source of frustration and increasing dissatisfaction. Self-management could help accomplish aspirations of fulfillment and self-realization. In Yugoslavia too, the increasing number of work stoppages and strikes during the 1970s indicates how expectations raised by the egalitarian rhetoric of self-management of the previous decades were blocked. As a result, the lack of exercise of real power and economic equality among workers created the need for reevaluation, as well as an extension of the self-management system.

IMPACT OF OUTSIDE FACTORS AND MODELS

Specific socioeconomic circumstances endemic in each country promote the need for workers' participation schemes. Outside political or economic factors and developments can also have a significant impact in this respect. A country's experience with worker participation can serve as a learning experience and can create an indirect pressure for another country to consider the participative approach to management. Since its application, the Yugoslav self-management system has been studied and analyzed by scholars and elites in a number of countries all over the world. In the midst of the 1968 Czechoslovakian reform, for instance, the Yugoslav notion of self-management was examined and contested, and the first councils established had functions similar to their counterparts in Yugoslavia. Based on the negative aspect of the Yugoslav experience regarding the domination of councils by technocratic elites and thus the unequal distribution of power, objections and criticisms were raised as soon as the same pattern seemed to emerge in Czechoslovakia. The Yugoslav experience with self-management has also inspired research and influenced developments in the West.

Gorbachev's recent efforts to restructure the economy and introduce worker participative structures have been watched carefully in both West and East and have encouraged developments for more democracy throughout Eastern Europe. In 1990, the world anxiously observed the daring macroeconomic experiment Poland launched, as the country attempted to immediately transform its economy through the so-called shock therapy from a centrally planned economy to an open market economy. This plan, which is the brainchild of Jeffrey Sachs, a Harvard economist, entails among other measures, cutbacks in government subsidies, closing down inefficient firms, and stabilizing the currency. According to some projections, 30 percent of the workforce could be temporarily out of work. Although some optimists argue that most of these people will find more productive work, others caution about the possibility of increased worker unrest, as workers once again have to face the contradictions of market reforms (Weschler, 1990: 207–208).

These are not the only national experiences that have aroused interest and have served as models to other countries. The German codetermination model has also been studied extensively worldwide. It was closely studied in England and in the Scandinavian countries, for instance, when debates regarding the merits and disadvantages of worker representation on the board of directors emerged in those countries. Furthermore, in Norway in the early 1960s, Thorsrud and Emery, after a careful evaluation of the Yugoslav, German, British, and Norwegian experiences with worker representation at the board level, argued that worker representation at that level would not be an effective way to increase workers' power. Instead, evaluating in more positive terms the developments that were undertaken at the Tavistock Institute, they recommended autonomous group activities and more direct worker participation at the plant level. Their suggestion was put into practice, and the second phase of the Industrial Democracy Program started. Practices in Sweden, on the other hand, such as semiautonomous work teams and job enlargement and enrichment schemes, were also publicized and applied in the United States and in the Soviet Union.

The Japanese system of management, especially the practice of quality control circles, has been studied and applied by other countries, especially the United States, since these practices are perceived to contribute to Japan's strong competitive position within the world market. Finally, developments in the European Economic Community regarding workers' participation also show that practices in one country or area might have an impact on another. As mentioned above, EEC legislation on industrial democracy influenced French and English developments regarding workers' representation at the board level.

POWER, RESOURCES, AND SCHEMES OF WORKER PARTICIPATION

Worker participation in management of any type and at any level inherently contains the notion of power, since its application requires that workers gain some influence in decision-making processes and that traditional managerial prerogatives be eroded by the newly acquired worker rights. This is true even if we consider QWL projects, consultation schemes, and human relations tactics, such as job enlargement and job enrichment schemes.

Experiments have been conducted even in the United States, where participative schemes are generally very limited in terms of the influence workers exercise. There the initial goal was to make workers happy and eventually increase productivity. Yet, some of them reached the point (the Polaroid experiment being one of them) when workers' influence was perceived as undermining managerial prerogatives, and they were abruptly interrupted. The different types of participative mechanisms from simple consultation, to codetermination, to labor board representation merely reflect the degree of influence exercised by workers and the scope of issues covered under a specific scheme.

Worker participation in management challenges the traditional principle that managers must manage and workers must obey. It further contests the legitimacy and effectiveness of traditional technocratic and authoritarian work structures. We have also argued that redistribution of power among industrial actors, so that workers and their representatives can influence decisions that affect their working lives, cannot take place unless existing industrial practices, relations, and interests are challenged. It should also be emphasized that participation, whether the result of a rational choice or the outcome of a spontaneous demand, is variable and dynamic. Participation encompasses a variety of value orientations, assumptions, or ideologies that, in retrospect, inform a number of goals and objectives that participation schemes can serve. With this in mind, we can begin to understand the variety of participation schemes in the countries under consideration.

The initiative to introduce workers' participation in both Japan and the United States rests with management. Management in Japan, however, had a strong interest in initiating changes, given the tight labor market of the 1960s and early 1970s. Management in the United States, on the other hand, did not face similar challenges and therefore, did not have a strong incentive to innovate. Therefore, diffusion and institutionalization of participation schemes in the United States did not extend to the degree they did in Japan. Since management was in charge in Japan, it carefully controlled the work restructuring process by allowing workers to get involved, share information, and integrate themselves to accomplish company objectives. Union-management cooperative relations, rooted in the special conditions of industrialization and emergence of unionism in Japan, and the fact that union interests were not threatened by the new developments, help us understand why unions did not challenge the managerial initiatives and why participation did not manifest itself in forms other than joint consultation.

In the United States, because of the specific mode of industrial unionism and traditional union orientation toward control of job opportunities, managerial efforts to introduce QWL strategies have been perceived as threatening to the basic labor prerogatives and as a way to undermine union power. Traditional adversarial labor-management relations, and the fact that most of the new work systems were introduced in new, nonunionized plants, has further reinforced such union positions. Because of union skepticism and suspicion and because managerial leadership in the United States is neither ideologically committed nor forced to introduce new work structures, an organizational infrastructure has not been developed in the United States as in Japan. Therefore, participative work structures have been limited. However, the new structural and technological changes discussed above pose a real threat to the unions' survival. This possibility becomes more acute in cases where management initiates such participatory systems. In those cases the unions' legitimacy is seriously eroded. The recent tendency for joint union-management participation in QWL experiments reflects the need to protect union legitimacy and survival.

The Swedish unions during the 1960s also faced legitimacy problems and decided to collaborate with management toward participatory goals. The Swedish trade union movement, however, was in a very advantageous position in contrast to its American counterpart, since it was politically and organizationally very powerful. It was therefore able to influence management and advance its own demands. Since in the United States the goal of managerially initiated participation schemes is to improve quality of working life and hence productivity, rather than to increase industrial democracy, we can understand why such schemes have been introduced at the plant level. Given the traditional adversarial labor-management relations, we can understand why unions considered expansion of the scope of collective bargaining, to include matters once considered managerial prerogatives, to be a more appropriate way to expand workers' influence than worker representation at the board level. The labor movement's goal is not to take part in management and thus share the responsibility of such a strategy. Instead, by keeping their distinct and opposing position, the assumption is that unions can be more effective in protecting workers' interests.

In Germany, unions are ideologically committed to the goal of employee representation at the board level, and despite strong employer opposition, over the years they have pushed for legislation to accomplish such a goal. The national preoccupation with order and authority, and the tendency to resolve differences by integrating forces with conflicting interests within the context of a predictable institutional framework, have also had an impact in regard to the highly legalistic approach of workers' participation. Since the board is the higher level of managerial authority, a successful establishment of representation at that level could be accomplished by utilizing the strongest existing formal means available, such as legislation, rather than relying on bargaining.

Similar considerations can shed some light on the development of worker participative schemes in Scandinavian countries as well. Overall, the first participation schemes introduced in these countries, such as production committees and works councils, had primarily advisory and consultative functions regarding the immediate everyday aspects of management. Given the long tradition of collective bargaining in these countries, it was easy to establish them on a voluntary basis through bargaining. However, as unions changed their objectives and aspired to higher goals, the means to accomplish such goals changed too. Demands escalated beyond the everyday aspects of management to include critical, long-term objectives that challenged traditional managerial prerogatives and capital's interests. It was imperative, therefore, to institute such demands through higher means.

Indeed, as unions demanded codetermination rights and representation of labor interests at higher managerial levels, the bargaining approach was abandoned and legislation was sought instead. Of course, the political climate facilitated such development. The Social Democratic party had been in power continuously for many years and was supportive of participatory goals. In England, too, despite the traditional bargaining approach to industrial relations, when the TUC attempted to introduce worker representation on the supervisory boards, it pushed for legislation in sharp opposition to its long voluntaristic approach. As discussed above, structural and technological developments had made the bargaining approach inadequate. The defensive union position could not be helpful in enabling unions to affect those developments that had a great impact on working-class lives and interests.

What differentiates Europe from the United States most is that in Europe not only has the issue of workers' participation been pushed by the unions, but it has also become a political issue debated at the national level. The issue there is not so much whether, but *how*, to introduce workers' participation. State intervention is far more common in Europe than in the United States, and therefore reliance on the legislative approach to introduce participation schemes can be expected there, especially given the strong affiliation of political parties with labor unions. In the United States, the state's traditional laissez-faire position, the unions' and government's lack of ideological commitment, the fact that the unions are on the decline have prevented the application of a legislative approach. The most important initiatives, therefore, come from managers influenced by the human relations tradition, who are not the most likely candidates to push for legislation.

Since free collective bargaining is not allowed in the state socialist countries, the legislative approach to workers' participation has also been followed there. Ideologically, the party plays the most important role by controlling and satisfying society's needs. Therefore, the state must intervene in order to institutionalize and control basic aspects of life, including industrial relations. As discussed above, the Yugoslav case differs substantially from the other state socialist countries with respect to the party's role in the society. Although a basic reason for introducing self-management was to legitimize its own existence, the party has not lost its leading position in the society. However, the whole ideology of self-management is based on decentralizing state authority and control through the direct participation of people in the decision-making process of self-managed political and economic units. The Basic Law enacted in 1950 indicated that the state ceased to be the formal owner of the means of production. Instead, workers were the formal owners of social property and were responsible through their councils for managing that property. Therefore, far-reaching changes affecting the whole fabric of the society, like those introduced since the early 1950s in Yugoslavia, required a powerful institutional means to accomplish them.

There is a big difference between the legislative approach adopted in European capitalist and that adopted in the state socialist countries. Unions in Western Europe, depending on their ideological orientation, political strength, and mobilizing activity, can push for enactment of legislation to introduce workers' participation and can also safeguard the formally given rights and press for further changes. In the state socialist countries, such changes are unlikely to occur through the formal union structure, since unions are incorporated into the formal power structure dominated by the party. Unions are expected to further the interests of the enterprise as a whole, and harmony of interests is assumed regarding the industrial actors.

There are exceptions to this rule. During the 1968 crisis in Czechoslovakia, the labor movement was put in a strained position to support participatory goals and mobilize the working class toward that goal, since its legitimacy was seriously threatened. The theme of legitimacy thus comes up in both state socialist and market economies, though for different reasons. The Solidarity movement in Poland is another exception to the rule. In the 1980–1981 period, Solidarity was able to mobilize about 10 million Poles around issues of economic and political democratization, including self-management. With all the dramatic changes that are currently taking place in Poland, the union's legitimacy is under question again, as the Solidarity-backed, first democratic government begins its austerity measures to ameliorate the serious economic conditions. Solidarity itself has been trapped into supporting and taking responsibility for economic austerity, especially for keeping wages down and increasing food prices. In contrast, we can observe a completely different situation in Yugoslavia, where the recently won democratic freedoms have allowed the unions in that country to become increasingly militant. Without taking responsibility for economic austerity, their role has instead been to make sure that austerity is equitably distributed among all social strata (Denitch, 1990c: 151). It remains to be seen how the newly democratic rights in the Soviet Union and Eastern Europe will change the structure and traditional functions of the unions in those countries. Thus far, the first signs seem promising for a greater role of unions in advancing workers' interests.

In Western Europe, the initiative for workers' participation has come primarily from the unions in an effort to curtail management's unilateral decision-making prerogatives and to establish democracy in the workplace. The ideological commitment to this goal, as well as the organizational capacity and political strength of unions, however, differ from one country to another, and this has a strong impact on the extent as well as the degree of workers' participation in each country. In France, for instance, the union movement is numerically weak and is divided politically and organizationally. These conditions, and the fact that CGT, the biggest union, opposes reformist solutions such as workers' participation, explains why the spread of participatory work structures is limited and workers' rights in the existing schemes are confined mostly to consultation and information. In England, it could be argued that the existing shopfloor job control preempted the need for further participative schemes. The long tradition of voluntarism in industrial relations worked against the utilization of legislation to expand workers' control. Given the long history of opposition, collective bargaining is the major form of workers' participation there. Worker participation in management is generally viewed with suspicion, as a way to co-opt workers and undermine unions. In order to avoid these problems, when TUC considered worker representation at the board level, it favored parity representation on a single-tier board. The labor movement was divided on the issue, however. The fact that unions are not particularly strong, and are unable to mobilize support for the independent incumbency of the Labor party in government, worked against such a goal.

In contrast to English unions, unions in Germany have pushed for the legislative approach to workers' participation. Despite the long tradition of worker participation at the plant/company level, as well as supervisory boards via statutory regulations, the labor movement's weakness, its inability to supply the Social Democrats with the support needed to hold an exclusive position in government, and its lack of a common ideological base to mobilize workers explain the limited success of the codetermination model. Codetermination regarding parity representation has not expanded to the degree envisaged. For the reasons just mentioned, and because of the successful mobilization of capital's political and economic power, the participation model has been designed to protect the employer's ultimate decision-making power. Furthermore, works councils, despite their formally approved rights, have served primarily as a way to integrate workers, rather than to expand their power, mostly because unions have failed to mobilize workers' support toward accomplishing real codetermination.

The opposite has happened in Scandinavia. Because of the powerful role of unions, integration was avoided there. When, upon the employers' resistance, negotiations to expand workers' control rights failed in the 1960s, the strong, centralized, politically powerful labor movement was able to escalate its demands and mobilize workers' support. It also succeeded slowly through the years in enacting legislation that expanded workers' decision-making power. The transfer of control rights to workers (and recently, in Sweden, of income rights as well) is impressive, and we would perceive it as threatening to employers' interests. Unions did face strong opposition from the employers. However, we also have to remember that all these reforms have taken place progressively through the years, and at no particular point in time have they seriously threatened the stability of the enterprise or the economy. Therefore, employers did not view them with great fear.

This safe element of reform plays an important role in regard to the extent and outcome of participative schemes, not only in Western industrialized countries, but also in state socialist countries. There is, of course, a difference. In the state socialist countries the threat of the reform is perceived mostly in political rather than economic terms. The workers' councils that emerged in Poland in 1956, for example, assumed managerial responsibilities that undermined party control, and this basically caused their demise. In Hungary during the same year, demands for self-management expanded to political demands and therefore threatened the crucial strategic and political interests of the Soviet Union, especially because Nagy's leadership followed the popular demand for national independence. The result is very well known: The country was invaded and the councils were dissolved.

These political constraints were well understood in Poland in 1980, as Solidarity carefully set up the boundaries of its self-limiting revolution. The deepening of the economic and political crisis, however, inevitably politicized the self-management movement and caused its failure. In Hungary, on the other hand, the initiative of reform since the mid-1960s comes from the party, which slowly throughout the years has controlled the extent of change. Similarly, until very recently at least, in the Soviet Union reforms were not introduced because of major political or economic crisis. The party was the chief manipulator of the reform, and changes there never seriously challenged its power.

This does not necessarily mean that opposition to the introduced reforms does not exist. Gorbachev's recent attempts to decentralize the economy and reform the workplace, for instance, have met with skepticism and resistance ranging from the general public to members of the Communist party and bureaucrats, thus causing delays in implementing the reform. Recent market reforms, including participative reforms in other Eastern European countries, Yugoslavia, and China, have met resistance from various social groups, whose interests are threatened by the proposed changes. Beyond the *nomenklatura* system's resistance in all these societies, a new element that has to be taken into account with regard to the reforms is the increasing rate of discontent and opposition within the workforce and the overall population there.

As people in Soviet-type societies increasingly face the contradictions of market reforms, the more potential exists in these societies to see more demands for reforms stemming from below. Recently, in East Germany angry farmers brought their cows inside the Parliament to protest high prices and unfair competition from imported Western products. Meanwhile, factory workers, being accustomed to employment security, were protesting the increasing unemployment rates that market reforms had brought. In Czechoslovakia, the euphoria of Havel's democratically elected government aside, workers in the steel and coal mines are skeptical about the results of the planned changes (Blumberg, 1990). In China effective organized resistance has not been in evidence since Tiananmen Square, but there is no doubt that the seeds of discontent and popular dissatisfaction with austerity measures do exist. There is no question, too, that the regime cannot ignore the increasing popular discontent and low worker morale. The question is whether the government will address the deep economic problems through democratic changes, given the risks those changes entail for its entrenched interests. As of this writing, the future does not seem bright. As we have argued many times throughout this book, workers' participation is a political issue in both market-oriented and plan-based societies. It remains to be seen how the increased international competition and the huge transformations that take place in both West and East will transform the power relations within the societies and thus affect the future development of participative mechanisms.

Bibliography

Afanasyev, Yuri, and Tatyana Zaslavskaya
1990 "Socialist Voices in the Soviet Union." *Dissent* 37: 192–193.
Aganbegyan, Abel
1989 "What Perestroika Means for Soviet Enterprises." *International Labour Review* 128: 85–101.
1988 *The Economic Challenge of Perestroika*. Bloomington and Indianapolis: Indiana University Press.
Albrecht, Sandra
1981 "Preconditions for Increased Workers' Influence: Factors in the Swedish Case." *Sociology of Work and Occupations* 8: 252–271.
1980 "Politics, Bureaucracy, and Worker Participation: The Swedish Case." *Journal of Applied Behavioral Science* 16: 299–315.
Albrecht, Sandra, and Steven Deutsch
1983 "The Challenge of Economic Democracy: The Case of Sweden." *Economic and Industrial Democracy* 4: 287–320.
Allen, Christopher
1987 "Worker Participation and the German Trade Unions: An Unfulfilled Dream?" in Carmen Sirianni (ed.), *Worker Participation and the Politics of Reform*, pp. 174–197. Philadelphia: Temple University Press.
Andors, Stephen (ed.)
1977 *Workers and Workplaces in China*. White Plains, N.Y.: M. E. Sharpe, Inc.
Arzenšek, Vladimir
1978 "Managerial Legitimacy and Organizational Conflict," in Josip Obradović and William N. Dunn (eds.), *Workers' Self-Management and Organizational Power in Yugoslavia*, pp. 374–389. Pittsburgh: Center for International Studies.
Åsard, Erik
1986 "Industrial and Economic Democracy in Sweden: From Consensus to Confrontation." *European Journal of Political Research* 14: 207–219.

Azumi, Koya, et al.

1985   "Technology and Organization Design in Japan Versus the West: Woodward Transplanted and Revised." Paper presented at the Annual Meetings of the American Sociological Association, Washington, D.C.

Bachaman, David

1988   "Politics and Political Reform in China." *Current History*, September 1988: 249–252, 275–277.

Batstone, Eric, et al.

1983   *Unions on the Board: An Experiment in Industrial Democracy*. London: Basil Blackwell.

Bean, R.

1985   *Comparative Industrial Relations. An Introduction to Cross-National Perspectives*. London: Croom Helm.

Beijing Review

1980   "Hua Guofeng's Speech at the Third Session of the Fifth National People's Congress." Reprinted in *Beijing Review* 38: 12–29.

Bell, Daniel

1990a   "As We Go into the Nineties." *Dissent* 37: 171–176.

1990b   "On the Fate of Communism." *Dissent* 37: 187–188.

1973   *The Coming of Post-Industrial Society*. New York: Basic Books.

Bellace, Janice, and Howard Gospel

1983   "Disclosure of Information to Trade Unions: A Comparative Perspective." *International Labor Review* 122: 57–75.

Bennett, Gordon

1985   "Economy, Polity, and Reform in China." *Comparative Politics* 18: 85–100.

Blazejczyk, M., et al. (eds.)

1978   *Workers' Participation in Management in Poland*. International Institute for Labour Studies, Research Series No. 30.

Bluestone, Barry, and Bennet Harrison

1982   *The Deindustrialization of America. Plant Closings, Community Abandonment, and the Dismantling of Basic Industry*. New York: Basic Books, Inc.

Bluestone, Irving

1980   "How Quality-of-Worklife Projects Work for the United Auto Workers." *Monthly Labour Review* 103: 39–41.

Blumberg, Abraham

1990   "Happiness in Czechoslovakia." *Dissent* 37: 213–218.

Blumberg, Paul

1971   *Industrial Democracy: The Sociology of Participation*. London: Constable.

Bornstein, M. (ed.)

1974   *Comparative Economic Systems: Modes and Cases*. Homewood, Ill.: Richard D. Irwin, Inc.

Bornstein, Stephen, and Keitha Fine

1977   "Worker Control in France: Recent Political Developments," in G. David Garson (ed.), *Worker Self-Management in Industry*. The West European Experience, pp. 152–191. New York: Praeger Special Studies.

Bouvin, Ake

1977   "New Swedish Legislation on Democracy at the Workplace." *International Labour Review* 115: 131–143.

Bowers, Stephen
1983   "An Assessment of the Polish Crisis: The East European View." *Journal of Social, Political and Economic Studies* 7: 257–268.
Brannen, Peter
1983a   *Authority and Participation in Industry*. New York: St. Martin's Press.
1983b   "Worker Directors—An Approach to Analysis: The Case of the British Steel Corporation," in C. Crouch and F. Heller (eds.), *Organizational Democracy & Political Processes*, vol. 1 in *International Yearbook of Organizational Democracy*, pp. 121–138. New York: John Wiley and Sons.
Brannen, Peter, E. Batstone, D. Fatchett and P. White
1976   *The Worker Directors: A Sociology of Participation*. London: Hutchinsan.
Braverman, Harry
1984   "The Real Meaning of Taylorism," in Frank Fischer and Carmen Sirianni (eds.), *Critical Studies in Organization and Bureaucracy*, pp. 79–85. Philadelphia: Temple University Press.
1974   *Labor and Monopoly Capital: The Degradation of Work in the Twentieth Century*. New York: Monthly Review Press.
Brecher, Jeremy
1978   "Uncovering the Hidden History of the American Workplace." *Review of Radical Political Economy* 10: 1–23.
Breslauer, George
1989   "Linking Gorbachev's Domestic and Foreign Policies." *Journal of International Affairs* 42: 267–282.
Briggs, Pamela
1988   "The Japanese at Work: Illusions of the Ideal," in Mike Parker and Jane Slaughter (eds.), *Choosing Sides: Unions and the Team Concept*, pp. 60–64. Boston: South End Press.
Brody, David
1980   *Workers in Industrial America. Essays on the Twentieth Century Struggle*. New York: Oxford University Press.
Brumberg, Abraham
1989   "Poland: State and/or Society. The See-Saw Between Government and Solidarity." *Dissent* Winter 1989: 47–55.
Bruyn, Severyn and Litsa Nicolaou
1988   *International Issues in Social Economy: Studies in the United States and Greece*. New York: Praeger Publications.
Burawoy, Michael
1983   "Between the Labor Process and the State: The Changing Face of Factory Regimes Under Advanced Capitalism." *American Sociological Review* 48: 587–605.
Burawoy, Michael, and János Lukács
1985   "Mythologies of Work: A Comparison of Firms in State Socialism and Advanced Capitalism." *American Sociological Review* 50: 723–737.
Burks, R. V.
1973   "The Political Implications of Economic Reform," in Morris Bornstein (ed.), *Plan and Market: Economic Reform in Eastern Europe*. New Haven, Conn.: Yale University Press.
Burns, John
1989   "China's Governance: Political Reform in a Turbulent Environment." *The China Quarterly* 119: 481–518.

Burns, Tom, et al.
1979   *Work and Power. The Liberation of Work and the Control of Political Power.*
       London: Sage Studies in International Sociology.
Business Week
1981   "The New Industrial Relations," in U.S. Department of Labor, 1985, *Perspectives on Labor-Management Cooperation*, pp. 1–8. (Reprinted from the May issue of *Business Week*.)
Carnoy, Martin, and Derek Shearer
1980   *Economic Democracy: The Challenge of the 1980s.* New York: M. E. Sharpe, Inc.
Carroll, Glenn, and Karl Mayer
1985   "Job-Shift Patterns in the Federal Republic of Germany: The Effects of Social Class, Industrial Sector, and Organizational Size." Paper presented at the Annual Meeting of the American Sociological Association, Washington, D.C.
Case, John, and Rosemary C. R. Taylor (eds.)
1979   *Co-ops, Communes and Collectives. Experiments in Social Change in the 1960s and 1970s.* New York: Pantheon Books.
Central Committee of the Communist Party of China
1984   Decision of the Central Committee of the Communist Party of China on Reform of the Economic Structure, adopted by the 12th at its Third Plenary Session on October 20, 1984, reprinted in *Beijing Review*, 27: III–XVI.
Charlton, Jacqueline
1984   "The Rise and Fall of Employee Participation in British Public Administration." *Economic and Industrial Democracy* 5: 261–272.
Cheng, Chu-Yuan
1988   "China's Economy: New Strategies and Dilemmas." *Current History*, September 1988: 253–256; 281–302.
Clarke, Christopher
1986   "Rejuvenation, Reorganization and the Dilemmas of Modernization in Post-Deng China." *Journal of International Affairs* 39: 119–132.
Clegg, Hugh Armstrong
1976   *Trade Unionism under Collective Bargaining.* London: Basil Blackwell.
1960   *A New Approach to Industrial Democracy.* Oxford: Basil Blackwell.
Coates, K., and T. Topham
1974   *The New Unionism. The Case for Workers' Control.* London: Penguin.
Coates, K., and T. Topham (eds.)
1970   *Workers' Control.* London: Panther Modern Society.
Cohen, Mitchell
1990   "Creating the New-Old Europe." *Dissent* 37: 161–170.
Cole, Robert
1987   "The Macropolitics of Organizational Change: A Comparative Analysis of the Spread of Small-Group Activities," in Carmen Sirianni (ed.), *Worker Participation and the Politics of Reform*, pp. 34–66. Philadelphia: Temple University Press.
1985   "The Macropolitics of Organizational Change: A Comparative Analysis of the Spread of Small-Group Activities." *Administrative Science Quarterly* 30: 560–585.

1982 "Diffusion of Participatory Work Structures in Japan, Sweden and the United States," in Paul Goodman and Associates (eds.), *Change in Organizations*, pp. 184–185, San Francisco: Jossey-Bass.

1980 "Will QC Circles Work in the U.S.?" *Quality Progress* 8: 30–33.

1979 *Work, Mobility, and Participation: A Comparative Study of American and Japanese Industry*. Berkeley: University of California Press.

Cole, Robert, and Dennis Tachiki

1983 "A Look at U.S. and Japanese Quality Circles: Preliminary Comparisons." *The Quality Circles Journal* 6: 10–16.

Cole, Robert, and Andrew Walder

1984 "The Macropolitics of Organizational Change: A Four-Nation Comparative Analysis of the Spread of New Work Structures." (Unpublished manuscript.)

Coleman, R. J.

1978 "Employee Participation in the U.S. Enterprise." *British Journal of Industrial Relations* 16: 175–195.

Comisso, Turkish Ellen

1987 "Industrial Relations and Economic Reform in Socialism: Hungary and Yugoslavia Compared," in Carmen Sirianni (ed.), *Worker Participation and the Politics of Reform*, pp. 224–266. Philadelphia: Temple University Press.

1985 "Industrial Relations and Economic Reform in Socialism: Yugoslavia and Hungary Compared." University of California. (Unpublished manuscript.)

1981 "Workers' Councils and Labor Unions: Some Objective Tradeoffs." *Politics and Society* 10: 251–279.

1980 "Yugoslavia in the 1970s: Self-Management and Bargaining." *Journal of Comparative Economics* 4: 192–208.

1979 *Workers' Control Under Plan and Market. H Implications of Yugoslav Self-Management*. New Haven, Conn.: Yale University Press.

Comisso, Turkish Ellen, and P. Marer

1986 "The Economics and Politics of Reform in Hungary." *International Organization* 40: 421–455.

Constitution of the People's Republic of China

1982 Constitution of the People's Republic of China. Adopted by the Fifth National People's Congress of the People's Congress of the People's Republic of China, reprinted in *Beijing Review*, December 27: 10–18.

Cordova, E.

1982 "Workers' Participation in Decisions Within Enterprises: Recent Trends and Problems." *International Labour Review* 121: 125–141.

Cornfield, Daniel

1987a "Labor-Management Cooperation or Managerial Control," in Daniel Cornfield (ed.), *Workers, Managers, and Technological Change*, pp. 331–353. New York: Plenum Press.

Cornfield, Daniel (ed.)

1987b *Workers, Managers, and Technological Change. Emerging Patterns of Labor Relations*. New York: Plenum Press.

Coser, Lewis

1990 "The Intellectuals in Soviet Reform." *Dissent* 37: 181–183.

Cressey, Peter, et al.

1985 *Just Managing: Authority and Democracy in Industry*. Milton Keynes: Open University Press.

Crocker, L. Olga, et al.
1984   *Quality Circles: A Guide to Participation and Productivity*. New York: New American Library.
Cross, Gary
1983   "Redefining Workers' Control: Rationalization, Labor Time, and Union Politics in France, 1900–1928," in James Cronin and Carmen Sirianni (eds.), *Work, Community, and Power*, pp. 143–173. Philadelphia: Temple University Press.
Crouch, C., and F. Heller (eds.)
1983   *Organizational Democracy and Political Process*. New York: John Wiley and Sons, Ltd.
Dachler, Peter, and Bernhard Wilpert
1978   "Conceptual Dimensions and Boundaries of Participation in Organizations: A Critical Evaluation." *Administrative Science Quarterly* 23: 1–25.
Dahl, Robert
1990   "Social Reality and Free Markets." *Dissent* 37: 224–228.
1974   "Power to the Workers?," in B. Silverman and M. Yanowitch (eds.), *The Worker in "Post-Industrial" Capitalism*. New York: Free Press.
Davis, Louis, and Charles Sullivan
1980   "A Labor-Management Contract and Quality of Working Life." *Journal of Occupational Behavior* 1: 29–41.
Dawisha, Karen
1988   *Eastern Europe: Gorbachev and Reform, the Great Challenge*. Cambridge: Cambridge University Press.
Deem, Rosemary, and G. Salaman (eds.)
1985   *Work, Culture and Society*. Milton Keynes: Open University Press.
Delamotte, Yves
1977   "The 'Reform of the Enterprise' in France." *Annals of the American Academy of Political and Social Sciences* 431: 54–62.
1976   "Working Conditions and Government Policy: Some Western European Approaches." *International Labour Review* 114: 139–154.
Della Rocca, Giuseppe
1987   "Improving Participation: The Negotiation of the New Technology in Italy and Europe," in Carmen Sirianni (ed.), *Worker Participation and the Politics of Reform*, pp. 140–173. Philadelphia: Temple University Press.
DeMasi, Guido, and Giacomo Marramao
1976   "Councils and State in Weimar Germany." *Telos* 28: 3–35.
Denitch, Bogdan
1990a   "The Triumph of Capitalism?" *Dissent* 37: 177–180.
1990b   "First Free Elections in Yugoslavia." *Dissent* 37: 303–305.
1990c   "Reform and Conflict in Yugoslavia." *Dissent* 37: 151–153.
1989   "Yugoslavia: The Limits of Reform." *Dissent*, Winter 1989: 78–85.
1976   *The Legitimation of a Revolution: The Yugoslav Case*. New Haven, Conn.: Yale University Press.
Derber, Charles, and William Schwartz
1983   "Toward a Theory of Worker Participation." *Sociological Inquiry* 53: 61–78.
de Weydenthal, Jan
1981   "Poland: Workers and Politics," in Jan Triska and Gati (eds.), *Blue-Collar Workers in Eastern Europe*, pp. 187–209. London: George Allen and Unwin.

Diamant, Alfred
1977   "Democratizing the Workplace: The Myth and Reality of *Mitbestimmung* in the Federal Republic of Germany," in G. David Garson (ed.), *Worker Self-Management in Industry. The West European Experience*, pp. 25–47. New York: Praeger Special Studies.

Dickens, William, and J. Leonard
1985   "Accounting for the Decline in Union Membership, 1950–1980." *Industrial and Labor Relations Review* 38: 323–334.

Dienstbier, Jiri
1989   "Gorbachev and Czechoslovakian Reform." *New Politics* 2: 137–151.

Draper, Theodore
1987   "Soviet Reformers: From Lenin to Gorbachev." *Dissent* 34: 287–301.

Dubofsky, Melvyn
1985   *Technological Change and Workers' Movements. Explorations in the World-Economy*. Beverly Hills, Calif.: Sage Publications, Inc.

Edwards, Christine, and Elmund Heery
1985   "The Incorporation of Workplace Trade Unionism? Some Evidence from the Mining Industry." *Sociology* 19: 345–363.

Edwards, Richard
1979   *Contested Terrain. The Transformation of the Workplace in the Twentieth Century*. New York: Basic Books.

Eiger, Norman
1986   "Education for Workplace Democracy in Sweden and West Germany," in R. N. Stern and S. McCarthy (eds.), *The Organizational Practice of Democracy*, vol. 3, in *International Yearbook of Organizational Democracy*, pp. 105–124. New York: John Wiley and Sons.

Elvander, Nils
1990   "Incomes Policies in the Nordic Countries." *International Labour Review* 129: 1–21.

Emery, F. E., and E. Thorsrud
1976   *Form and Content in Industrial Democracy*. London: Tavistock Publications.
1969   *Democracy at Work*. Nijhoff: Leiden.

Ericson, Richard
1989   "Soviet Economic Reforms. The Motivation and Content of Perestroika." *Journal of International Affairs* 42: 317–331.

Esping-Andersen, Gösta
1981   "From Welfare State to Democratic Socialism: The Politics of Economic Democracy in Denmark and Sweden." *Political Power and Social Theory* 2: 11–140.
1978   "Social Class, Social Democracy, and the State." *Comparative Politics* 11: 42–57.

Espinosa, Juan, and Andrew Zimbalist
1978   *Economic Democracy. Workers' Participation in Chilean Industry 1970–73*. New York: Academic Press.

Feher, Yuri
1990   "Versions of Economic Reform." *Dissent* 37: 348–352.

Fischer, Frank, and Carmen Sirianni
1984   *Critical Studies in Organization and Bureaucracy*. Philadelphia: Temple University Press.

Fišera, Vladimir
1978 *Workers' Councils in Czechoslovakia 1968–1969*. London: Allison and Busby.
Fisher, Malcolm
1978 "Labor Participation in the Management of Business Firms in Great Britain," in Svetozar Pejovich (ed.), *The Codetermination Movement in the West*, pp. 47–57. Lexington, Mass.: Lexington Books.
Flakierski, Henryk (ed.)
1985–1986 "Economic Reform and Income Distribution: Problems and Issues." *Eastern European Economics* 24: 3–44.
Foy, Nancy, and Herman Gadon
1976 "Worker Participation: Contrasts in Three Countries. *Harvard Business Review* 54: 71–83.
Frankenstein, John
1988 "Chinese Foreign Trade in the 1980s." *Current History*, September 1988: 257–260, 272–275.
Fraser, Steve
1983a "Industrial Democracy in the 1980s." *Socialist Review* 13: 99–122.
1983b "The 'New Unionism' and the 'New Economic Policy', " in James Cronin and Carmen Sirianni (eds.), *Work, Community, and Power*, pp. 173–197. Philadelphia: Temple University Press.
Freund, A. Richard
1980 "Quality Technology—A Bridge to International Cooperation." *Quality Progress* 13: 32–33.
Fry, John (ed.)
1979 *Industrial Democracy and Labour Market Policy in Sweden*. Oxford: Pergamon Press.
Fuller, Stephen
1980 "How Quality-of-Worklife Projects Work for General Motors." *Monthly Labor Review* 103: 37–39.
Furstenberg, Friedrich
1977 "West German Experience with Industrial Democracy." *The Annals of the American Academy of Political and Social Science* 431: 44–53.
Gallie, Duncan
1983 *Social Inequality and Class Radicalism in France and Britain*. Cambridge: Cambridge University Press.
Garson, G. David (ed.)
1977 *Worker Self-Management in Industry. The West European Experience*. New York: Praeger Publications.
Gevers, J.K.M.
1983 "Worker Participation in Health and Safety in the EEC: The Role of Representative Institutions." *International Labour Review* 122: 411–428.
Goetschy, Janine
1983 "A New Future for Industrial Democracy in France?" *Economic and Industrial Democracy* 4: 85–101.
Gold, Charlotte
1986 "Labor-Management Committees: Confrontation, Coaptation, or Cooperation?" No. 29. *New York State School of Industrial and Labor Relations*. Ithaca, N.Y.: Cornell University, ILR Press.

Gold, Evan Michael
1989   "An Introduction to Labor Law." ILR Bulletin 66. *New York State School of Industrial and Labor Relations*. Ithaca, N.Y.: Cornell University.

Goldman, Marshall
1990a   "The Soviet Economy and the Need for Reform." *The Annals of the American Academy of Political and Social Science* 507: 26–43.

1990b   "Party Meeting Has Gorbachev on the Wire." *The Boston Sunday Globe*, July 8: 67, 70.

1987   *Gorbachev's Challenge: Economic Reform in the Age of High Technology*. New York: W. W. Norton and Co.

Gorbachev, Michail
1987   *Perestroika: New Thinking for Our Country and the World*. New York: Harper and Row (in Greek).

Gordon, David, Richard Edwards, and Michael Reich
1982   *Segmented Work, Divided Workers. The Historical Transformation of Labor in the United States*. Cambridge: Cambridge University Press.

Gorlice, Josef
1986   "Introduction to the Hungarian Democratic Opposition." *Berkeley Journal of Sociology* 31: 117–165.

Graham, Gregory
1985   "QWL: Progress or Retreat for Trade Unions." Paper presented at the Annual Meetings of the American Sociological Association, Washington, D.C.

Granick, David
1974   "The Hungarian Economic Reform," in M. Bornstein (ed.), *Comparative Economic Systems*. Homewood, Ill.: Richard D. Irwin.

Greenberg, S. Edward
1986   *Workplace Democracy. The Political Effects of Participation*. Ithaca, N.Y.: Cornell University Press.

1983   "Context and Cooperation: Systematic Variation in the Political Effects of Workplace Democracy." *Economic and Industrial Democracy* 4: 191–225.

Griffin, Larry, et al.
1986   "Capitalism and Labor Organization." *American Sociological Review* 51: 147–167.

Grunberg, Leon
1986   "Workplace Relations in the Economic Crisis: A Comparison of a British and a French Automobile Plant." *Sociology* 20: 503–529.

1985   "Safety, Productivity and the Social Relations in Production: An Empirical Study of Worker Co-operatives." Paper presented at the Annual Meetings of the American Sociological Association, Washington, D.C.

Grzybowski, Kazimierz
1957   "Polish Workers' Councils." *Journal of Central European Affairs* 17: 272–286.

1956   "Trade Unions in Communist Poland." *Problems of Communism* 5: 16–21.

Guest, David
1986   "Workers' Participation and Personnel Policy in the United Kingdom: Some Case Studies." *International Labour Review* 125: 685–702.

Gunn, Christopher Eaton
1984   *Workers' Self-Management in the United States*. Ithaca, N.Y.: Cornell University Press.

Gustavsen, Bjorn
1986   "Training for Work Environment Reform in Norway," in R. N. Sterns and S. McCarthy (eds.), *The Organizational Practice of Democracy*, vol. 3 of *International Yearbook of Organizational Democracy*, pp. 125–139. New York: John Wiley and Sons.

Gustavsen, Bjorn, and Gerry Hunnius
1981   *New Patterns of Work Reform: The Case of Norway*. Oslo: Universitetsforlaget.

Hall, J. R. Carby
1977   *Worker Participation in Europe*. London: Croom Helm.

Hammond, Kenneth
1982   "Rise and Fall of a Chinese Version of Solidarity." *New York Times*, February 18: 24.

Hanami, Tadashi
1981   *Labor Relations in Japan Today*. Tokyo: Kodansha International.

Hancock, M. Donald
1978   "Productivity, Welfare, and Participation in Sweden and West Germany." *Comparative Politics* 11: 4–23.

Hardt, John, and Carl H. McMillan (eds.)
1988   *Planned Economies Confronting the Challenges of the 1980s*. Cambridge: Cambridge University Press.

Harrington, Michael
1989a   "Markets and Plans. Is the Market Necessarily Capitalist? Could It Work with a Democratic Socialist Economy?" *Dissent*, Winter 1989: 56–70.
1989b   "Toward a New Socialism." *Dissent*, Spring 1989: 153–163.

Harrison, Roger
1976   *Workers' Participation in Western Europe*. London: Institute of Personnel Management.

Hearn, June
1977   "W(h)ither the Trade Unions in China?" *Journal of Industrial Relations* 19: 158–172.

Heclo, Hugh, and Henrik Madsen
1987   *Policy and Politics in Sweden*. Philadelphia: Temple University Press.

Helburn, B. I., and John C. Shearer
1984   "Human Resources and Industrial Relations in China: A Time of Ferment." *Industrial and Labor Relations Review* 38: 3–15.

Herrick, Neal Q.
1986   "Workplace Democracy: Learning from Mistakes." *Transaction of Social Science and Modern Society* 23: 30–36.

Hethy, L., and C. Mako
1977   "Workers' Direct Participation in Decisions in Hungarian Factories." *International Labour Review* 116: 9–21.

HEW (Health Education and Welfare) Report
1973   *Work in America*. Cambridge, Mass.: MIT Press.

Hewett, A. (ed.)
1988   *Reforming the Soviet Economy. Equality Versus Efficiency*. Washington, D.C.: The Brookings Institution.

Hill, Stephen
1981   *Competition and Control at Work. The New Industrial Sociology*. Cambridge, Mass.: MIT Press.

Hirschhorn, Larry
1984 *Beyond Mechanization: Work and Technology in a Post-Industrial Age.* Cambridge, Mass.: MIT Press.

Hirszowicz, Maria
1982 *Industrial Sociology: An Introduction.* New York: St. Martin's Press.

Hoagland, Jim
1987 "A Stagnating System Gropes for Solutions." *Washington Post*, April, 5, pp. A1, A20.

Hoffmann, Eric, and Robbin Laird
1985 *Technocratic Socialism. The Soviet Union in the Advanced Industrial Era.* Durham, N.C.: Duke University Press.

Hohmann, Hans-Hermann, et al. (eds.)
1975 *The New Economic Systems of Eastern Europe.* Berkeley: University of California Press.

Holland, David
1984 "Self-Management Without Solidarity." *Labour Focus on Eastern Europe* 7: 16–17.

Hollander, Paul
1975 "Comparing Socialist Systems: Ends and Results," in Carmelo Mesa-Lago and Carl Beck, *Comparative Socialist Systems: Essays on Politics and Economics.* Pittsburgh: University of Pittsburgh Center for International Studies.

Hong, Sek Neg
1984 "One Brand of Workplace Democracy: The Workers' Congress in the Chinese Enterprise." *Journal of Industrial Relations* 26: 57–75.

Howard, Robert, and Leslie Schneider
1987 "Worker Participation in Technological Change: Interests, Influence, and Scope," in Carmen Sirianni (ed.), *Worker Participation and the Politics of Reform*, pp. 67–93. Philadelphia: Temple University Press.

Howe, Irving
1990 "Soviet Transformation." *Dissent* 37: 133, 134.

Hunnius, Gerry, et al.
1973 *Workers' Control: A Reader on Labor and Social Change.* New York: Vintage Books.

Ichiyo, Muto
1983 "Interview with Muto Ichiyo: The Crises in the U.S.–Japan Relations, Japanese Labor and the Japanese Left." *The Insurgent Sociologist* 11: 23–36.

Industrial Democracy in Europe (IDE) Industrial Research Group
1981a *Industrial Democracy in Europe.* Vol. 1. Oxford: Clarendon Press.
1981b *European Industrial Relations.* Vol. 2. Oxford: Clarendon Press.

IDE (Industrial Democracy in Europe)
1977 *Industrial Democracy in Europe (IDE): An International Comparative Study. Social Science Information* 15: 177–203.

Inglehart, Ronald
1971 "The Silent Revolution in Europe: Intergenerational Change in Post-Industrial Societies." *American Political Science Review* 65: 991–1017.

International Labor Office (ILO)
1981 *Workers' Participation in Decisions Within Undertakings.* Geneva: International Labour Organization.

Ishikawa, Akihiro
1984   "Japanese Trade-Unionism in a Changing Environment." *International Social Science Journal* 36: 271–285.
Jacobson, Julius
1989   "Beijing to Moscow: The Cracks Widen." *New Politics* 2: 101–107.
Jain, Hem (with the collaboration of Genevieve Laloux Jain)
1980   *Worker Participation: Success and Problems*. New York: Praeger Publishers.
Jaruzelski, Wojciech
1988   "Socialism Is Not a Gift Workers Receive from History." *World Marxist Review* 31: 5–29.
Jecchinis, Chris
1986   *Preconditions for the Success of Workers' Participation in Management*. Athens, Greece: Manpower Employment Organization.
Jenkins, David
1974   "Industrial Democracy," in B. Silverman and M. Yanowitch (eds.), *The Worker in "Post-Industrial" Capitalism*. New York: Free Press.
1973   *Job Power: Blue and White Collar Democracy*. New York: Doubleday.
Jones, Derek
1977   "Worker Participation in Britain: Evaluation, Current Developments, and Prospects," in David Garson (ed.), *Worker Self-Management in Industry. The West European Experience*, pp. 97–152. New York: Praeger Publishers.
Jovanov, Neca
1978   "Strikes and Self-Management," in Josip Obradović and William N. Dunn, *Workers' Self-Management and Organizational Power in Yugoslavia*, pp. 339–374. Pittsburgh: Center for International Studies.
Junkerman, John
1982   "We Are Driven: Life on the Fast Line at Datsun." *Mother Jones* 7: 21–41.
Juran, J. M.
1978   "International Significance of the QC Circle Movement. Can Non-Japanese Cultures Apply This Concept of Using Workforce Creativity to Improve Performance?" *Quality Progress* 8: 18–21.
Kalleberg, Raqnvald
1985   "Work Environment Reform as Participatory Democratization. A Sociological Analysis of the Norwegian Work Environment Act." Paper presented to the American Sociological Association Congress, Washington, D.C.
Kanter, Rosabeth Moss
1983   *The Change Masters*. New York: Simon and Schuster.
1978   "Work in a New America." *Daedalus* 107: 47–78.
Karabel, Jerome
1990   "Why Gorbachev's Economic Reforms Won't Work." *The Boston Sunday Globe*, July 1: 88.
Kendall, Walter
1972   "Workers' Participation and Workers' Control: Aspects of the British Experience." First International Sociological Conference on Participation and Self-Management, Zagreb, vol. 3, pp. 57–69.
Kerr, C., et al. (eds.)
1962   *Industrialization and Industrial Man*. London: Heinemann.

Kesselman, Mark
1982   "Prospects for Democratic Socialism in Advanced Capitalism: Class Struggle and
       Compromise in Sweden and France." *Politics and Society* 11: 397–438.
King, Charles, and Mark van de Vall
1978   *Models of Industrial Democracy: Consultation, Co-determination and Workers'
       Management.* New York: New Babylon.
Kingston-Mann, Esther
1988   "Perestroika with a Human Face?" *Socialist Review* 1: 7–30.
Kiraly, Belace
1986   "The Armed Forces and the Working Class in the Hungarian Revolution, 1956."
       New Politics 1: 193–212.
Kis, Janos
1989   "Turning Point in Hungary." *Dissent*, Spring 1989: 235–241.
Klingel, Sally, and Ann Martin (eds.)
1988   *A Fighting Chance. New Strategies to Save Jobs and Reduce Costs. New York
       State of Industrial and Labor Relations.* Ithaca, N.Y.: Cornell University, ILR
       Press.
Kochan, Thomas (ed.)
1985   *Challenges and Choices Facing American Labor.* Cambridge, Mass.: MIT Press.
Kochan, Thomas, Harry Katz, and Robert McKersie
1986   *The Transformation of American Industrial Relations.* New York: Basic Books.
Kochan, Thomas, Harry Katz, and Nancy Mower
1985   "Worker Participation and American Unions," in Thomas Kochan (ed.), *Chal-
       lenges and Choices Facing American Labor*, pp. 271–306. Cambridge, Mass.:
       MIT Press.
1984   *Worker Participation and American Unions: Threat or Opportunity.* W. E. Upjohn
       Institute for Employment Research.
Kohak, Erazim
1990   "Can There Be a Central Europe?" *Dissent* 37: 194–197.
Kohn, Melvin (ed.)
1989   *Cross-National Research in Sociology.* Newbury Park, N.J.: Sage Publications.
Kolankiewicz, George
1982   "Employee Self-Management and Socialist Trade Unionism," in Jean Woodall
       (ed.), *Policy and Politics in Contemporary Poland*, pp. 129–148. New York: St.
       Martin's Press.
1981   "Poland 1980: The Working Class under Anomic Socialism," in J. Triska and
       C. Gati (eds.), *Blue-Collar Workers in Eastern Europe*, pp. 136–157. London:
       George Allen and Unwin.
1973   "The Polish Industrial Manual Working Class," in David Lane and George Kola
       (eds.), *Social Groups in Polish Society*, pp. 88–152. New York: Columbia Uni-
       versity Press.
Kostopoulos, Sotiris
1984   *Self-Management.* Athens, Greece: Stochastis (in Greek).
Kovanda, Karel
1977   "Works' Councils in Czechoslovakia, 1945–47." *Soviet Studies* 29: 255–269.
1976   "Czechoslovak Workers' Councils (1968–69)." *Telos* 28: 36–54.
Kusin, Vladimir
1972   *Political Grouping in the Czechoslovak Reform Movement.* New York: Columbia
       University Press.

236   BIBLIOGRAPHY

Kuttner, Robert
1986 "Unions, Economic Power and the State: New Problems, New Strategies, as Unions Regroup." *Dissent* 10: 33–44.
Kyn, Oldrich
1975 "Czechoslovakia," in Hans-Herman Hohmann et al., *The New Economic Systems in Eastern Europe*. Berkeley: University of California Press.
Laaksonen, Oiva
1984 "Participation Down and Up the Line: Comparative Industrial Democracy Trends in China and Europe." *International Social Science Journal* 36: 299–319.
Lafferty, William
1984 "Workplace Democratization in Norway: Current Status and Future Prospects with Special Emphasis on the Role of the Public Sector." *Acta Sociologica* 27: 123–138.
Lane, David
1985 *Soviet Economy and Society*. New York: New York University Press.
1976 *The Socialist Industrial State: Towards a Political Sociology of State Socialism*. London: George Allen and Unwin.
Lane, David, and George Kolankiewicz (eds.)
1973 *Social Groups in Polish Society*. New York: Columbia University Press.
Lee, Gary
1987 "Opposition Blunts Gorbachev's Efforts." *The Washington Post*, April 8, p. A16.
Lee, M. Mark
1985 *ESOPs in the 1980s*. New York: AMA Membership Publications Division.
Lee, Yung Hong
1986 "The Implications of Reform for Ideology, State and Society in China." *Journal of International Affairs* 39: 77–89.
Levinson, Charles (ed.)
1974 *Industry's Democratic Revolution*. London: George Allen and Unwin.
Lewin, Moshe
1989 "Perestroika: A New Historical Stage." *Journal of International Affairs* 42: 299–316.
Licht, Sonja
1989 "Yugoslavia: Reform Without Democracy." *New Politics* 2: 152–165.
Lijphart, Arend
1971 "Comparative Politics and the Comparative Method." *American Political Science Review* 65: 682–693.
Lind, Olof
1979 "Training and the Swedish Law on Employee Participation in Decision-Making," in John Fry (ed.), *Industrial Democracy and Labor Market Policy in Sweden*. Oxford: Pergamon Press.
Linden, Ronald
1986 "The Impact of Interdependence: Yugoslavia and International Change." *Comparative Politics* 18: 211–234.
Lindenfeld, Frank, and Joyce Rothschild-Whitt (eds.)
1982 *Workplace Democracy and Social Change*. Boston: Porter Sargent Publishers.
Linz, Susan
1988 "Managerial Autonomy in Soviet Firms." *Soviet Studies* 40: 175–195.

Lipski, Jan Josef
1990   "Poland: The State and Markets." *Dissent* 37: 338–339.

Long, Richard
1986   "Recent Patterns in Swedish Industrial Democracy," in R. N. Stern and S. McCarthy (eds.), *The Organizational Practice of Democracy*, vol. 3 of *International Yearbook of Organizational Democracy*, pp. 375–386. New York: John Wiley and Sons.

Ludlow, Howard
1975   "The Role of Trade Unions in Poland." *Political Science Quarterly* 90: 315–324.

Macy, Barry
1980   "The Quality-of-Worklife Project at Bolivar: An Assessment." *Monthly Labor Review* 103: 41–43.

Mallet, Serge
1972   "Movement Social et Structures Syndicates en Europe Occidentale." *First International Sociological Conference on Participation and Self-Management*, Zagreb, vol. 3, pp. 5–10.

Marsh, Robert, and Hiroshi Mannari
1988   *Organizational Change in Japanese Factories*. Greenwich, Conn.: JAI Press, Inc.

Martin, Andrew
1987   "Unions, the Quality of Work, and Technological Change in Sweden," in Carmen Sirianni (ed.), *Worker Participation and the Politics of Reform*, pp. 95–139. Philadelphia: Temple University Press.

1979   "From Joint Consultation to Decision-Making: The Redistribution of Workplace Power in Sweden," in John Fry (ed.), *Industrial Democracy and Labor Market Policy in Sweden*, pp. 5–14. Oxford: Pergamon Press.

1977   "Sweden: Industrial Democracy and Social Democratic Strategy," in G. David Garson (ed.), *Worker Self-Management in Industry. The West European Experience*, pp. 49–95. New York: Praeger Special Studies.

Maslow, Abraham
1954   *Motivation and Personality*. New York: Harper Bros.

Matejko, Alexander, and E. Alberta
1984   "The Nature of the Polish Crisis." *Sociologia Internationalis* 22: 59–110.

1972   "The Sociotechnical Principles of Workers' Control. Industrial Democracy: Myth and Reality." *First International Sociological Conference on Participation and Self-Management*, Zagreb, vol. 3, pp. 25–55.

McForan, D. W.
1988   "Glasnost, Democracy, and Perestroika." *International Social Sciences Review* 63: 165–175.

Meidner, Rudolf
1981   "Collective Asset Formation Through Wage-Earner Funds." *International Labour Review* 120: 303–317.

Mesa-Lago, Carmelo, and Carl Beck (eds.)
1975   *Comparative Socialist Systems: Essays on Politics and Economics*. Pittsburgh: University of Pittsburgh for International Studies.

Misztal, Bronislaw (ed.)
1985   *Poland After Solidarity*. New Brunswick, N.J.: Transaction Books.

Mlinar, Zdravko, and Henry Teune
1972 "Development and Participation." *First International Sociological Conference on Participation and Self-Management*, Zagreb, vol. 2, pp. 114–136.
Monissen, Hans
1978 "The Current Status of Labor Participation in the Management of Business Firms in Germany," in Svetozar Pejovich (ed.), *The Codetermination Movement in the West*, pp. 57–85. Lexington, Mass.: Lexington Books.
Montgomery, David
1979a *Workers' Control in America. Studies in the History of Work, Technology, and Labor Struggles*. Cambridge: Cambridge University Press.
1979b "The Past and the Future of Workers' Control." *Radical America* 13: 7–23.
1976 "Workers' Control of Machine Production in the Nineteenth Century." *Labor History* 17: 485–509.
Muqiao, Xue
1980 "On Reforming the Economic Management System." *Beijing Review* 231: 16–21.
Murphy, W. John
1986 "Yugoslav Self-Management and Social Ontology." *East European Quarterly* 20: 75–89.
Muto, Ichiyo
1983 "The Crises in U.S.-Japan Relations, Japanese Labor and the Japanese Left." *The Insurgent Sociologist* 11: 23–36.
Mydral, Hans-Goran
1981 "Collective Wage-Earner Funds in Sweden: A Road to Socialism, the End of Freedom of Association." *International Labour Review* 120: 319–331.
Nel, P. S., and P. H. van Rooyen
1985 *Worker Representation in Practice in South Africa*. Pretoria: Academica.
Neuberger, Egon, and Estelle James
1973 "The Yugoslav Self-Managed Enterprise," in M. Bornstein, *Plan and Market: Economic Reform in Eastern Europe*. New Haven, Conn.: Yale University Press.
Nicolaou-Smokoviti, Litsa
1988 *New Institutions in Labor Relations. Participation and Self-Management*. Athens, Greece: Papazissis Pbs. (in Greek).
Norr, Henry
1987 "Self-Management and the Politics of Solidarity in Poland," in Carmen Sirianni (ed.), *Worker Participation and the Politics of Reform*, pp. 267–297. Philadelphia: Temple University Press.
1985 "Poland: Solidarity and Self-Management." (Unpublished Manuscript.)
1983 "Quite a Frog to Eat: Self-Management and the Politics of Solidarity." (Unpublished Manuscript.)
1981 "Socialist Perspectives in Poland." *Socialist Review* 59: 147–179.
Nove, Alec
1983 *The Economics of Feasible Socialism*. London: George Allen and Unwin.
1980a "The Soviet Union: Problem and Prospects." *New Left Review* 119: 2–19.
1980b *The Soviet Economic System*. London: George Allen and Unwin.
Nove, Alec, et al. (eds.)
1982 *The East European Economies in the 1970s*. London: Butterworths.

Nove, A., and D. M. Nuti (eds.)
1972   *Socialist Economics: Selected Readings*. London: Penguin Books.
Nuti, Domenico Mario
1981a   "Poland: Economic Collapse and Socialist Renewal." *New Left Review* 130: 23–36.
1981b   "The Polish Crisis: Economic Factors and Constraints," in Ralph Miliband and John Saville (eds.), *The Socialist Register, 1981*, pp. 104–143. London: The Merlin Press Ltd.
Nyers, Rezso
1988   "The Hungarian Lessons of Four Decades." *World Marxist Review* 31: 17–28.
Obradović, Josip, and William N. Dunn (eds.)
1978   *Workers' Self-Management and Organizational Power in Yugoslavia*. Pittsburgh: University Center for International Studies.
Odaka, Kunio
1975   *Toward Industrial Democracy: Management and Workers in Modern Japan*. Cambridge, Mass.: Harvard University Press.
Ogden, S. G.
1982   "Trade Unions, Industrial Democracy and Collective Bargaining." *Sociology* 16: 544–563.
Olcott, Martha
1989   "Gorbachev's National Dilemma." *Journal of International Affairs* 42: 399–421.
Ouchi, William
1981   *Theory Z: How American Business Can Meet the Japanese Challenge*. New York: Avon Books.
Palmer, Thomas
1989   "Solidarity Activist Is Asked to Form Government." *Boston Globe*, August 20: 1, 22.
Pankin, Robert
1985   "A Union Organized Democratic ESOP at the Atlas Chain Company." Paper presented at the Annual Meetings of the American Sociological Association, Washington, D.C.
Parker, Mike
1985   *Inside the Circle: A Union Guide to QWL*. Boston: South End Press.
Parker, Mike, and Jane Slaughter
1988   *Choosing Sides: Unions and the Team Concept*. Boston: South End Press.
Pastuović, Nicola
1978   "Education and Training for Self-Management," in Josip Obradović and William N. Dunn (eds.), *Workers' Self-Management and Organizational Power in Yugoslavia*, pp. 435–477. Pittsburgh: University Center for International Studies.
Pateman, Carole
1970   *Participation and Democratic Theory*. Cambridge: Cambridge University Press.
Pejovich, Svetozar
1990   "A Property-Rights Analysis of the Yugoslav Miracle." *The Annals of the American Academy of Political and Social Science* 507: 123–132.
Pejovich, Svetozar (ed.)
1978   *The Codetermination Movement in the West*. Lexington, Mass.: Lexington Books.
Pelikan, Jiri
1978   "Reforme ou Revolution? Les Perspectives et les Possibilites de Changement dans les Pays de l'Est," in Pierre Kende and Krzysztof Pomian (eds.), *1956 Varsovie-*

Budapest: La Deuxieme Revolution d'Octobre, pp. 215–230. Paris: Editions du Seuil.

1973   "Workers' Councils in Czechoslovakia." *Critique* 401: 7–19.

Persky, Stan, and Henry Flam (eds.)

1982   *The Solidarity Sourcebook*. Vancouver: New Star Books.

Piore, Michael

1985   "Computer Technologies, Market Structures, and Strategic Union Choices," in Thomas Kochan (ed.), *Challenges and Choices Facing American Labor*, pp. 193–204. Cambridge, Mass.: MIT Press.

Piore, Michael, and Charles Sabel

1984   *The Second Industrial Divide*. New York: Basic Books.

Pipkorn, Jorn

1984   "Employee Participation in the European Community: Progress and Pitfalls," in B. Wilpert and A. Sorge (eds.), *International Perspectives on Organizational Democracy*, vol. 2 of *International Yearbook of Organizational Democracy*, pp. 49–69. New York: John Wiley and Sons.

Pomeranz, Ken

1990   "China Since the Square." *Dissent* 37: 243–246.

Poole, Michael

1986   "Participation Through Representation: A Review of Constraints and Conflicting Pressures," in R. N. Stern and S. McCarthy (eds.), *The Organizational Practice of Democracy*, vol. 3 of *International Yearbook of Organizational Democracy*, pp. 235–257. New York: John Wiley and Sons.

1982   "Theories of Industrial Democracy." *Sociological Review* 30: 181–207.

1981   "Industrial Democracy in Comparative Perspective," in Michael Poole and Roger Mansfield (eds.), *International Perspectives on Management Organization*, pp. 23–53. Farnborough: Gower.

1978   *Workers' Participation in Industry*. 2nd ed. Boston: Routledge and Kegan Paul.

Poole, Michael, and Roger Mansfield (eds.)

1981   *International Perspectives on Management Organization*. Farnborough: Gower.

Popovic, Mihailo

1984   "Causes of Economic and Sociopolitical Instability in Yugoslavia." *Eastern European Economics* 23:5–16.

Porket, J. L.

1978   "Industrial Relations and Participation in Management in the Soviet-Type Communist System." *British Journal of Industrial Relations* 16: 70–85.

1977   "The Soviet Model of Industrial Democracy." *The Annals of the American Academy of Political and Social Science* 431: 123–140.

1975   "Participation in Management in Communist Systems in the 1970s." *Journal of Industrial Relations* 13: 371–387.

Poznanski, Kazimierz

1986   "Economic Adjustment and Political Forces since 1970." *International Organization* 40: 455–486.

Pravda, Alex

1979   "Industrial Workers: Patterns of Dissent, Opposition and Accommodation," in Rudolf Tokes (ed.), *Opposition in Eastern Europe*, pp. 209–261. Baltimore: Johns Hopkins.

1973   "Some Aspects of the Czechoslovak Economic Reform and the Working Class in 1968." *Soviet Studies* 25: 102–124.

Pravda, Alex, and Blair A. Ruble
1986   *Trade Unions in Communist States*. Boston: Allen and Unwin.

Provisional Regulations
1981   Provisional Regulations Concerning Congresses of Workers and Staff Members in State-Owned Industrial Enterprises, reprinted in *Beijing Review*, September 7: 16–19.

Prybyla, Jan
1990   "Economic Reform of Socialism: The Dengist Course in China." *The Annals of the American Academy of Political and Social Science* 507: 113–121.

Putnam, W. George
1985   "Market Socialism and Economic Cleavages in the Working Class: The Yugoslavian Experience." Paper presented at the 1985 Annual Meetings of the American Sociological Association, Washington, D.C.

Quinn-Judge, Paul
1990a   "Soviet Power Shift Reshapes Politburo." *The Boston Sunday Globe*, July 15: 1, 12.
1990b   "Gorbachev Urges Wide Coalition." *The Boston Globe*, July 14: 1, 7.

Qvale, Thoralf Ulrik
1976   "Norwegian Strategy for Democratization of Industry." *Human Relations* 29: 453–469.

Ramsay, Harvie
1983   "Evolution or Cycle? Worker Participation in the 1970s and 1980s," in C. Crouch and Heller (eds.), *Organizational Democracy and Political Processes*, vol. 1 of *International Yearbook of Organizational Democracy*, pp. 203–223. New York: John Wiley and Sons.
1977   "Cycles of Control: Worker Participation in Sociological and Historical Perspective." *Sociology* 11: 481–506.

Reagan, Kathleen
1985   "Quality Circles in Action." Elms College, Chicopee, Massachusetts. (Unpublished Manuscript.)

Reich, Robert
1983   *The Next American Frontier*. New York: Penguin Books.

Révész, Gábor
1979   "Enterprise and Plant Size of the Hungarian Industry." *Acta Oeconomica* 22: 47–68.

Riddell, D. S.
1968   "Social Self-Government: The Background of Theory and Practice in Yugoslav Socialism." *British Journal of Sociology* 19: 47–75.

Rosen, Corey, et al. (eds.)
1986   *Employee Ownership in America*. Lexington, Mass.: Lexington Books.

Rosen, Stanley
1988   "Dissent and Tolerance in Chinese Society." *Current History*, September 1988: 261–164, 278–281.

Rosenthal, Philip
1977   *Co-determination: Worker Participation in German Industry*. New York: German Information Center.

Ross, George
1987   "Autogestion Coming and Going: The Strange Saga of Workers' Control Movements in Modern France," in Carmen Sirianni (ed.), *Worker Participation and the Politics of Reform*, pp. 198–223. Philadelphia: Temple University Press.
Roucek, Libor
1988   "Private Enterprise in Soviet Political Debates." *Soviet Studies* 40: 47–63.
Roussis, George
1983   *Workers' Participation*. Athens, Greece: Sinchroni Epochi (in Greek).
Roustang, Guy
1983   "Worker Participation in Occupation Safety and Health Matters in France." *International Labour Review* 122: 169–182.
Rubinstein, Sidney
1980   "QWL and the Technical Societies." *Quality Progress* 8: 28–31.
Runciman, W. G.
1985   "Contradictions of State Socialism: The Case of Poland." *The Sociological Review* 33: 1–19.
Rus, Velko
1984   "The Future of Industrial Democracy." *International Social Science Journal* 36: 232–254.
Rusinow, D.
1977   *The Yugoslav Experiment: 1948–1974*. Berkeley: University of California Press.
Russell, Raymond
1985   *Sharing Ownership in the Workplace*. Albany: State University of New York Press.
Ryden, Rune
1978   "Labor Participation in the Management of Business Firms in Germany," in Svetozar Pejovich (ed.), *The Codetermination Movement in the West*, pp. 85–113. Lexington, Mass.: Lexington Books.
Sabel, Charles
1982   *Work and Politics. The Division of Labor in Industry*. Cambridge: Cambridge University Press.
Sabel, Charles, and David Stark
1982   "Planning, Politics, and Shop-Floor Power. Hidden Forms of Bargaining in Soviet Imposed State-Socialist Societies." *Politics and Society* 11: 439–473.
Schiller, Bernt
1977   "Industrial Democracy in Scandinavia." *The Annals of the American Academy of Political and Social Science* 431: 63–73.
Schneider, Leslie
1983   "Technology Bargaining in Norway." Unpublished paper presented for the Ministry of Local Government and Labor, Oslo, Norway.
Scholl, Wolfgang
1986   "Codetermination and the Quality of Working Life," in R. N. Stern and S. McCarthy (eds.), *The Organizational Practice of Democracy*, vol. 3 of *International Yearbook of Organizational Democracy*, pp. 153–174. New York: John Wiley and Sons.
Schregle, Johannes
1981   "Comparative Industrial Relations: Pitfalls and Potential." *International Labour Review* 120: 15–30.

1978   "Co-determination in the Federal Republic of Germany: A Comparative View."
        International Labour Review 117: 81–98.
1976   "Workers' Participation in Decisions Within Undertakings." *International Labour
        Review* 113: 1–15.
1974   "Labour Relations in Western Europe: Some Topical Issues." *International La-
        bour Review* 109: 1–22.
Schuller, Tom
1985   *Democracy at Work.* New York: Oxford University Press.
Selden, Mark, and Victor Lippit
1982   *The Transition to Socialism in China.* New York: M. E. Sharpe, Inc.
Shaiken, Harley
1980   "The New 'World Car.' Detroit Downsizes U.S. Jobs." *The Nation,* October 11:
        345–348.
Shalev, Michael
1980   "Industrial Relations Theory and the Comparative Study of Industrial Relations
        and Industrial Conflict." *British Journal of Industrial Relations* 18: 26–43.
Shenfield, Arthur
1978   "Labor Participation in Great Britain," in Svetozar Pejovich (ed.), *The Code-
        termination Movement in the West,* pp. 23–47. Lexington, Mass.: Lexington
        Books.
Shimada, Haruo
1980   *Japanese Industrial Relations Series: The Japanese Employment System.* The
        Japan Institute of Labour. Series 6.
Siegel, Irving, and Edgar Weinberg
1982   *Labor-Management Cooperation: The American Experience.* Michigan: W. E.
        Upjohn Institute for Employment Research.
Silver, Marc
1981   "Worker Management: A Power-Dialectic Framework." *Sociology of Work and
        Occupations* 8: 145–165.
Silverman, B., and Murray Yanowitch (eds.)
1974   *The Worker in "Post Industrial" Capitalism. Liberal and Radical Responses.*
        New York: Free Press.
Simmons, John, and William Mares
1985   *Working Together: Employee Participation in Action.* New York: New York
        University Press.
Singleton, Fred
1970   "Workers' Self Management and the Role of Trade Unions in Yugoslavia," in
        K. Coates and T. Topham, *Workers' Control.* London: The Merlin Press, Ltd.
Sirianni, Carmen (ed.)
1987a   *Worker Participation and the Politics of Reform.* Philadelphia: Temple University
        Press.
1987b   "Worker Participation in the Late Twentieth Century: Some Critical Issues," in
        Carmen Sirianni (ed.), *Worker Participation and the Politics of Reform,* pp. 3–
        33. Philadelphia: Temple University Press.
1983   "Workers' Control in Europe: A Comparative Sociological Analysis," in James
        Cronin and Carmen Sirianni (eds.), *Work, Community and Power,* pp. 254–310.
        Philadelphia: Temple University Press.

1982   *Workers' Control and Socialist Democracy: The Soviet Experience*. London: Verso Editions.

Skilling, H. Gordon

1976   *Czechoslovakia's Interrupted Revolution*. Princeton, N.J.: Princeton University Press.

Skocpol, Theda (ed.)

1984   *Vision and Method in Historical Sociology*. Cambridge: Cambridge University Press.

1983   "Methods of Comparative Sociology." Didactic Seminar Presentation at the Annual Meetings of the American Sociological Association, Detroit, Michigan.

1979   *States and Social Revolutions*. Cambridge: Cambridge University Press.

Skocpol, Theda, and Margaret Somers

1980   "The Uses of Comparative History in Macrosocial Inquiry." *Comparative Studies in Society and History* 22: 174–197.

Solinger, Dorothy

1986   "Industrial Reforms: Decentralization, Differentiation, and the Difficulties." *Journal of International Affairs* 39: 105–118.

Sorge, Arndt

1976   "The Evolution of Industrial Democracy in the Countries of the European Community." *British Journal of Industrial Relations* 14: 274–294.

Staniszkis, Jadwiga

1989   "The Obsolescence of Solidarity." *Telos* 80: 37–49.

1984   *Poland's Self-Limiting Revolution*. Princeton, N.J.: Princeton University Press.

1981   "The Evolution of Forms of Working-Class Protest in Poland: Sociological Reflections on the Gdansk-Szczecin Case, August 1980." *Soviet Studies* 33: 204–231.

Stark, David

1985   "Market Inside the Socialist Firm: Internal Subcontracting in Hungarian Enterprises." Paper presented at the Annual Meetings of the American Sociological Association, Washington, D.C.

1980   "Class Struggle and the Transformation of the Labor Process." *Theory and Society* 9: 89–129.

Stefanowski, Roman

1977   "Workers' Councils: 1956–1977." *Radio Free Europe Report*, No. 160: 1–22.

Stephens, Huber Evelyn

1980   *The Politics of Workers' Participation: The Peruvian Approach in Comparative Perspective*. New York: Academic Press.

Stephens, Huber Evelyn, and John D. Stephens

1982   "The Labor Movement, Political Power, and Workers' Participation in Western Europe." *Political Power and Social Theory* 3: 215–249.

Stern, Robert, and Sharon McCarthy (eds.)

1986   *The Organizational Practice of Democracy*, vol. 3 of *International Yearbook of Organizational Democracy*. New York: John Wiley and Sons.

Stern, Robert, and William F. Whyte

1981   "Economic Democracy: Comparative Views of Current Initiatives." *Sociology of Work and Occupations* 8: 139–143.

Stokes, Bruce

1978   *Worker Participation-Productivity and the Quality of Work Life*. Worldwatch Paper 25.

Strauss, George
1979   "Workers' Participation: Symposium Introduction." *Industrial Relations. A Journal of Economy and Society* 18: 247–262.
Street, John
1983   "Socialist Arguments for Industrial Democracy." *Economic and Industrial Democracy* 4: 519–539.
Sturmthal, Adolf
1977   "Unions and Industrial Democracy." *The Annals of American Academy of Political and Social Science* 431: 12–21.
1964   *Workers' Councils: A Study of Workplace Organization on Both Sides of the Iron Curtain.* Cambridge, Mass.: Harvard University Press.
Svejnar, Jan
1975   "Workers' Participation in Management in Czechoslovakia." Paper presented at the 1975 International Conference on Self-Management, Cornell University, Ithaca, N.Y.
Tagliabue, John
1989   "Parties in Poland Will Ask Walesa to Form a Cabinet." *New York Times*, August 17: 1, A14.
Tardos, Marton
1984   "A Development Program for Economic Control and Organization in Hungary." *Eastern European Economics* 22: 3–32.
Teague, Elizabeth
1988   "Perestroika: The Polish Influence." (Survey.) *A Journal of East & West Studies* 30: 39–58.
Thalheim, Karl
1975   "Balance Sheet," in Hans-Herman Hohmann et al., *The New Economic Systems of Eastern Europe.* Berkeley: University of California Press.
Thomas, J. Robert
1985   "Quality and Quantity? Worker Participation in the U.S. and Japanese Automobile Industries," in M. Dubofsky (ed.), *Technological Change and Workers' Movements*, pp. 162–188. Beverly Hills, Calif.: Sage Publications.
Thompson, E. P.
1967   "Time, Work-Discipline, and Industrial Capitalism." *Past and Present* 38: 56–93.
Thomson, Andrew
1977   "New Focus on Industrial Democracy in Britain." *The Annals of the American Academy of Political and Social Science* 431: 32–43.
Thorsrud, E.
1972   *Workers' Participation in Management in Norway.* Geneva: Institute for Labour Studies.
Tomlins, Christopher
1985   *The State and the Unions: Labor Relations, Law, and the Organized Labor Movement in America, 1880–1960.* Cambridge: Cambridge University Press.
Tomlinson, J. D.
1984   "Economic and Sociological Theories of the Enterprise and Industrial Democracy." *British Journal of Sociology* 35: 591–605.
Touraine, Alain, F. Dubet, M. Wieviorka, and J. Strzelecki
1983   *Solidarity: The Analysis of a Social Movement: Poland 1980–1981.* Cambridge: Cambridge University Press.

Triska, Jan, and Charles Gati (eds.)
1981   *Blue-Collar Workers in Eastern Europe.* London: George Allen and Unwin.
Triska, Jan, and Paul M. Johnson
1975   "Political Development and Political Change," in Carmelo Mesa-Lago and Carl
        Beck, *Comparative Socialist Systems: Essays on Politics and Economics.* Pitts-
        burgh: University of Pittsburgh Center for International Studies.
Trist, E. L., G. W. Higgin, H. Murray, and A. B. Pollock
1963   *Organizational Choice.* London: Tavistock.
Tsiganou, Helen
1982   "Greek Migration to Europe in the Last Twenty Years: Causes and Effects."
        Unpublished Master's Thesis, Northeastern University.
Tyler, Gus
1986   "Labor's Vatican II: Search of New Goals, New Methods." *Dissent* 33: 505–
        513.
Ursell, Gill
1983   "The Views of British Managers and Shop Stewards on Industrial Democracy,"
        in C. Crouch and F. Heller (eds.), *Organizational Democracy and Political Pro-
        cesses*, vol. 1 of *International Yearbook of Organizational Democracy*, pp. 327–
        387. New York: John Wiley and Sons.
U.S. Department of Labor
1985a   *Selections from the Second National Labor-Management Conference.* Washing-
        ton, D.C.: Bureau of Labor-Management Relations and Cooperative Programs.
1985b   *Handbook of Labor Statistics: Bureau of Labor Statistics* pp. 64–430.
Valenta, Jiri
1981   "Czechoslovakia: A Proletariat Embourgeoise," in Jan Triska and C. Gati (eds.),
        Blue-Collar Workers in Eastern Europe, pp. 209–223. London: George Allen and
        Unwin.
Vallier, Ivan (ed.)
1971   *Comparative Methods in Sociology. Essays on Trends and Applications.* Berkeley:
        University of California Press.
Vitak, Robert
1971   "Workers' Control: The Czechoslovak Experience." *The Socialist Register* 245–
        264.
Vogel, Ezra
1979   *Japan as Number 1: Lessons for America.* New York: Harper Torchbooks.
Vogel, Ezra (ed.)
1975   *Modern Japanese Organization and Decision-Making.* Berkeley: University of
        California Press.
Volgyes, Ivan
1981   "Hungary: The Lumpenproletarianization of the Working Class," in Jan Triska
        and C. Gati (eds.), *Blue-Collar Workers in Eastern Europe*, pp. 224–236. London:
        George Allen and Unwin.
Walder, Andrew
1986   *Communist Neo-Traditionalism. Work and Authority in Chinese Industry.* Berke-
        ley: University of California Press.
1984   "China's Industry in Transition: To What?" *The Annals of the American Academy
        of Political and Social Science* 476: 62–73.

1982   "Some Ironies of the Maoist Legacy in Industry," in Mark Selden and Victor Lippit (eds.), *The Transition to Socialism in China*, pp. 215–238. New York: M. E. Sharpe, Inc.

Walker, F. Kenneth
1977   "Toward the Participatory Enterprise: A European Trend." *The Annals of the American Academy of Political and Social Science* 431: 1–11.

Walters, Roy
1982   "The Citibank Project: Improving Productivity Through Work Redesign," in Robert Zager and Michael Rosow (eds.), *The Innovative Organization: Productivity Programs in Action*, pp. 109–125. New York: Pergamon Press.

Walton, Richard
1982   "The Topeka Work System: Optimistic Visions, Pessimistic Hypotheses, and Reality," in Robert Zager and Michael Rosow (eds.), *The Innovative Organization: Productivity Programs in Action*, pp. 261–291. New York: Pergamon Press.
1979   "Work Innovations in the United States," pp. 24–34, in *Perspectives on Labor-Management Cooperation*, U.S. Department of Labor, 1985 (reprinted from the July/August issue of *Harvard Business Review*).

Wells, Don
1986   "Soft Sell: 'Quality of Working Life' Programs and the Productivity Race." Ottawa, Ontario. The Canadian Centre for Policy Alternatives.

Weschler, Lawrence
1990   "Poland Takes the Plunge." *Dissent* 37: 207–212.

Wilpert, Bernhard, and A. Sorge
1984   *International Perspectives on Organizational Democracy*. Vol. 2 of *International Yearbook of Organizational Democracy*. New York: John Wiley and Sons.

Wilson, Jeanne
1987   "The Institution of Democratic Reforms in the Chinese Enterprise since 1978," in Carmen Sirianni (ed.), *Worker Participation and the Politics of Reform*, pp. 299–327. Philadelphia: Temple University Press.

Windmuller, John
1977   "Industrial Democracy and Industrial Relations." *The Annals of the American Academy of Political and Social Science* 431: 22–31.

Witte, John
1980   *Democracy, Authority, and Alienation in Work: Workers' Participation in an American Corporation*. Chicago: University of Chicago Press.

Woodall, Jean
1982a   *The Socialist Corporation and Technocratic Power*. Cambridge: Cambridge University Press.
1982b   *Policy and Politics in Contemporary Poland*. New York: St. Martin's Press.
1982c   "Introduction: The Construction of a 'Developed Socialist Society' and 'Socialist Renewal', " in Jean Woodall, *Policy and Politics in Contemporary Poland*. New York: St. Martin's Press, pp. 1–23.
1981   "New Social Factors in the Unrest in Poland." *Government and Opposition* 16: 37–57.

Woodward, Susan
1986   "Orthodoxy and Solidarity: Competing Claims and International Adjustment in Yugoslavia." *International Organization* 40: 505–547.

Woodworth, W., et al. (eds.)
1985   *Industrial Democracy: Strategies for Community Revitalization*. Beverly Hills, Calif.: Sage Publications.

Wu, Yu-Shan
1990   "The Linkage Between Economic and Political Reform in the Socialist Countries: A Supply-Side Explanation." *The Annals of the American Academy for Political and Social Science* 507: 92–102.

Yamamoto, Kiyoshi
1981   "Labor-Management Relations at Nissan Motor Co., Ltd. (Datsun)." *Annals of the Institute of Social Science* 21: 24–44.

Yamamoto, Mititaka
1980   "The Japanese Homogeneity Promotes Ikigai." *Quality Progress* 8: 18–21.

Yanaev, I. G.
1987   "Soviet Restructuring: The Position and Role of the Trade Unions." *International Labour Review* 126: 703–712.

Yanowitch, Murray
1985   *Work in the Soviet Union: Attitudes and Issues*. Armonk, N.Y.: M. E. Sharpe, Inc.
1978   "Pressures for More 'Participatory' Forms of Economic Organization in the Soviet Union." *Economic Analysis and Workers' Management* 12: 403–417.
1977   *Social and Economic Inequality in the Soviet Union*. New York: M. E. Sharpe, Inc.

Zager, Robert, and Michael P. Rosow
1982   *The Innovative Organization: Productivity Programs in Action*. New York: Pergamon Press.

Zaslavsaya, Tatyana
1988   "Perestroika and Sociology." *Social Research* 55: 267–276.

Zaslavsky, Victor
1987–1988   "Three Years of Perestroika." *Telos* 74: 31–42.
1985   "The Soviet World System: Origins, Evolution, Prospects for Reform." *Telos* 65: 3–21.

Zdravomyslov, A. G., et al. (eds.)
1970   *Man and His Work*. New York: International Arts and Sciences Press, Inc.

Zielinski, Janusz
1973   *Economic Reforms in Polish Industry*. London: Oxford University Press.

Zimbalist, Andrew
1975   "The Limits of Work Humanization." *Review of Radical Political Economy* 7: 50–59.

Ziyang Zhao
1981   "The Present Economic Situation and the Principles for Future Economic Construction." Report delivered at the Fourth Session of the Fifth National People's Congress, reprinted in *Beijing Review*, December 21: 6–36.

Zukin, Sharon
1981   "The Representation of Working-Class Interests in Socialist Society: Yugoslav Labor Unions." *Politics and Society* 10: 281–316.

Zwerdling, Daniel
1980   *Workplace Democracy*. New York: Harper Colophon Books.

Index

About the Author

HELEN A. TSIGANOU is a Lecturer in the Sociology Department at North-eastern University. Specializing in the sociology of work, organizations, and industry, she is currently conducting a longitudinal study of help wanted ads in the *New York Times* and the *St. Louis Post-Dispatch*.